REREADING
William Styron

REREADING
William Styron

GAVIN COLOGNE-BROOKES

LOUISIANA STATE UNIVERSITY PRESS
BATON ROUGE

Published with the support of the Bath Spa University
Contemporary Writing Research Centre.

Published by Louisiana State University Press
Copyright © 2014 by Louisiana State University Press
All rights reserved
Manufactured in the United States of America
First printing

DESIGNER: *Mandy McDonald Scallan*
TYPEFACE: *Whitman*
PRINTER AND BINDER: *Maple Press*

Library of Congress Cataloging-in-Publication Data
Cologne-Brookes, Gavin, 1961–
 Rereading William Styron / Gavin Cologne-Brookes.
  pages cm
 Includes bibliographical references and index.
 ISBN 978-0-8071-5287-4 (cloth : alk. paper) — ISBN
978-0-8071-5288-1 (pdf) — ISBN 978-0-8071-5289-8
(epub) — ISBN 978-0-8071-5290-4 (mobi) 1. Styron,
William, 1925–2006—Criticism and interpretation. I.
Title.
 PS3569.T9Z6247 2014
 813'.54—dc23

2013014278

For Nicki, and for Matt Martin, a good friend for many years

We do not go, we are driven; like things that float, now leisurely then with violence, according to the gentleness or rapidity of the current.

—MICHEL DE MONTAIGNE

Good criticism is a creative act.

—WILLIAM STYRON

CONTENTS

ACKNOWLEDGMENTS

I began to reread William Styron after a suggestion that I should write an essay discussing a manuscript page of *Sophie's Choice*. This essay appeared in *The Mississippi Quarterly* in 2009 along with a conversation Styron and I recorded in 1998. Recalling the conversation led me to combine personal experience and scholarly analysis in this critical memoir. I am therefore grateful to James L. W. West III, both for suggesting the essay and for his help over the years, and Noel Polk, who encouraged me to expand the essay and combine it with the conversation. My subsequent research led to renewed correspondence with Rose Styron and with Bill and Rose's daughter, Alexandra, and I thank them both for their cooperation. Thanks are due, too, to all staff at the Louisiana State University Press who were involved in the project, including John Easterly, Lee Sioles, Margaret Lovecraft, Joanne Allen, and Mandy Scallan. Once again, I am indebted to the British Academy for a research grant. This enabled me to examine archive material at Columbia University, the Library of Congress, and Duke University and to visit places relevant to Styron's novels in New York, Washington, DC, North Carolina, and Virginia. In New York, Matt Martin, Elizabeth Reingold, Daniel, and Erin provided their customary hospitality. I thank the staff at Columbia University, particularly Karla Nielsen, and at the Library of Congress for their help. Elizabeth Dunn, of Duke University, deserves a special thank-you for tremendous support during my visit and with later queries. While visiting Courtland and Newport News I appreciated the helpfulness and courtesy of everyone I met, not least Betty Anne Beard, of the Walter Cecil Rawls Library, who put me in touch with Rick Francis; Rick himself, who gave me the time of day, along with useful historical information; and James W. Lash III, the current owner of Styron's childhood home. I also thank Ben Camardi for permission to view the Harold Matson Papers; Shira Schindel, of International Creative Management, for securing permission to quote from a Ted Geisel letter; Barry Hannah Jr., Ray Lane, JoAnne Prichard Morris, and David Rae Morris for permitting me to quote from archived letters; Rebecca Parry for a particular insight into Styron's writing; Ekwueme Mike Thelwell and Henry Louis Gates Jr. for swift and friendly responses to queries; Hanna Gruszczyńska, who made a brave attempt to improve my Polish; and Amy Cliff, Dan Disch, Bill Heyen, and Susan Shillinglaw as American friends who have, one way or another, informed my writing.

I received significant input from Bath Spa University colleagues, past and present. Each spring Fiona Peters organizes a student field trip to Poland. Those trips and her insights on reading the manuscript helped to shape the chapter on *Sophie's Choice*. I am also grateful to Ellen McWilliams and Richard Kerridge for reading the manuscript, to Beth Wright and Ian Gadd for supplying information, to Tracy Brain and Tessa Hadley for reminding me that criticism can be creative, and to Ron George for mounting an exhibition of my paintings, including a Styron portrait. Tim Middleton, Tracey Hill, and Steve May engineered funding or teaching relief at important junctures. I gave two presentations to colleagues while writing the book, and I thank them for their responses. Many BSU students, too, have helped shape my views on Styron's work.

Without thought for the family we grow up in we amount to very little, so my father, Philip, and my brother and sister, Bruce and Amelia, deserve mention, along with my mother, Bobbi, who died in 2008. As ever, my love for my wife, Nicki, is accompanied by gratitude for her unparalleled support through the years. As for my daughters, love mingles increasingly with admiration for the way their own lives are shaping up. But I thank Xenatasha especially for showing me, at age nine, when we visited the U.S. military cemetery above Omaha Beach in Normandy, the power of recording individual names to personalize mass tragedies, and Anastasia for her wit and good humor during my time spent writing the book.

REREADING
William Styron

CHAPTER 1

The Meaning of Rereading

> The writer must criticize his own work as a reader. Every day I pick up
> the story or whatever it is I've been working on and read it through. If I
> enjoy it as a reader then I know I'm getting along all right.
> —STYRON, *Paris Review* interview, 1954

Rereading William Styron is a critical memoir. It involves two kinds of
rereading, just as it was born of two impulses, one more objective and
critical, the other more personal and passionate. *Rereading* refers to
close critical reading. My concerns here involve showing how and why
the best of Styron's writing rewards this activity. But to reread Styron is
also, for me, to reflect on the impact of the man and his writing during
my twenties and thirties, up to and beyond *The Novels of William Styron*
(1995). Although my earlier book contains an appendix of conversations
with Styron, it's a conventional critical analysis, treating the novelist
as a kind of disembodied persona. But now that Bill Styron the man is
dead, my memories of him may contribute a different kind of insight
into the work.

Perhaps to write another book about the same author is a strange
thing to do. Like Jorge Luis Borges's Pierre Menard, who manages to
compose pages of *Don Quixote* that were not copied yet coincide with
Cervantes's "word for word and line for line,"[1] I might have ended up
writing a book that already exists. But as we age we change both as
people and as readers. Different issues concern us. One subterranean
subject here, therefore, is the labyrinthine network of identities—those
of the author, of the characters, and of the reader—and our changing
perspective on them. To reread, in this sense, is to reflect upon a body of

writing with a heightened awareness of the passing years. The impulses to read closely and to reflect both involve explicating the writing. But to reread while acknowledging passing time has the added dimension of reflecting on the nature of an attachment to a writer and his work and on the experience of rereading from different perspectives and in different circumstances. Moreover, I return to Styron's work very aware—from years of discussing the novels with students—that that same process occurs in all readers open to the possibility of multiple perspectives. This book, therefore, doesn't provide the kind of all-encompassing, chronological scrutiny of the major works attempted in the earlier book. Rather, it offers fresh perspectives on Styron's fiction and nonfiction within the context of my sense of his personality.

To expand, first, on the main, critical impulse: the book assesses Styron's oeuvre on its own terms and, depending upon what's under discussion, in differing degrees of detail. What matters to me here is his craft. To borrow Henry James's phrase about Balzac, I think of Styron's best novels as having achieved "saturation" in the sense of being integrated and textured on many different levels.[2] Such art repays scrutiny, rewarding focus on specific details, and on a multitude of elements. If you contemplate *The Merchant of Venice* or *Moby-Dick* or *Buddenbrooks* or the poetry of Emily Dickinson, you are rarely disappointed. The writer, or at least the writing process, has invariably got there first. This quality is evident in great painting and music too. Look at a Caravaggio and concentrate on the color blue, and it will reward you with a very different yet equally rich experience compared with concentrating on the color red, the tonal balance, or the brushwork. Equivalent rewards occur in listening to Mozart or Beethoven. If the work is inferior (whether it's by the same artist or by others), these patterns will be sparser and less consistent and may merely result from our pattern-making minds. Analysis increases appreciation of Styron's best writing even as it explains why aspects of the work are less than successful. My aim is thus to show how and why Styron's two novels of artistic maturity, *The Confessions of Nat Turner* (1967) and *Sophie's Choice* (1979), are so integrated that they "anticipate" a spectrum of responses and reward rereading in the manner of classic literature.

Lie Down in Darkness (1951) is no less remarkable, and not just as a first novel, but its qualities are less evenly spread. Styron saw this during composition. "What I've written so far on this book is good," he told his father, but "far from maturity or perfection." Indeed, he was noticing "the maturation process" even as he wrote. But the fact that he was aware of this is itself an indication of how mature his approach already was, even while he also acknowledged that he didn't yet "know enough about people" to produce a mature work.[3] Although I feel that in important ways Styron's other full-length novel, *Set This House on Fire* (1960), is an advance on his first, it's also of interest as a work of uneasy transition. Its failings have to do, in part, with experiments that both anticipate and highlight the later triumphs.

Of Styron's other writing I agree with James L. W. West III that Styron's nonfiction is one of his "unrecognized achievements."[4] With exceptions, I'm less sure of the comparative literary value of his short fiction, including the novel fragments published as autonomous tales. Collected in *This Quiet Dust and Other Writings* (1982, rev. 1993), *Darkness Visible: A Memoir of Madness* (1990), and the posthumous, *Havanas in Camelot: Personal Essays* (2008), his nonfiction is a considerable contribution to literature. His mature writing is in any case a complex blend of the dramatic and the essayistic, so an examination of his essays in terms of both subject matter and literary qualities is as apt as it is overdue. As for his short fiction, the point is that his creative vision required a large canvas. The complexity of the novels means that close reading of them most rewards—or with *Set This House on Fire* reveals—when we consider parts in terms of the whole. Styron was at his best creating novels the minutiae of which related to what he called the "architecture."[5] He managed to achieve this architecture in at least three of his four full-length novels but couldn't build a fifth. While assessment of the completed novels illustrates his thoughts on fiction in his essays, to analyze the fragments of unfulfilled endeavor would be a letdown after considering *The Confessions of Nat Turner* and *Sophie's Choice*. I therefore treat most of this work as marginalia. The stories, in particular in *Letters to My Father* (2009) and *The Suicide Run: Five Tales of the Marine Corps* (2009), seem, for the most part, less worthy of close reading and (unlike *Set This House on Fire*) add little to our understanding of his intellectual journey.

Three narratives that are neither juvenilia nor related to Styron's attempts to write a long Marine Corps novel are *The Long March* (1952), in that it was written to stand alone, and two of the three stories in *A Tidewater Morning: Three Tales from Youth* (1993): "Shadrach" and the title story. Following the practice of other book-length studies, I devoted a chapter of *The Novels of William Styron* to *The Long March*, but this novella is not substantial enough to bear the weight of further extended analysis. Passing reflections on it, as with "Shadrach," feel sufficient.

"A Tidewater Morning," though, is as powerful as anything Styron wrote, and not least in terms of the insight it provides into the impact of losing his mother to cancer when he was only just fourteen. These observations may explain where and why my emphasis falls in terms of critical rereading.

To return to Styron's writing in critical terms has its risks. I knew that what once seemed fabulous writing might feel sadly diminished. I knew I might have been fooled by youthful fervor as surely as Stingo believes that Nathan is something other than a madman. Had I indeed found that to be the case, I'd not have decided on this second study. But it's also true that one of the usually unspoken facts about the academic profession is that critics of individual writers have a vested interest in advancing the cause of their subject. For this reason, contemporary writers of dubious quality receive extended boosts to their literary longevity because their profile suits the needs of the academy of the day. It takes time for the truly remarkable writings to become regarded as classic, and the canon—or "posterity"—is formed less by critics than by a writer's influence on later writers and by readers. No one now disputes the quality, significance, or impact of *Pride and Prejudice*, *Walden*, *The Trial*, *L'Etranger*, or *Invisible Man*, but posterity will decide whether writing by Styron or his contemporaries is with these books a hundred years from now. Honesty, in sifting for the best, has therefore been my watchword.

To write a critical memoir, however, is to admit a loyalty to the memory of the man and a predisposition to appreciate the work. For this book is not just about rereading but also about remembering a novelist. Viewed more objectively in later life, *friendship* is too weighty a word. Our acquaintance—yet that's too light a word—was sporadic. It included correspondence between 1987 and 2003; a visit to Connecticut in 1988; a summer spell in Connecticut and then on Cape Cod in 1990; a drive across England in 1991; weekends on Cape Cod in 1998 and in Connecticut in 2001; and evenings in London in 2002, leading to a final letter from him in 2003, on the cusp of what his daughter, Alexandra, would describe at his memorial service in 2007 as his "epic, wretched descent." But such relatively scant contact can provide a young person with a lifetime of emotional and intellectual capital. For many of those years Styron was a frequent presence in my mind even if our encounters were episodic. As different as my concerns now are, rereading him still involves recalling my first encounters with the work and conversations with the man himself.

It would be fair to query the relevance of including the personal at all, arguing that we should not confuse life and literature. But another view convinces me more. From Nietzsche through William James to Wittgenstein to Richard Rorty, there are those who argue for life's inescapable aestheticism. "Reality," wrote Wallace Stevens, "is an Activity of the Most August Imagination." This being the case, it's more honest to confess subjectivity than to feign objectivity. I take it as a given that we create and re-create rather than merely experience reality. We are all, as David Bromwich neatly puts it, "Novelists of Every Day Life."[6] The German author Christa Wolf provides an apt description of the complex relationship between life and literature. "To begin writing you must first be someone to whom reality is no longer self-evident," she argues. To show that "there is a truth outside the important world of facts," she describes a "rainy afternoon in the world of Dostoevsky's Raskolnikov," which can be uncovered "like an archaeological stratum" in modern-day St. Petersburg. During the day, Dostoevsky's grandson shows her the moneylender's house, and as they climb the stairs "the grisly deed" seems "on the point of being committed again." "Here's where it happened," he tells her. Wolf wonders what business they have being there, but the woman living there not only lets them in but also tells Wolf she's "where the moneylender stood when Raskolnikov delivered the blow." Wolf recalls involuntarily stepping back, "caught up in the tangle of reality and fiction."[7]

The tangle tightens when she and the grandson visit Raskolnikov's lodgings. For Wolf, "the different levels of reality" now come together. The old man's research leaves "no doubt that Dostoevsky himself" hid here from his creditors while working "like a demon on his book." She feels, therefore, "solid ground" in that "a certifiably real author, a historical figure and flesh-and-blood human being, had lived here a century ago, and saw no other escape from the trouble that assailed him within and without than to project his conflict onto an invented character." Indeed, she muses, perhaps *invented* is the wrong word, for Raskolnikov inhabited the same room, "took the possessions of both to the same pawnbroker, and was able to carry out the act which must have begun as a grisly mental experiment in the brain of the author." "The fusion of 'author' and 'subject,'" writes Wolf, "once achieved, generates a third element, the new reality of the book, which effortlessly implies 'real' houses, streets, apartments, and staircases, without needing to prove, of course, that these particular houses and rooms can be found in the world in the exact form in which the book describes them."

Hence "the reality of *Crime and Punishment* goes beyond the topography of a city. It is certainly St. Petersburg. But can anyone doubt that the Petersburg we know—this dreary human Babylon—would never have existed if the overheated imagination of an unhappy writer had not seen it?" Wolf therefore reminds us that authors don't simply use settings but shape them. Dostoevsky created our St. Petersburg. Hence, in terms of both settings and characters, an author can create a world to such an extent that the likes of "Raskolnikov, Anna Karenina, and Julien Sorel" become "as much our companions in this world as are Napoleon or Lenin."[8]

Wolf's overall point is that "literature and reality do not stand to each other in the relation of mirror to what is mirrored."[9] Styron's writing, in turn, is often about the reality of the imagination, or the imagined element inherent in our notions of reality. He sought to enable readers to experience what he had experienced, or what he imagined people in history experiencing. "I don't think very well unless I relate it to historical events," he said. Fiction was his vehicle for meditating upon "real" places, "real" people, "real" life, but always with awareness that our concept of reality is bound up with imagination. It's therefore implicit that, in the fiction itself, the actual and the imagined merge. The initial impulse was personal and intensely imagined, but his work's connection with a wider reality accounts for its power and endurance. "I never began as a writer in order to become an operative," he said in 1988. "But I'm beginning to realize, almost in retrospect, that my work has addressed large social issues, and for some reason, in various contexts in other countries, this has reached out and grabbed people."[10] His obsessions catch our imaginations because, among other reasons, his writing homes in on historical moments that reflect wider social preoccupations.

In keeping with the intertwining of imagination and reality, his immersion in the subject matter involved visiting, or revisiting, the locations of the historical events to enable him to render the scenario convincingly. In "This Quiet Dust," he writes of visiting the Virginia locale of Nat Turner's 1831 insurrection, even though the place no longer much resembled the one Nat would have known. In "Auschwitz," he discusses his visit to Cracow and the death camps to write *Sophie's Choice*, even though no part of the immediate action occurs within the camp boundaries. Styron's purpose was to get a feel for the geography and the atmosphere. In turn, I have felt it important to familiarize myself with these and other settings and to make this part of the experience of rereading. My visits were not systematic, and I was never sure what I hoped to discover. Like Wolf, I sometimes wondered what business I had in a place where what happened could only be imagined, and where other occurrences were purely fictional. But these visits provided surprising insight into Styron's depictions of places and events. Elements of the work's creation suddenly revealed themselves. In a phrase from *Sophie's Choice*, these on-site experiences therefore "seem to have a place in this narrative."[11]

Styron's work is especially interesting with regard to actual settings and historical facts in that he does not simply use realist techniques nor merely wed actual settings and historical figures with fiction. He also merges drama and essay. This further complicates the relationship between fiction and fact even as it adds authenticity, and relevance, to the experience of reading his novels. To plunge into *Lie Down in Darkness*, *The Confessions of Nat Turner*, and *Sophie's Choice* is not to plunge into mere fiction, but into a contemplation of historical moments and the complexities of actual lives. They are novels not of escape but of engagement. To read them is to contemplate wartime America in a southern coastal town, antebellum Virginia, and 1940s Poland and postwar New York, and in the latter two novels we witness dramatizations of real people, augmented by historical documentation and/or memory, and, in the case of *Sophie's Choice*, overt essayistic commentary. This solidifies their status as fusions of different "levels of reality" beyond "the important world of fact." Unlike Julien Sorel or Anna Karenina, a man named Nat Turner did live as a slave in Southampton County. He did instigate an insurrection, and he probably did kill Margaret Whitehead. Beyond that is surmise, but Styron's is an informed but also intuited surmise not tied to every supposed fact, or, in other words, to the fallible written record. Sophie may be a fiction (though Styron did meet an Auschwitz survivor named Sophie), but, like her, you can enter St. Mary's Church in Rynek Główny, Cracow's Grand Square. You can hear the bugler play the *Hejnał Mariacki* from the higher tower every hour. On a visit to Auschwitz I today you enter the gas chamber a few hundred yards from the commandant's villa, stand amid the vast bleakness of Birkenau, and trudge the desolate path to the crematoriums. To witness these places is to know that these things happened and where. But Styron, among many others, has helped to make their role in history all the more vivid, just as he has provided us with characters who seem "as much our companions in this world" as historical figures like Nat Turner and Rudolph Höss.

So with Styron's work, if not with all artists', the relationship between art and life (not just the writer's but also the reader's) seems a valid part of the discussion. This was Styron's own approach. He writes, for instance, of Stingo's encounters with Leslie Lapidus that while "this saga, or episode, or fantasia" had "little direct bearing on Sophie and Nathan," it was "bound up into the fabric of that summer" (119–20). Styron's writing is part of a continuum in that it grows from and contributes to a zest for life and in turn feeds and informs the lives of its readers. Narrative scholarship has thus seemed the best approach. Moreover, it suits my experience of his work in discussing it with students. The seminar is the arena in which these two forms of rereading meet. When you discuss a book in class the two elements work together. Discussion soon reveals whether or not a work of art is saturated. Unsaturated art soon dries it up. Saturated art enables you simultaneously to discover through close observation and to witness new readers' refreshing visions not just of the novelist's craft but of their own lives as well. As Pearl Bell puts it, Styron's "genuine strength" is less "as a philosophic mind meditating on history" than in how he brings worlds and characters to life. Sophie, for instance, "seems less imagined than remembered. As we read her story, we bear witness to her fatality, and it is the word made flesh that remains with us in the end."[12]

As for having known the author, much time has passed and I can see my youthful admiration in perspective, but again I'm aware of the pitfalls. In a review of *The Second Flowering,* Styron praises Malcolm Cowley's observations about writers of the Lost Generation but provides a warning to anyone in such a position. "A lesser commentator," he writes, "might have made a terrible botch of it just because of this propinquity and friendship, giving us one of those familiar works of strained observation, at once fawning and self-flattering, where the subject is really victimized as if by a distorting lens held scant inches from the nose." Valuable criticism, Styron implies, balances admiration with clear observation and concise critique. Cowley expresses "honesty and devotion to what they stood for" but never assumes "a posture of adulation."[13] So I will draw on the personal because it's "bound up into the fabric" of rereading, but my focus is the work itself and the rewards of critical rereading.

One further thing I should explain in this introduction is my own frequent reference, with regard to Styron's work, to the kind of writer that Wolf cites. Rather than Styron's American forebears or contemporaries, my yardsticks are often those masters of nineteenth-century European realism, Flaubert, Dostoevsky, and Tolstoy. Styron has many literary forefathers, citing among others Hawthorne, Melville, Twain, and Faulkner. Other critics will continue to discuss Styron's work primarily in the contexts of American literature, as may I. But Sophie's story, in Bell's words, is "told in the grand manner of nineteenth-century fiction," and she possesses "something of the tragic stature and self-defeating complexity of such classic heroines as Tolstoy's Anna Karenina and Hardy's Sue Bridehead." Styron's obvious grounding in European literature as much as American, together with my own background, inclines me to such comparisons. Along with the twentieth-century triumvirate of Orwell, Koestler and Camus, whom I wrote about in *The Novels of William Styron,* they add an otherwise largely untapped dimension to discussion of Styron's achievement. He followed Flaubert's sense of the power of *le mot juste,* Tolstoy's view that "art begins where the little bits begin," and Dostoevsky's adherence to psychological realism, sometimes at the expense of outer realism.[14]

In terms of the book's structure, the two forms of rereading will most notably merge where close reading is informed by conversations with Styron or descriptions of an actual setting. The book involves visiting, or revisiting in some cases, the world of William Styron and the worlds about which he wrote. Thus chapter 2 is not about the books as such but about the man himself, at least as I knew him. I outline the context of my youthful reading of his work and explain the context out of which this rereading takes place. In doing so I argue that personality is an integral rather than subsidiary quality in the writing. Chapter 3 is about Styron's nonfiction, which, as already noted, has received far less attention than his novels yet is very much part of his achievement.[15] I argue that the essays—which one might take to be an author's most direct form of writing for publication—display great craft even as they elucidate some of the values, preoccupations, and complexities of a body of fiction that, in turn, incorporates an essayistic approach. Not least significant here, too, is *Darkness Visible,* both in literary terms and in terms of the fact that elements of Styron's writing can now be see in light of his struggles with clinical depression.

Both chapters 4 and 5 draw on *Sophie's Choice* as the culmination of Styron's art in the context of his two early novels. In chapter 4 I reflect, first, on the letters and stories in *Letters to My Father* as a way into assessing the significance of *Lie Down in Darkness.* A novel of huge artistic ambition if thematic bleakness, it combines realist, modernist, and most significantly—both for the novel form and for Styron's subsequent novels—cinematic techniques. But I also consider it in terms of the clinical depression Styron documents in *Darkness Visible* and in its relationship to *Sophie's Choice*. Chapter 5 begins with a commentary on *The Long March* but is mainly concerned with *Set This House on Fire*. It might have been nice to have visited the southern Italian landscape he writes about so vividly and sensuously in this novel, but one reason why this is a less successful novel is that there is less integration of character, place, and historical moment than we find in his major works. For all the evocation of a postwar setting amid the landscape of the Amalfi coast, the actual events of Sambuco seem superimposed. The narrator, Peter Leverett, is a lawyer involved in the Marshall Plan for the reconstruction of Europe, and the novel is a satire, among other things, on American materialism. But my dual interpretation reflects the novel's split nature and uncertainty of tone. The first reading highlights its clear faults when it is assessed as a realist novel, not least by comparing specific passages with similar ones in *Sophie's Choice*. The second reading, however, shows how focus on the novel as a psychological drama in the Dostoevskian mode, particularly with reference to *The Brothers Karamazov*, produces a more illuminating reading.

Chapter 6 and 7 concern Styron's two most important novels. Chapter 6 rereads *The Confessions of Nat Turner* in terms of his description of it in the author's note as "less an 'historical novel' in conventional terms than a meditation on history." Focusing on it primarily as a novel, rather than on the cultural contexts that so often shape discussion, my aim is to pinpoint its innovations and articulate some of the subtler reasons for its continued influence. It may in recent years have been viewed as a document from a past era, but it's also itself concerned with "the relativity of time" and our rereading of the past. The notion of the past haunting the present and the present returning through imagination to the past—all connected with the inextricable relationship between "reality" and imagination—is never far from the surface in Styron's world. I thus use Carlos Fuentes's observation that the novel is "a meeting place" between Styron and Nat Turner to show this to be true in more ways than might first be seen. The chapter ends with discussion of Styron's Marine Corps fiction in *The Suicide Run*, along with "Love Day" from *A Tidewater Morning*. Focusing on Styron's portrayal of masculinity, I assess ways in which these fragments of an unrealized vision contribute to our understanding of his achievement, and not least with regard to the portrayal of masculinity in *The Confessions of*

Nat Turner and *Sophie's Choice*. Chapter 7 then opens with a description of what it's like to visit Auschwitz today. The fact that Auschwitz still exists, with all its evidence, frames my rereading of *Sophie's Choice* in terms of how specific scenes relate to the novel's architecture. When I first wrote about the novel, I had never visited the camps. To have done so has changed elements of my perspective, not least in terms of driving home the realities that Styron's novel has helped to keep alive in our imaginations. Folding my rereading of the novel into the fact of Auschwitz, I seek to bring out the patterns of tenderness and terror that make up this depiction, not just of postwar New York and prewar and wartime Poland, but of human experience.

Just as chapter 2 breaks with scholarly convention by explaining the personal motivation for this book, while chapter 7 includes a memoir of visiting Auschwitz, so I return to critical memoir in the final chapter. Styron's career is framed by a train south to start *Lie Down in Darkness* and Stingo's train north near the end of *Sophie's Choice*. Chapter 8 mimics this in being built around an account of taking that same route during a research trip to Columbia University, the Library of Congress, and Duke University. In between reflections on these journeys many decades after those recounted by Styron, I describe visiting the Manhattan, Brooklyn, and Washington locations of *Sophie's Choice*, the Courtland and Southampton County setting of *The Confessions of Nat Turner*, and Styron's boyhood town, Newport News, the model for Port Warwick in *Lie Down in Darkness*. The Hilton Village area of Newport News is also the setting of Styron's title story in the final collection published in his lifetime, *A Tidewater Morning*. My discussion of "Shadrach" and the title tale concludes the critical rereading and leads, by way of an unpublished essay, "State of Writers in America," to reflections pondered on the train north to New York on Styron's literary legacy in terms of such contemporaries as Philip Roth, Norman Mailer, Joyce Carol Oates, Toni Morrison, and Cormac McCarthy. In sum, my aim in the book as a whole is to reflect on Styron the man and Styron's world, as well as on the work, and so to give a rounded assessment of his place in American writing and of his continued relevance to readers and writers in the twenty-first century.

CHAPTER 2

His Heart Laid Bare

Personality, Craft, Compassion, Intimacy

> If any ambitious man have a fancy to revolutionize, at one effort, the universal world of human thought, human opinion, and human sentiment, the opportunity is his own—the road to immortal renown lies straight, open, unencumbered before him. All that he has to do is write and publish a very little book. Its title should be simple—a few plain words—"My Heart Laid Bare." But this little book must be *true to its title*. No man dare write it. No man *could* write it, even if he dared. The paper would shrivel and blaze at every touch of the fiery pen.
>
> —EDGAR ALLAN POE, 1848

In *Rereading William Styron* I have in mind both the writing and the man. This chapter is ultimately a memoir, but the two forms of rereading I have outlined are entwined. The prose reflects the person. Styron's mature writing creates in many a reader a remarkable sense of intimacy. As the reams of letters among his papers testify, he was a writer with whom readers sought personal contact. This has to do with a combination of subject matter and voice. As Styron put it of F. Scott Fitzgerald, a true writer has "a distinctive and identifiable voice," which "is not really the same thing as a style; a style can be emulated, a voice cannot."[1] That voice need not suggest intimacy, but Styron's did, and this sense of an engaging personality is as much an objective quality of his writing as is any other.

Such a statement needs qualification. As Borges writes, "Fame is a form of incomprehension, perhaps the worst." Styron's readers may have been mistaken about the personality behind the words. Obviously, too, the writing is not the person. Edgar Allan Poe warns that the core self is inexpressible. Mikhail Bakhtin writes that it would be easier to pick yourself up by your own hair than to put yourself on the page. Moreover, those close to Styron commonly observe that the personality apparent in the writing is rather different from the man himself, or displays a very different side of him. Bill Styron, they tend to say, was not given to emotional intimacy, while "William Styron" was far more open. Of walking and talking with him, West explains in *William Styron, A Life* that "if one has taken these walks over many years and has listened to these talks before, one knows by now that Styron will have revealed very little about himself in what he has said." By this, West means that Styron gave "no real glimpse of" such things as "ambitions and desires," "obsessions and fears," "fantasies and dreams." For West, Styron was "the most private of authors," perhaps "too private a man to be approached directly," and best understood through his "immensely and painfully self-revealing" writing. Styron's neighbor and friend Arthur Miller went so far as to suggest that the work and the man were distinct. "He's a very subterranean person," Miller said in a 1982 documentary. "I don't necessarily equate the books with him. There are two guys in there, and that's a good thing. It generally makes for a more interesting writer."[2] Meanwhile, Alexandra Styron's *Reading My Father* seems to confirm William James's view that personality is in no sense unitary, but dependent upon the relationship of each of us to one another and upon the given moment of a given life.

Such viewpoints intrigue me. I knew the man in what his daughter calls "his mellow phase," when he'd evidently become more self-revealing. But my feeling that the man and his writing were closely linked raises questions about what "knowing" someone—especially an author—might mean. Borges famously articulates the writer/writing paradox in a brief statement titled "Borges and I." "I live, let myself go on living," he writes, "so that Borges may contrive his literature, and this literature justifies me. It is no effort for me to confess that he has achieved some valid pages, but those pages cannot save me, perhaps because what is good belongs to no one, not even to him, but rather to the language and to the tradition." Borges was speaking here for all who write anything remotely personal. There is the person an instant of whom is recorded on the page or screen, and there is the flesh-and-blood being who exists, ages, and dies. At the end of the essay Borges encapsulates our paradoxical sense of "personality" in the written word with the statement, "I do not know which of us has written this page." To read is to hear a voice. We may consider it brilliant or stupid, cruel or compassionate, distant or intimate, but if it's in any way personal we sense personality, just as we do in getting to "know" someone. Might the physical being's outward personality be very different from the personality we witness in the writing? There are those who see our inner selves as our truer selves, and our social selves are an act. But despite such complexities, my view remains that one of the strengths of Styron's later writing is that he doesn't masquerade; he doesn't toy with the reader; he is not a trickster, but bares his heart and mind—to the extent that such a thing is possible—in expressing his sense of the truth. In my limited experience, he was like that as a man too, and this may suggest the spirit in which his works were written.[3]

The difference between West and Miller's perspective and mine may be wholly explicable. I was young, inexperienced, in awe of getting to "know" a writer I admired. I may well have paid too little attention to our actual interaction. Perhaps I didn't really get to know him at all. Perhaps my sense that the man and the work converged was the result of befriending him after reading it, and only as a youth meeting someone in late middle age, and only at intervals. Perhaps, victim of the "form of incomprehension" known as "fame," I simply projected the personality of his writing onto him and approached him in that light. Yet still, I can't ignore that experience. Moreover, that urge to testify is rooted as deeply in critical writing as in "creative" writing. To reread a writer might involve the desire to reevaluate his work, but if one knew the writer, there's also the inevitable recalling of the person. Whether or not these two meanings are distinct, the brutal, tragic truth is that artistic enterprise, which seems a sideshow (the "ridiculous profession," as Styron described novel writing to Donald Harington), remains solidly there, while life itself turns out to be ephemeral.[4] Our "real" lives— so tangible minute by minute, as we breathe and taste and talk and tap our keyboards—slip away, while the written word, or any kind of construction from a painting to a symphony, a front stoop to a space ship, remains. As Styron writes in *Selected Letters*, citing a Hippocrates aphorism, *Ars longa, vita brevis,* "Art is long, life is short" (78, 141).

Nevertheless, my premise is that in the case of Styron an understanding of the man aids an understanding of the work. Primo Levi observes that "what we commonly mean by 'understand' coincides with 'simplify,'" but simplification can still involve accuracy.[5] Bill Styron produced the work he did because of the man he was. In keeping with his ruminative nature, he "*carved* those novels," as Miller put it in the documentary, with painstaking care and indifference to literary fashions. He never rushed to produce. He probably could not have even had he wanted to. He crafted a voice, in his best work, every word of which had been pondered, and so created a sense of intimacy that readers still respond to. But while the personality, craft, compassion, and sense of intimacy exist in the books, we do have testimony that the work matched the man. The evidence is in memories of the man and in the urge, on the part of his friends and associates, to record them. About seven hundred people packed St. Bartholomew's Church in Manhattan for the memorial service on 2 February 2007, and readings and speeches came from an array of names. But the pews were filled with ordinary folk. William Styron was an admired author, and Bill Styron a much-loved and respected man. So it's by way of a portrait of the man himself—a portrait, that is, of one side of him, as seen by me and by others who approached him as a well-known novelist—that I've chosen to begin my rereading of his work.

Of the two kinds of rereading I outlined in chapter 1, the first has to do with the time we spend immersed in a given work, bringing it to life in our minds and in terms of our own experiences and dispositions and—through writing and/or teaching—helping to nuance it for others. The second kind of rereading is an activity we engage in on different levels through our lives. Any kind of reflective life involves re-creating and rereading past experiences. So far as reflecting on literature is concerned, this kind of rereading involves a contextual temporality. Weeks, months, years go by while we read, get to know, reflect on, and move away from or return to a writer, just as we do with people, places, and ideas. This second kind of rereading is "personal" in the sense of applying on different levels to all readers in ways usually known only to the individual concerned. We encounter our key writers in specific, usually formative moments. For Malcolm Cowley there were the writers of the Lost Generation. For Nicholson Baker, author of *U and I: A True Story* (1991), it was John Updike. For Styron himself there was, West notes, "a fixation" on Irwin Shaw in his Paris heyday, or, as Styron expresses it in *Sophie's Choice*, "an author of the stature of John O'Hara," who, while not his most "illustrious" literary hero, represents for Stingo "the kind of writer a young editor might go out and get drunk with" (5).

Two examples of how Styron's work, too, demonstrably inspires a sense of intimacy and identification appear in Joe McGinniss's *Heroes* (1976) and Michael Mewshaw's *Do I Owe You Something?* (2003). For McGinniss, Styron "seemed a hero" thanks to *Lie Down in Darkness*. "I had read it four times," he writes. "It was a fine, rare, desperate book; one that scared me more the older I got. I could not imagine how Styron could have written it at twenty-five." Ostensibly McGinniss seeks out Styron "to talk about heroes, and illusion, and the heroic effort required to live without illusion, or beyond the boundaries of the illusions one has been conditioned to accept." He wants "to feel a closeness to Styron, a degree of intimacy, a sense of shared experience," even if, beyond being writers, "there had been none." He turns up at Styron's summer home in Vineyard Haven, gets drunk with him, and rises in the morning to make a pie with Styron's last tin of expensive crabmeat. Within the "false intimacy" induced by alcohol, they've discussed *Sophie's Choice,* and Styron has told him that "the idea for it had come to him one night during a dream in which he had seen writing on the wall." "So that was it," comments McGinniss: "Joyce Carol Oates heard voices; William Styron saw writing in his dreams."[6]

No great revelation comes from this meeting, and McGinniss ends the book deciding that "hand-me-down solutions" and "prefabricated myths" no longer suffice. He cites Joseph Campbell writing in *The Hero with a Thousand Faces* that "the problem is nothing if not that of rendering the modern world spiritually significant—or rather—nothing if not that of making it possible for men and women to come to full human maturity through the conditions of contemporary life."[7] Like Campbell, McGinniss thinks that to achieve this one must construct one's "own mosaic," or "own myth, slowly, painfully, piece by piece." On the other hand, he deftly captures aspects of Styron's disarming mixture of gruffness, surliness, vulnerability, and, ultimately, amiability in a portrait that reminded me of the comment of Styron's editor, Bob Loomis, at the memorial service that Styron "was fully, intensely human." McGinniss discovers this, although as my next chapter illustrates, there's not a little of Styron in the notion of the individual, shorn of illusions, slowly and painfully constructing a personal "mosaic." McGinniss learns what Styron learned through reading the likes of Camus. The paradox of finding self-authenticity is that it may take a personal hero or two to remind you that you must do it alone.

Michael Mewshaw, no less than McGinniss, was drawn to Styron through a sense of wonder at the novels and the personality they suggested. "In Styron's case," he writes, "I had always had trouble separating the man from his work." *Set This House on Fire* left Mewshaw "longing to live in Italy, praying to publish a novel," and "eager to meet" Styron. As with McGinniss, Styron befriended Mewshaw and gave writerly advice. Mewshaw writes of how on every rereading of one letter he is moved by "Styron's generosity of spirit, his collegiality and readiness to assume an obligation to a neophyte for no better reason than that we both, though vastly different in talent and temperament, were committed to writing." Al Styron testifies that her father "responded to almost everyone who wrote him," and his generosity toward aspiring writers in particular shows itself in numerous letters among his papers, not the least engaging of which are to Donald Harington.[8] But McGinniss's and Mewshaw's accounts are remarkably similar not only in revealing that generosity but in the way both are drawn to the idea of "intimacy" with Styron. Equally, however, in all three cases the feeling of a bond with the man they imagine Styron to be arises directly from qualities in his prose; the reading came before the meeting. So while, like McGinniss, Mewshaw, Harington, and others, I was lucky enough to have Styron accommodate my youthful fantasy of befriending a famous author, my purpose in including this personal element in the book is to emphasize it as an important aspect of his work. The later writing, if not perhaps all the earlier writing, is infused with qualities—sensitivity, vulnerability, humanity, compassion—that readers respond to under the guise of the "personal." True as it obviously is that the written self is not the living self, Styron at least sought to write as directly as possible—in his novels no less than in his letters and essays—about life as he saw it.

Perhaps we are drawn to certain writers through our own circumstances or disposition, but the evocation of intimacy is not a quality of the prose of all writers. Perhaps the writers who tend to create this sense of intimacy are those who write most directly about pressing issues rather than aslant (even though, as Emily Dickinson reminds us, indirection has its place). Writers of this kind, such as Orwell, Koestler, and Baldwin, along with Camus, all temper Styron's modernist influences. Rima Reck's account of Camus in *Literature and Responsibility*, for instance, echoes my sense of Styron. As Reck notes, Camus said in his Nobel Prize speech that "in my eyes, art is not a solitary pleasure" but a way of offering readers "a privileged image of common sufferings and common joys. Thus art forces the artist not to isolate himself." In turn, toward the end of his career Styron said that he treasured the ability not only "to have been able to transport people" but also to have produced something that they "regard as important in their lives." "In the end," he continued, "you realize you have gotten yourself involved in that world for an ulterior motive—to make other people feel that ultimate emotional and intellectual effect."[9]

For all Stingo's grandiose dreams, *Sophie's Choice* makes it clear that the writers he sought to emulate were those who inspired a passionate engagement in the process of living. Stingo aims for the "ardor and soaring wings of the Melville or the Flaubert or the Tolstoy or the Fitzgerald who had the power to rip my heart out and keep a part of it and who each night, separately and together, were summoning me to their incomparable vocation" (12–13). While an awareness, even in Stingo, of the sadness of "all ambition—especially when it came to literature" (24) tempers such flights of fancy (undercut, too, by the repetition of "the," which turns the authors into inanimate objects of worship), nevertheless, the novel's whole tone and nature testify to Styron's belief that such aspirations can produce great art. "The aim of an artist is not to solve a problem irrefutably but to make people love life in all its countless, inexhaustible manifestations," wrote Tolstoy. "If I were told that I could write a novel whereby I might irrefutably establish what seemed to me to be the correct point of view on social problems, I would not devote even two hours to such a novel; but if I were to be told that what I should write would be read in about twenty years' time by those who are now children and that they would laugh and cry over it and love life, I would devote all my own life and all my energies to it."[10] Such a sentiment helps explain the aim and effect of both *The Confessions of Nat Turner* and *Sophie's Choice,* as well as the difference in perspective between those who admire these novels and those who baulk at Styron's refusal to seek to "irrefutably establish" a supposedly "correct point of view" (in other words, the critic's point of view) on the social problems dramatized.

Most of the writers mentioned not only create this sense of intimacy but also are consummate stylists who ensure that the smallest nuance informs the whole. Styron's advice to aspiring writers invariably emphasizes this quality of what, following Henry James, I have called "saturation." Styron wrote to Mewshaw that words were "not lumpish things to fling on the paper but units of the thought-process to be used meticulously." He advised Harington that writing about childhood required "hairbreadth precision." Of a draft of *The Cherry Pit* (1965), he admonished Harington for "loss of control," explaining that "monologs must be *action*" and "kept at a fever pitch of narrative excitement," but later he added that "the secret of art" was providing the reader with "the supremely necessary" rather than, as Harington was doing, "gobs and gobs of the totally unnecessary." Hence, Styron's novels at their best are built page by page, scene by scene, into integrated wholes.[11]

Clearly, Flaubert and Tolstoy are models. As with his "master Flaubert," a word or phrase often reveals far more than it at first suggests. Where Tolstoy writes of "how the artist Bryullov had transformed a pupil's drawing with a slight alteration and had explained to him that 'Art begins where the tiny bit begins,'" so Styron's attention to detail reaps constant reward and the unending prospect of surprise. In Tolstoy, wrote Dmitri Merejkowski, "one quiver of a muscle in the face" can "express the unutterable."[12] The same is so in Styron at his best. The intimacy he creates through voice is matched by the rewards of intimate knowledge of the work itself. As with the brushstrokes of a masterful painting, an attentive reader is drawn ever closer to minutiae and rewarded with fresh insight. Clarity and directness, therefore, do not preclude the need for close reading, or rereading. In the best writers it goes hand in hand with subtleties that even several readings may miss.

So the construction of the intimate voice encourages close reading but can also lead to seeking out the writer himself. I didn't know that I was following the footsteps of McGinnis, Mewshaw, Harington, and others, but we each experienced the same impulse, and Styron's no less generous response to me is the basis of the following portrait. This insight into the man behind the books contextualizes *Rereading William Styron* as a reassessment of his writing that draws whatever authority it has from a mixture of personal subjectivity and scholarly objectivity. Styron's openness toward me as a young scholar—or would-be writer, as, in common with many young people, I presented myself to be—was startling, and this book is in part a journey back to the friendship that grew from my painfully earnest introductory letter. Since the journey is cyclical, so too is the structure of this book. I became interested in Styron the man through his work. Now that the man has gone, and we have nothing but his "monument to time's attrition," as he put it in passing, I return to it unencumbered by concerns about what he might think of my assessment. In a very real sense, therefore, this book can now be more overtly subjective but also more objective than *The Novels of William Styron*.

My journey through the writing to the man himself began in a place as strange as Brockport, a town on the Erie Canal in upstate New York. It was August 1985, and I was about to return to Britain after studying for an MA. I told Professor Edward Murray, author of *The Cinematic Imagination* (1972), about my plans to start a PhD at the University of Nottingham on postwar American writers.

"Don't forget William Styron," he said as I was leaving his office. "He wrote *The Confessions of Nat Turner.*"

I must have looked quizzical because he went on to tell me that Turner was a slave who led an insurrection in 1831, that Styron was a white southerner, and that his novel, told from Turner's viewpoint and published in the late sixties, caused quite a controversy. "But read *Lie Down in Darkness* and *Sophie's Choice,* too," he said. "Novelists don't come much better."

As an undergraduate in Britain, I had heard of Styron only in passing. Our American literature lecturer pointed out a joke about *The Confessions of Nat Turner* in Kurt Vonnegut's *Slaughterhouse-Five.* During a radio discussion about "whether the novel was dead or not," one critic says that "it would be a nice time to bury" it "now that a Virginian, one hundred years after Appomattox, had written *Uncle Tom's Cabin.*" Styron's work was not on the module, and the lecturer expressed incredulity when, back in Britain, I told him that the novelist would feature in my thesis. This was a routine British response to Styron. When, in our first exchange of letters, I explained that to write on his work was to forge a lonesome trail through the Sceptered Isle, Styron replied that while he didn't "feel quite like Edmund Wilson, who called your countrymen 'the despicable English,'" it was true that he'd "felt no warmth" toward Britain over the years "and plainly the feeling is mutual."[13] But then the lecturer was only following the crowd, and hadn't, aged twenty-four, as I had that late summer and autumn, read Styron's four novels in successive weeks. Literature never felt the same again, not just because of *Lie Down in Darkness, The Confessions of Nat Turner,* and *Sophie's Choice* as novels, but because the first sent me to, or back to, Fitzgerald, Joyce, Woolf, Faulkner, Robert Penn Warren, and others; the second to Douglass, Booker T. Washington, Du Bois, Baldwin, Ellison, Malcolm X, Morrison, Henry Louis Gates Jr., and beyond; while the third drew me not merely to Holocaust testimonies and the history of totalitarianism but also to the writings of Melville, Dickinson, Wolfe, McCullers, and others, the music of Mozart, Brahms, Bach, and questions about art and aspiration, food and drink, parents and friendship, sex and death. My spirit of intellectual and emotional inquiry received a seismic boost. It was this experience—stemming from one person but flowing out to embrace the perspectives of so many others—that brought about the change of emphasis after Murray's recommendation.

In response to my hesitancy, Murray had told me that I'd find the novels in the Drake Memorial Library on the Brockport campus. Perhaps because he mentioned *The Confessions of Nat Turner* first, the novel's opening comes to mind when I think of that day. Just as Nat dreams of suspended time, so I recall crossing a deserted campus in high summer, the sun seeming "to cast no shadow anywhere." Nat, alone in a boat, sees only the distant shore, "unpeopled, silent," and senses that everything will "exist forever unchanged like this beneath the light of a motionless afternoon sun."[14] The novels were in the basement, which, in the nature of library basements, was windowless, weatherless, timeless. Only the hum of air-conditioning accompanied my footsteps. I fingered the stacks and found the two later novels: one black, the other pale blue, both with Styron's signature embossed in gold, low and small, on the front cover. I read those opening pages and then the start of *Sophie's Choice*. "In those days cheap apartments were almost impossible to find in Manhattan so I had to move to Brooklyn" (3). And so began "my voyage of discovery" (25).

At the Strand Book Store on Broadway, I found first editions of the four novels, including a signed copy of *Lie Down in Darkness* that set me back eighty dollars; then I flew home and quickly narrowed my studies exclusively to Styron. Serendipity struck again. Jim West, a long time before *William Styron, A Life,* happened to be in Cambridge that winter of 1985–86, so I caught a bus and traveled through the snowy Midlands to meet him. At the end of the two days, he told me, out of the blue, precisely what I wanted to hear: that I resembled the young Styron. This naturally reinforced whatever sense of identification and fate was already beginning to glow within me. I had to be the author's long-lost son, destined not only to write about him but to have my fate somehow join with his. Having stumbled upon the essays of Michel de Montaigne as a teenager, I knew that the Frenchman grossly understated the case when he observed that "the fortunes of above half the world, for want of a record, stir not from their place, and vanish without duration."[15] But I imagined that if I could achieve the humble yet real status of befriending this great author, my presence on earth would, for a time at least, be justified. Once again, Styron's words echo in my ear: "Oh Stingo, how I envy you! So long before the slack tides of inanition, the pooping out of ego and ambition!" (12).

Before I left Cambridge, Jim advised me to attend the Seventh Annual Symposium on Modern American Writers at Winthrop College, South Carolina, that April. More serendipity: there had never before been a conference on Styron, and there hasn't been one since. Indeed, whereas conferences regularly contain panels arranged by The Philip Roth Society or The Cormac McCarthy Society and panels on many other writers, there is never one on Styron, and he has no society. He would have grunted at such a notion. Asked if he would like to attend the Winthrop Symposium, he told the organizer, Eva Mills, that it would feel like attending his own wake. The fact that he's never attracted the *cult* of personality, and that years have passed since anyone put together even a panel on his work, may simply be because his profile is less marked, but it might be that his readers don't think in such terms. Responses seem personal rather than group-orientated. Despite being a family man with many friends, he was at heart a solitary Sisyphus, self-condemned to roll his rock: "hunted and haunted," as Al Styron describes him,[16] but by the burden of talent and vision, and unreconciled guilt and grief, rather than by symposia envy.

"I can't tell you how bored I am by academic criticism in general," he would warn me in 1988, admitting that, having read an essay of mine on his "reputation," he'd begun "to wonder what really" could "be gained by our getting together."

> "Reputation" seems to be a critical conceit, with no connection to the literary reality that means anything to me. You say, for instance, that my reputation in the U.S. is "far from settled." But what the hell does that mean? I have long been aware, through the grapevine, that my work here, while far from neglected in academe, has never really received the high-powered attention that some of my colleagues have received, with the 28 books written about them, or the 2,001 articles or the 12 symposia, their reputations presumably more settled than my own. I find all this nauseating. When is a "reputation" "settled"?
>
> Perhaps I would not be quite so insouciant if there were not many other more palatable signs that my reputation (always excluding England), for want of a better word, is alive and well. I get letters almost every day from all over the world about my work; a passionate letter of solidarity from a reader in Poland or Chile is worth about 47 condescending blowjobs from an assistant professor at Kansas State. Also, if my ego needed further stroking (which it doesn't) I could point to the fact that in the past three months I've received news of being given the two highest honors an American writer can receive from his *peers*—the only other group, aside from readers, that a writer should care about in

terms of approbation. (My well-known modesty prevents me from naming the source of these accolades, they will be made public.) No academic critics were involved, thank God.

What I think I'm objecting to in all the above is connected with something you alluded to in your essay—not simply my "hatred" of critics (hatred being a more youthful emotion) but my present mellow conviction that they are totally irrelevant.[17]

Naturally I thenceforth avoided any suggestion that I was a critic rather than an interested reader, or would-be writer, or even an illegitimate son, who had somehow wandered off the beaten track into Styron's farmhouse on Rucum Road. Whatever mountain Styron was heaving his existential boulder up, it was evidently not for academic applause. Literary glory may have been a youthful impulse; later he cared only for the respect of peers and the "solidarity" of readers. But equally there was, in Al's words, his "monumental"—even "all-consuming— artistic imperative." Since his mother's death from cancer when he was fourteen, he had sought "to do that Camusian thing, which in effect is merely saying, 'Kilroy was here,' but to do it with a sense of nobility and dignity."[18] Perhaps, too, without quite realizing it until his later years, he had sought through his writing to stave off the clinical depression that may in part have stemmed from early bereavement but was also perhaps genetic.

Yet there it was: a symposium on William Styron. Like Stingo, I was "fortune's darling." "It is true," goes the voice in my head once more, "that I had traveled great distances for one so young, but my spirit had remained landlocked, and I was unacquainted with love and all but a stranger to death" (24). This was my first conference and a heady experience. Giddy with the conversations, the debates, papers, opinions, and the beer and wine, I barely slept, and paced the lush green quads beneath pink cherry blossom with fevered energy. Eva Mills told me that the Winthrop library housed the papers of Nathan Asch, author of a 1930s memoir, *The Road: In Search of America*, and that I should take a look. I recall fingering a letter to Asch from Malcolm Cowley with the reverential awe that, in Styron's words on Stingo's certitude, "I only ever recall feeling up to the aged of twenty-two, or perhaps twenty-five" (67). As Pascal counsels, "A trifle consoles us because a trifle upsets us." There and then, aware of Styron's writing habits and inspired by Asch's manuscripts, I crossed the blossom-speckled quads, purchased 2B Venus Velvet pencils and yellow legal pads, and began writing. Not that I got much done. My happiness, to quote Fitzgerald, "approached such an ecstasy" that I "had to walk it away in quiet streets and lanes with only fragments of it to distill into little lines in books."[19]

The next thing, it became as clear to me as it had to McGinniss, Mewshaw, and Harington, was that I must meet the man. His decline of the symposium invitation at least made contact seem possible. More tantalizing yet, a guest speaker, the French novelist Thérèse de Saint Phalle, not only had his phone number but called the house in Roxbury while I was with her. (In retrospect, it was surely a good thing that he was away at the time.) I gathered all the information about him I could. Beyond a certain age, a reader or critic of this kind would resemble a stalker, but I was innocent in my interest and, not much beyond Stingo's age, could trade on the charm of youth. I read everything, and then read it all again. As homework on how to behave on meeting a famous writer, I supplemented it both with McGinniss's book and with Philip Roth's *The Ghost Writer.* McGinniss's Styron was a cantankerous, heavy-drinking, but not unkind man, certainly someone I could crack a beer with, even if I'd need to stay on his right side. Meanwhile, *The Ghost Writer* became my training manual. I would be Nathan Zuckerman to Styron's E. I. Lonoff, or Philip Roth to Bernard Malamud. From Winthrop I headed north for Durham and Duke University to examine the *Sophie's Choice* holograph. I merely leafed through the 985 hand-written pages—rejected material and all—but I knew, in my Churchill-inspired British spiritedness, that this could not be the end, or even the beginning of the end, but must in fact be only the end of the beginning.

The Winthrop Symposium brought my first academic publication. Not yet knowing Styron's attitude toward huge swathes of literary academia, I considered it a vital credential. With a degree of wisdom, I see in hindsight, I had accepted the invitation to contribute to a volume from the symposium by opting to write on *Set This House on Fire*, not because it was reviewed in Britain on the day I was born—though I was not unconscious of such coincidences—but as the least discussed of the novels. My paper "The British Reception to the Work of William Styron" had itself been a masterpiece of gap-filling. As the attitude of the lecturer who laughed at Vonnegut's joke indicated, it was a bit of a non-subject. Indeed, with one paper and an invitation to submit an essay for publication, I was now Britain's "leading Styron scholar." So, when the volume finally arrived, I turned with excitement and trepidation to the notes on contributors to check that I was indeed a scholar of significance, and that they had spelt my name correctly, only to read of the contributor in question that "her dissertation is on Styron." Regendered at a stroke, I should have seen right then the distance between the written and the living self. Still, it gave me an excuse to show off my triumph in a self-deprecating manner. Moreover, I found my name right beneath Styron's on the title page, and this gave me the kind of "consoling proximity" to glamor that Nick Carraway speaks of at the start of *The Great Gatsby*.[20]

I embarked with Raskolnikovian intensity upon my study of Styron in dingy lodgings that, situated beneath the rock of Nottingham Castle, were as perpetually in shadow as the valley of Tramonti Styron depicts in *Set This House on Fire*. My version of Stingo's "grime-encrusted window" (10) faced Castle Boulevard, a main city thoroughfare. To open it was to invite gritty traffic fumes in on the November wind. Envisaging the Connecticut greenery as my escape route from this suffocating, sunless existence, I now wrote Styron a letter requesting an interview. The reply might as well have been an invitation from Zeus to hang out on Mount Olympus. Handwritten in blue ink, it arrived in a classy, cream envelope with "William Styron" printed on the back. It announced that he "would welcome the opportunity" of meeting me and hoped for "a fruitful and enjoyable get-together."[21] In my grim room I dedicated a bottle of 1981 Bulgarian Cabernet Sauvignon to my potential savior. Within days I had booked my flight for the following April.

It was then that I nearly made that fatal error of sending not only my *Papers on Language and Literature* essay but one called "William Styron and the Critical Canon," which drew on my Winthrop talk and referred to his British reputation as "far from settled." Even as I forged ahead with my writing, anticipating my climb up Mount Olympus, that second letter dropped onto the doormat. Fortunately, it softened in tone. He didn't, it turned out, feel "hatred" for critics, and at least I wasn't an assistant professor at Kansas State. Moreover, he found the "cultural chasm" I spoke of "fascinating." "Why is a great writer like Chateaubriand virtually unknown in the English-speaking world? Why is John Cowper Powys unknown in America? Why is Anthony Powell such a dull drag to me and most of my friends? Why do we find Anita Brookner weird? Why is Goethe so opaque in English?" He ended with, "Looking forward to seeing you," and I realized that my plans were alive.[22] Nowadays I'm aware of the irony of the exchange in terms of the mismatch between my immature agenda and the viewpoint of the man I would meet. On the train south, Stingo talks to Sophie of what they will do when they "get settled." "How do you mean 'get settled,'" asks Sophie

(460). Naturally, since being in the text of life—having a profile, a status, standing, prominence, a *reputation*—was my own great concern, I assumed that it would be Styron's. But perhaps my wrongheadedness, my very diction, was a blessing. Perhaps he latched onto that word *settled* precisely because it was Stingo's word to Sophie, and so a sign of forgivable naivety. At any rate, the bruise the letter left had long faded by the time I packed my suitcases with books for him to sign, along with the dog-eared copy of Montaigne's essays that kept me company in those years, soared skyward, and hurtled toward the city of Sophie, Nathan, and Stingo, booted and spurred to face my fate.

Decades have passed since the red-and-black Bonanza bus wound out of a misty Manhattan and up through the Connecticut countryside to Danbury, but the memory remains as crisp as that spring morning. I arrived hours before the agreed time and spent them on a bench outside Danbury Library, listening on my Walkman to Mozart's *Prague* Symphony and the Sinfonia Concertante in E-flat Major, which so moves Sophie on pages 93 and 94 of the Random House hardback of *Sophie's Choice*. Dimly conscious of distant traffic, I read a limited edition of the novella-length tale "Shadrach" and, as the sunshine broke into fullness, gazed intermittently at the billowing clouds, which seemed whiter than any I had ever seen. In a dim liquor store, I bought Styron a bottle of Chianti (remembering that this is what E. I. Lonoff uncorks for his meal with Nathan Zuckerman at the start of *The Ghost Writer*). In the florist's next door, I bought Rose Styron an eight-dollar bouquet. Then I sat and waited until a pale green Mercedes slid to the curb. Out stepped a heavy-set, gray-haired, jowly man in slacks, a shirt open at the collar, with a slightly world-weary expression in his heavy-lidded eyes. Styron and I greeted each other warily, and he weaved the Mercedes almost silently through the verdurous, sun-dappled lanes up a hill to his yellow pre–Civil War farmhouse.

"Look at this crap," he said, pulling a wad from his mailbox on the small, gravel driveway. "Ninety percent of my mail is junk mail. You have a mailbox and they stuff it with junk." Pausing only to point to the initials *W.S.* on the doormat ("Well-known English writer," he chuckled), he led me through to the kitchen, introduced me to Rose, and disappeared upstairs. I liked Rose instantly. She had a sparkly smile and a fine bone structure and was altogether the most beautiful sixty-year-old I had ever encountered.

"I guess people come up here all the time," I ventured.

Rose frowned. "Oh no," she said. "This is real nice for Bill."

I tried again. "I've read your poems."

Rose beamed and we got talking. She told me about a disconcerting dinner they had had with President Reagan. As she did so, Styron came clumping down the old oak stairs and walked through into the kitchen.

"Reagan's a nice man," she said. "He just doesn't know anything. We asked serious questions and he just laughed them off and went back to telling stories about Hollywood. It was the time of the Libyan crisis, and he tried to joke about it. He's a nice *man*."

"He's *not* a nice man," Styron grumbled. "He's a complete jerk."

"Well, I was just saying how we went to dinner and he was likeable enough."

"Mmph." He disappeared again, this time down a narrow passage to some other part of the sprawling, L-shaped home.

"Maybe I'd better go in and talk with him."

"Maybe you had. I don't want to be found keeping you."

Styron sat reading the paper in the spacious lounge. A cigar smoldered in an ashtray on a table beside him. I looked around. The living room was as cozy, plain, and neat as Lonoff's; a large, beamy room with beige carpeting, armchairs, two cream-colored sofas at right angles around a square rug before the hearth, long, crowded bookshelves either side of the fireplace, a grand piano in the corner, a staircase and balcony, a CD-player, a dining table and chairs, every surface, chairs included, piled with books. The walls were bare but for a large painting of a faraway building on a flat horizon and, above a bar lined with empty bottles, a snapshot taped haphazardly to a beam, and what looked like a death mask. To the right there was a stained-glass window, and to the left, beyond the oak table, a wall-length window with French doors and a view of dark-limbed trees and a sloping lawn that stretched to fields and woodland. "Purity. Serenity. Simplicity. Seclusion. All one's concentration and flamboyance and originality reserved for the grueling, exalted, transcendent calling." I look around, mouthing Zuckerman's words. "This is how I will live."[23]

Only then did I notice Styron peering at me over his newspaper from the armchair that completed the wagon train around the hearth. He motioned for me to take a seat, picked up his cigar, and puffed at it with a strange, spluttering, popping sound, as if trying to expel all remnants of smoke as soon as he'd sucked it in. Its blue haze uncurled through the sunlight toward the shadows of the raftered ceiling, and the pleasant aroma began to fill the room.

I had with me thirty or so three-by-five cards. Whenever I thought I might dry up, I flipped to the next question. We talked all morning and for another hour after lunch, but all too soon I felt it was time to go.

"You're leaving?" Styron responded to my intimations. "I thought you'd at least stay over, since you've come all the way from foggy Albion. Still, I'll drive you to the bus."

"I'll stay then," I said.

"Good. When's your flight?"

"Monday."

"So you'll stay the weekend."

The days slid by. Over meals and on walks along the Shepaug River at Judd's Bridge, "Bill," Rose, and I discussed southern cooking, Herbert Aptheker, Eugene Genovese, Arthur Schlesinger (a friend!), Carly Simon (another friend!), Norman Mailer (they'd made up), summer camps, young love, youth being wasted on youth, extramarital sex, Humphrey Bogart, literary thieves, quail, risotto, caffeine, Italians, Chianti, Chablis, insomnia, soft-shell crabs, Michelob, English women, a career as a writer—"I have no regrets, none whatever"—whiskey, abortion, the Kennedys, Marilyn Monroe, Arthur Miller, Larry and Bertha (the Styrons' gardener and cleaner), the novel as a form of theater, the Styron's Irish au pair from the sixties, Mary Murphy, who worked for Pan Am, became chief stewardess, and died in the Lockerbie atrocity, Dublin "Colleens" who put their hands over their chests when men look at them, dogs, music, Brahms's *Alto Rhapsody*, the slow movement of Beethoven's Fourth Symphony, and no doubt other things I don't recall.

"Three years ago," Rose told me one day when Styron had disappeared to write, "you'd never have gotten to see him. You have good timing."

"You mean since his breakdown," I said nonchalantly, "he's looked up from his writing pad?"

I had no idea, at the time, what this "breakdown" amounted to, nor much inclination to find out. "Every one, knowing intimately all the complexities of his own circumstances," writes Tolstoy in *Anna Karenina*, "involuntarily assumes that these complexities and the difficulty of clearing them up are peculiar to his own personal condition, and never thinks that others are surrounded by similar complexities." So far as I was concerned, Styron just lived the life of a famous author, shielded by success from what Cass Kinsolving in *Set This House on Fire* calls "the *fleas* of life," let alone the hornets. "It might have appeared, to the untrained eye, that my father was coasting rather serenely into old age," writes Al Styron. My eye was as untrained as they come. Just as Al had done as a child, I viewed his "success as both varying and eternal," and a "breakdown" seemed to me to be merely an episode in the glamorous melodrama of a literary life. But the complex truth would surface eventually, and I'd grow old enough to see it. As a step toward that, Styron must soon after this have begun describing his illness in what would become *Darkness Visible,* the first copy of which I would see on his dining-room table on Martha's Vineyard in July 1990. Like Stingo, I was innocent of the shadows beside the sunlight, though aware that on some level, as with the story of Mary Murphy, fortune and misfortune wove a perpetual dance and either might pull any of us into their swirl toward delight or disaster.[24]

Meanwhile, I was on a different kind of alert. Styron had promised to read the opening to his new novel. I dared not be absent when he chose the moment. When he focused on me he really did focus, but when we were not talking he plodded the same dogged, inward-looking way through the creaking passageways of his house. Sometimes he cleared his throat as if to warn of his approach, but much of the time he just grunted in passing—and often we did pass unexpectedly at some intersection between rooms—or simply ignored me. In Al's phrase, at such times "he wasn't exactly *there.*"[25]

Then one late afternoon he said, "I've been writing. Would you like to hear some of it?"

Would I? "I'd love to, yes."

"Would you?" He looked concerned. "Just a few pages to see how it starts? It may be inflicting too much on you. I feel that since you're at least partially on a quest to see what I'm up to, this might be helpful. I haven't read a word of it to anyone. I'm trying to establish the voice, the tone, and it may be that I'll have to discard some of this." As the evening drew in, he switched on a lamp and I sat opposite while he shuffled his yellow legal sheets, cleared his throat, and began. "In the year following the end of World War II, having returned from the Pacific to my home in Tidewater Virginia, I was in moral and physical disarray. My existence had become so aimless as to give new meaning to that gray old phrase 'at loose ends.' For the first time in my life I was faced with what appeared to be almost nothing to occupy my hours intelligently, or enliven my days."[26]

"There," he said after reading for ten minutes or so. "Is it any good?"

On my last night, as the shadows of home lengthened toward me, Styron administered a new shock. "You should write something yourself," he said. "Why not write a book? You can use my cottage. It's where James

Baldwin wrote parts of *Another Country* and started his seminal essay, *The Fire Next Time*. It's where I wrote much of *Nat Turner* and *Sophie's Choice*. Romain Gary stayed there, and Jean Seberg, and my good friend, Carlos Fuentes. You can have it for a summer, just pay for your phone calls." Rose raised her eyebrows. "Let me know when you want it."

The evening floated away. I remember at one point Styron calling me a "friend." "When one is sitting here, as now, with friends," he said, perhaps aware that I was probably the loneliest junior academic currently in Connecticut. But I remember little else, except waving good-bye at the station—"Keep writing," I said, or some such inanity—and boarding the Amtrak for New York to fly home.

Two years later, in 1990, I therefore spent a few weeks from May into June in Styron's guest cottage. The evening of my arrival was one of the pleasantest of my life. "Sunny, mild, flower-fragrant," the days again seemed as "arrested in perpetual springtime" as they did for Stingo in the summer of 1947 (3). By six that evening, I rested on moss beneath a pine in a corner of the garden and opened a Michelob. A cardinal flashed red against the greenery. I leaned against the trunk, my feet held from slipping by some tangled roots around which a few large wood ants busied for the coming night. Ahead of me the yellow farmhouse stood solid as fact. To my left, the windows of my yellow cottage with its black shutters and white sills sparkled in the last glow of sunlight. Birds cheered and whistled among the trees. Rose had settled me. Styron had yet to appear. When he finally stomped up the path from his literary labors I drained the Michelob and stood to greet him.

"Got a car?" he barked. "You can't survive up here without a car. Got supplies? Come on. Let's get you some supplies."

In Southbury, Styron waited in his Mercedes while I purchased the kind of groceries I thought Stingo and Sophie would buy, including bagels, bread, cheese, meat, beans, butter, fruit, vegetables, beer, and a bottle of Five Highs.

"He's got no car," he told Rose on our return. "We'll leave him a Mercedes."

The Styrons were due to depart for Martha's Vineyard the next morning, and I was to look after their two dogs, Tashmoo the golden retriever and Dinah the black Labrador, and drive them out to the Vineyard in late June. So that night we sat in the kitchen over a farewell supper during which Rose recounted how she and Bill had met. The way I recall her telling it, though it differs slightly from the official version, was that Bill was reading at Johns Hopkins and Rose, knowing only that he was the author of *Lie Down in Darkness*, went to check the book out of the university library. The novel she pulled from the shelves was indeed called *Lie Down in Darkness*, but by H. R. Hays, published in 1944. Rose found it dull and nearly avoided the event, but she did go and was perplexed to find that she didn't recognize the book Bill was reading from. Because of this she went up to him afterwards and realized her mistake. The rest, so far as the Styron's marriage goes, is history.[27]

"By the way," said Styron, as supper ended, "when you drive out to the Cape, make a point of stopping at the Traveler Restaurant. It's a little establishment on Route 84, Exit 74, near Union, Connecticut. Eat a meal there and you get to choose a free book from a small collection at the back of the restaurant."

The weeks passed, with Styron's last comment to me before leaving still in my head. "Not afraid of ghosts, are you?" he called as I trudged up the moonlit path once used by James Baldwin. "A lot of people have lived in that cottage. A lot of time has passed."

I was not surprised that Al, in *Reading My Father*, refers to the cottage as giving out "a feeling of foreboding" and "a thoroughly haunted vibe."[28] From the narrow entrance hall to the cavernous lounge with its huge poster of an etching of Nat Turner to the small window I looked through daily from the desk in the upper room, I found the cottage utterly unnerving. Day after day, the rain blurred the luminescent foliage and tapped on the roof in percussive accompaniment to the groaning beams. I did get out my 2B pencils and my yellow legal pads and periodically wrote something about somewhere or someone in America, as well as compiling my critical study of Styron's novels. But more than once, startled by what sounded like footsteps, I turned, or even left my desk and opened the door to check the staircase. Paralyzed by the atmosphere of the cottage, its known literary history and unknown other history, I was finally spooked out and spent evenings in the main house. It's never locked, Styron had told me. The place is yours.

At dusk on my rainy final night in Roxbury I sat reading George E. Vaillant's *The Natural History of Alcoholism* in the lounge where I'd interviewed Styron two years before. The dogs lay beside me. On the terrace, against a backdrop of misty trees, droplets plopped on abandoned chairs. Beyond the bar across the dimming room empty decanters lined the wall where Styron's "death mask" had hung, made, said Rose, while "he was real sick." In its place now hung what looked like the death mask of James Baldwin, Styron's Legion of Honor medal slung around it on a red ribbon. I browsed the fireside shelves: Langer's

The Holocaust and the Literary Imagination, Malcolm X Speaks, Aptheker's *American Negro Slave Revolts,* Fuentes's *Where the Air is Clear,* Buchwald's *Buchwald Stops Here,* Malraux's *The Twilight of the Absolute,* Kemble's *Journal of a Residence on a Georgian Plantation,* Lester's *Look Out Whitey! Black Power's Gon' Get Your Mama!,* Plato's dialogues, Steiner's *Language and Silence,* the letters of Faulkner, the letters of Mencken, the complete works of Montaigne. . . .

Rain gusted against the wall-length windows. Night had turned them into mirrors reflecting the whole room. I felt as if the dogs and I were in a glass case, like one of those doll's-house interiors in the basement of the Art Institute in Chicago, this one entitled "American Lounge c. 1990." To a soundtrack of gentle canine snoring, time began to stretch. I imagined the room decades before and, sitting facing one another, lit by the glow of a blazing hearth on some snowbound night at the start of the sixties, a dark-haired Styron and the delicate figure of Baldwin, their shadows stretching across the carpet and up the walls. I pictured them, cigarettes in hand, cradling brandies that caught the light, and listened as if to snatches of chatter as imaginary snowdrifts piled up outside.

"My grandmother, Marianna," Styron was saying, "had two little slave girls, Drusilla and Lucinda."

"My own father was a victim of slavery," Baldwin replied, verbatim from "My Dungeon Shook." "He was defeated long before he died because, at the bottom of his heart, he really believed what white people said about him."[29]

In truth, I'd grown lonely in the house and rose with zest at dawn to usher Tashmoo and Dinah into the Mercedes and drive toward Massachusetts, stopping, as suggested, at the Traveler Restaurant on Route 84. Finishing my meal, I went to the back to a low case of used books. A small book with a tatty black cover caught my eye. "Lie Down in," was written in faded yellow letters. I picked it out to find that the final word of the title, in a dull green, was "Darkness." *Lie Down in Darkness,* I thought. Well I never. For a moment I assumed it was an edition I hadn't seen before, but it was almost immediately apparent what I held in my hands. It was a copy of *Lie Down in Darkness* by H. R. Hays, a first edition, 1944.

Thrilled at my extraordinary discovery, I sped on to Massachusetts, over the Bourne Bridge with its fabulous vista of the Cape and the blue Atlantic, onto the Wood's Hole Ferry to spend a couple of days on Martha's Vineyard, eager to tell the Styrons about this most unlikely of coincidences.

"Perhaps you'd sign it, Bill," I said, showing him the book as we drank Chablis on the porch and looked out over the lawn to the choppy water.

So he did. "To Gavin Cologne-Brookes," he scrawled, "who I hope will overlook the fact that that son of a bitch William Styron <u>stole my title!</u> H. R. Hays."

I have occasionally taken from my bookcase this most marginal of literary marginalia and pondered the coincidence of finding it at the restaurant. Only years later did it occur to me that Styron might have planted it. I think not. What if I'd missed it? What if someone else had taken it? But how could a first edition of a sixty-six-year-old novel that had been pivotal in the Styrons' first meeting, a novel that had been the subject of a conversation that included reference to the restaurant, turn up there on the one occasion that I passed by? If Styron had planted it, he would have to have been the most cunning of practical jokers, and there was still the need for me not only to stop there but also to go to the bookcase and to spot the book. Perhaps he was testing to see if I was alert to detail: one of those, as Henry James advises, "on whom nothing is lost."[30] This seems unlikely, but no more unlikely than for the book to have turned up there by sheer coincidence.

The years passed, and while we corresponded for the next thirteen years, I would only see Bill those four more times I noted earlier. In the winter of 1991, on his way to Paris, he gave a reading at the University of East Anglia. I picked him up from a murky Heathrow for lunch with his agent, Tessa Sayle, and drove him up to talk to students at my place of work at the time, Harlaxton College, Lincolnshire, and then to Norwich. After three fogbound days, we drove down through fog to London for his flight to Paris. Styron's visits to Britain were rare. On a 1952 trip, he told me, the fog had never once lifted, so the weather caused him no surprise, however unusual I insisted it was. "They say about Europe," he remarked, "that come winter a concrete ceiling fixes over the continent." It's not true, but he left believing it, and I bent my head toward the completion of *The Novels of William Styron*.

Five more years accumulated before we met again. In 1998 I was back in upstate New York, so I gunned my rented Mazda into Massachusetts. Once more the Cape burst before me over the breathtaking sweep of the Bourne Bridge. I caught the ferry, to be welcomed by Rose as if I'd never been away. But a decade had dissolved since our first meeting. The Styrons' grandchildren raced around the lawn between the house and the bay, where sailboats bobbed and cormorants shrieked and plunged.

Now seventy-three, Styron walked out onto the porch haltingly, not from decrepitude but from an eye complaint for which he was due an operation.

Early the next morning I awoke in a sky-blue room with white furniture and white curtains billowing in the dawn light. The Atlantic gusts carried the cries of seagulls. Photos of sand dunes and sunsets, along with a montage by Sylvia Cooper, decorated the walls. On a table stood a stack of Martha's Vineyard books, including one called *Vineyard Summer* inscribed to the Styrons—with a wink at history, their full names written in it—from Bill and Hillary Clinton. The signs of fame were everywhere. Styron had turned down an invitation to dinner with Margaret and Denis Thatcher and Nancy Reagan. I asked him why.

"Do you *blame* me?"

After a morning swim and a chat over breakfast with Daphne, the Styrons' Jamaican housekeeper, Rose found me mid-morning and said: "Come on, we're going to a farewell lunch for Dick Widmark and his new wife, Susan. She's lovely, as deaf as he is. She was once married to Henry Fonda. His daughter, Anne, will be there, too. She used to be married to the baseball player Sandy Koufax." So off Rose, Bill, and I went for lunch at the house of a painter named Kib Bramhall. Open-planned and adorned with seascapes, it was up a winding track and looked out over woodland to the sparkling Atlantic. Richard Widmark himself was about eighty, but slim and tanned, and remarkably fit and well so long after what happened to him at the Alamo. Looking much the same as in his movies, except for a pair of big spectacles that enlarged his eyes, he was as funny as he was deaf. Most of his career he found hilarious, not least *The Long Ships*, an unwatchable film he did with Sidney Poitier.

"Sid was a brave Moor with a great, curving scimitar to slice me up," laughed Widmark, "but I was an even braver Norseman." He clapped his hands. "And there was a golden bell made of plastic." "When it fell off the cart," he boomed, "it *bounced!*"

Lunch was lobster salad. The talk ranged from Hollywood to bus travel—a hazy memory for all except me since I'd spent many a recent summer on Greyhounds—but kept coming back to arthritis. "*Everyone* has arthritis," said Bramhall. Styron talked of getting drunk with Jackson Pollock and watching him paint. Widmark joked that maybe Styron had done one of the paintings and it hung somewhere, attributed to Pollock. Anne, a warm, blue-eyed woman of maybe fifty, talked about her time at Sarah Lawrence studying under Joseph Campbell.

"I didn't enjoy it," she said. "He was complicated, like most brilliant men."

I said I once heard Campbell's advice to the young. Follow your bliss: if you do that, you'll enjoy yourself and you're more likely to succeed. If you don't, it doesn't matter because you've been doing what you want to do. If you spend your life doing what you don't really want to do, you won't be happy, win or lose.

"Follow your *bliss!*" mocked Styron. "When I was recovering from my depression they said, Let it wash over you, Mr. Styron. *Woosh!* I don't like that stuff."

"You know what I don't like?" said Widmark. "Texans, and they don't like me. I'm walking down the street in San Antonio minding my own business when along comes this woman and, thwack! She whops me one. I despise you, she says. Another time I'm in a bar in Lubbock and this guy gives me the eye, and thud! *He* whops me one. You miserable, dirty coward, he says."

After watching *Saving Private Ryan* at the local cinema ("Shame about all the clichés," said Styron) on my final evening, he and I watched the yachts in the harbor across from his lawn and recorded a conversation about his career.[31] I asked him how he felt about life as "a grand old man of American literature."

"Ha-ha!" he said flatly.

"Well, you've got health, grandchildren, houses in Connecticut and Martha's Vineyard, the respect of your peers. Aren't you satisfied?"

"I'm bifurcated," he replied. "I'm both more dissatisfied than I thought I would be at this stage in my life, and more satisfied. I don't know how to describe it."

"Why are you dissatisfied?"

"Oh, I'm dissatisfied that I didn't turn out something else, but even as I say that I realize that you cannot look at your career as what you failed to do but what you *did* do. I've done far better than I thought I would ever be capable of doing. I also feel my work has at least acquired a kind of permanence. But, well, the world slips away from us all."

He sat there, looking out over the Sound as if into the past.

"It's the nature of the beast," I suggested, "that if you're ambitious to fulfill your potential you'll be dissatisfied because that's what drove you in the first place."

"Precisely," said Styron, "and I *am* dissatisfied. I'm *profoundly* dissatisfied. But it's combined with satisfied acceptance. It's a kind of schizoid feeling. Sometimes I feel a miserable insufficiency about myself, and other times I say, man, I've done this. Who else has done that? You see what I'm saying?"

When I last saw Styron on Martha's Vineyard, he raised a fist. "Don't let the bastards grind you down," he said.

Four years later, in March 2002, I visited Roxbury for the last time. Styron was now seventy-seven. His gait showed signs of Parkinson's, a hint of a shuffle, right leg always a little ahead of his left, right arm less than mobile. But he was the same cheerfully glum Bill with that same occasional, guttural cough now hacking at the icy Connecticut air. Late in the afternoon I drove him to one of his favorite walks, recalling it from the summer of 1990. In place of warm sunshine, and Tashmoo and Dinah chasing butterflies through the long grass, a grim, wintry wind now flapped our coats. The trees were skeletal against a salmon sky. The track was rutted solid and streaked with ice. In the ditches, clumps of snow slumped purple in the twilight.

Our walk was slow, dogged. While Styron's left arm swung normally, his right was close to his ribs and the hand that wrote the novels was clenched, raw red against the cold. We turned back. The sun blobbed beneath the stubble. We had no Tashmoo or Dinah with us now. Both had died two years previously, precipitating Styron's most recent depression.

"Not that the death of a dog leads to clinical depression," he said, "but these things lurk, and get triggered. You know I had shock treatment, don't you? Well, it was my decision, and it worked. But I feel spacey much of the time. It's hard to describe." He held both hands up, either side of his jowls, as if to represent a transparent mask or space helmet. "Oh, by the way, we've got dinner guests. I hope that's okay. You've met Arthur, haven't you? Arthur Miller? And Becky? She's staying with her father because Inge—did you meet Inge?" I'd met them during the 1990 summer. "Well sadly, she died. It happened only last month. She came back from a photography trip in Europe complaining of back pain that everyone assumed was the result of lugging cameras. But then she felt unwell, unable to get out of bed, and then she died, suddenly and shockingly. Lymphatic cancer." Our walk was now entirely in shadow. A pink line streaked the horizon, but otherwise it was that time of evening when your skin glows against the dying light. It was as if not just the darkening sky but the dismal news itself made the trees more skeletal, the wind more bitter, the road icier. "They were together so long," Styron was saying, "about forty years. His beloved Inge, with whom, one would guess, he found real happiness."

"One thing," he said as we reached the car in all but darkness, "I know you wouldn't do this, but please remember. I've been with Arthur on numerous occasions all over the country and in Europe. I can't think of a single time when someone hasn't brought up the subject of Marilyn Monroe. It *never* fails. You just wait for it to happen and someone says something like, 'Er, Mr Miller?' and your heart sinks."

"I wouldn't dream of mentioning her."

"Well, it honestly never fails but—especially at this sensitive time— let's hope it does. Also, don't expect anything of Arthur." The headlights of the Mercedes seemed to draw the bone-white trees toward us as we swept down the tunnel-like road. "He's eaten with us once a week or so since it happened. Up to now he's hardly spoken."

"You know him very well then?"

"We've been neighbors for years. But even when we came up here in the fifties Arthur was already a legend, even to himself." Styron laughed. "He was married to Monroe then. I drove by hoping to get a glimpse, same as everyone else."

"Did you ever meet her?"

"We invited them to a party, as you'd expect. They were supposed to be coming, but it got later and later and eventually Arthur turned up alone. He made his apologies for her. Apparently this happened a lot. She'd be getting ready but just never finished. I guess she didn't want to go out and be Marilyn Monroe. She didn't want to perform. As for Arthur, I know him, and I don't. Arthur is Mr. Enigma."

"He was very talkative the day I met him."

"Oh sure, Arthur'll talk all day. But what was it Nietzsche said? To talk a great deal about oneself can be a way of hiding oneself? Arthur is hard to fathom. There are areas you don't go into."

"That's what he said about you; that you're subterranean."

"Well, there you are: two behemoths of the deep dark sea. Anyway, just don't mention *Marilyn Monroe!*"

Arthur and Rebecca duly appeared that night. Rebecca was seven months pregnant, and, of course, she had lost her mother. She remained exceptionally beautiful. But this was the most terrible of times, and her blue eyes often filled with tears. Miller, whom I remembered as tall, striding, powerful, walked carefully and had a bent-over back. His beady eyes crinkled more than ever now behind his spectacles, as he edged through his eighties, reflective, scrutinizing, twinkling. We settled in candle glow at the kitchen table, Miller to my left, at the head, Rebecca to my right, Styron and Rose across the table, and an empty chair at the other end. Miller had two plays on in New York at the time. *The Crucible* had drawn packed audiences since 9/11. I asked him what he made of the War on Terror.

"We live," he said, as if allowing me time to write it down, "in Rome."

"What's the name of the other play you have on?" I asked.

Eyes twinkling, he replied as if dictating. "The Man Who Had All the Luck."

"Can one man be one thing and be it long?"

"I have no illusions left," he said. "None at all. I've seen so many people come and go, so many slide in and out of fortune, so many famous writers slip into oblivion, so many good people never achieve recognition, so many charlatans lauded."

"By other charlatans?"

"Not always. Well-meaning people do it too, and sincerely. You know, the first discovery of a planet orbiting a star beyond our own was less than twenty years ago. But since they found what they unromantically called 51 Pegasi B they can't *stop* finding new extra-solar planets. Soon enough they'll have found hundreds. They'll find an Earth-like planet in a year or two."

"Does Time really bend, do you think?"

The deep ridges around his eyes called to mind the cracked, icy crust of Europa, or perhaps just March in Connecticut. "They reckon that within a few years we could have proof." He touched my arm. "*Proof*, demonstrated in laboratories, that all our experience has been confined to a four-dimensional sheet floating in a higher-dimensional universe. Every educated person ought to know such things."

"Does it help?"

"To know the subjectivity of time is to accept that we really are a long time young and a short time old. Sure it helps."

"Joyce Carol Oates once wrote that time devours us in the name of wisdom."

"She's not kidding."

"So what matters is to live by heartthrobs, not by hours?"

"Did she say that?"

"Emily Dickinson."

"Ah yes! 'Opinion is a flitting thing but Truth, outlasts the Sun—If then we cannot own them both—Possess the oldest one—.'"[32]

"More wine?" Styron filled my glass with Merceaux.

Everything went swimmingly until Rose leaned across the table and said, "Did you say, 'Joyce Carol Oates'? He met her parents, Arthur. That must have been *fascinating!* What's that big, recent novel of hers?"

Before I could hold my tongue I said, "*Blonde.*"

"*Blonde?*" said Rose. "Isn't that the one about—?"

To my left sat an octogenarian dealing with the loss of his wife of forty years. To my right sat their pregnant, grieving daughter. Across sat Styron, looking at me.

"Oh my goodness," laughed Rose, who had not been privy to Styron's warning. "I was in Ireland with Joyce. She gave readings from *Blonde*. It was amazing! She looked down, brushed up her hair, gazed out at the audience and began to read. She had the voice, the mannerisms, everything! I've never seen such a performance! She simply *was* Marilyn Monroe."

I searched for something to say. Miller's eyes crinkled behind spectacles reflecting the candlelight that cast dancing shadows across the table to the empty chair. Rebecca gazed at her food. Rose grew thoughtful.

"Joyce approaches many subjects," winced Styron, "and occasionally bites off more than she can chew."

On the bus down into Manhattan the next day I had on my mind a parting conversation with Styron in which we had talked, once more, of *Sophie's Choice.*

"All that emotional chiaroscuro," I ventured, "is really quite operatic."

"I hate to tell you," said Styron, "but an opera is indeed in production for the Royal Opera House in Covent Garden this December. Want to come?"

The December 2002 premiere of *Sophie's Choice* at Covent Garden mingles with memories of Styron's memorial service in 2007. Each was a kind of ending, setting the seal on these reminiscences. After all, to sit in an auditorium watching an opera is perhaps not so very different from sitting amid a congregation watching the story of one man's life and achievements unspool ("with negligent haste" in the *Sophie's Choice* phrase [216]) before us as a screen of photographs from childhood to old age and a succession of testaments from family and friends.

In 2002, I sat with my wife, Nicki, high up in the darkness of the Royal Opera House, wearing a hired Moss Bros dinner jacket, my skin sore and sweating, my neck chafed, but wearing it out of respect, both for Styron and for the subject matter. I watched the drama unfold across the stage, in Brooklyn, Cracow, and Auschwitz. When Stingo, Sophie, and Nathan were in New York, I too was there, just as once I had been a kind of Stingo figure, entering a glamorous yet emotionally chiaroscuro world. But when Sophie screamed as her daughter was wrenched away, I knew that I was no longer the youth but the parent. All through the opera I pictured Styron with his family in the midst of the crowd. What must it have felt like to sit in old age watching your novel performed as opera? The babbling throng at the after-show party was like a gathering of characters from some idiosyncratic book—some famous, some talented, others just happy to be included. Over there stood the director, Trevor Nunn, and there the conductor, Simon Rattle, talking with Styron's biographer, Jim West, and look: over there Nathan, played by Rodney Gilfry! And over there, yet another Stingo imposter, Canadian Gordon Gietz (Stingo Canadian? Whatever next?)! And there, Sophie herself, the stunning mezzo-soprano Angelika Kirchschlager, engaged in a tête-à-tête with the operatic narrator, Dale Duesing.

I barely talked to Styron on this last occasion I would ever see him. We had chatted at a party the night before. He'd worn his Legion of Honor and announced that he was "getting so damned decrepit." Instead, a mere extra in the crowd scene, I touted my program for signatures. Framed now, it hangs on my study wall even as I write. "I've got those opening night blues. Bill," Styron wrote before the show, in a shaky yet still elegant hand. But that nervous comment came to be surrounded by the energetic after-show signatures of the composer, Nicholas Maw, of the operatic counterparts of Stingo, Sophie, and Nathan, of Trevor Nunn, and, most triumphantly of all, by the curling flourish of an impresario's hand across the center of the sheet, as if Simon Rattle were still conducting, even now.

"I've got those opening night blues," Styron repeats in the top left corner.

Rattle wraps a white-jacketed arm around the old man's shoulders and scrawls across the page: "What's wrong with the blues? Love Simon."

The last glimpse I caught of Styron, he was surrounded by family and friends, being hugged, fêted. Something felt complete when the crowd opened up and, arms outstretched, he shuffled forward to embrace Angelika. I thought of Stingo, finally old, being able to embrace Sophie and let her know that he had come to understand her, along with his own, dead mother, perhaps, as the young man never could have.

At this point we slipped away, but as I recall it now, it's as if I opened my eyes to find myself, this time with my younger daughter, Anastasia, amid the congregation at the memorial service in St. Bartholomew's five years later, on an overcast late afternoon that became a rainy night followed by brittle icy days and bright blue sky, as if the sun itself were the source of the freeze. The congregation ranged from close friends to people who had read but never met him, perhaps even to a few curious bystanders who had simply joined those filing in. And of course the turnout was international. Even before the service began, the poet Yevgeny Yevtushenko was urgently explaining to me just how important Styron was to Russian friends and readers. Pulling for me from his lumber jacket a crumpled copy of a speech given at a dinner the night before, he told me of how he would never forget the protection Styron had provided against the state's vengeance in the wake of Yevtushenko's protest against Brezhnev's tanks' entering Czechoslovakia in 1968.

During the service, Peter Matthiessen spoke of first meeting Styron in Paris in the fifties and of how, after too much plonk, his new friend fell face first, "lachrymose among the oysters." Al spoke of her father's "epic, wretched descent." Bill Clinton spoke of how "the Human Genome Project has shown us that ninety-nine percent of our genetic make-up is identical to every other human being on Earth" and that "all that we have that's different is mind and heart and what matters most is what we decide to do with these." "We become what we care about," he said. "William Styron was a great man." Styron's son, Tom, read "I was Dead" by Rumi, then looked out above the heads of the congregation and said, "Daddy, I forgive you." Other family members gave readings. Mike Nichols was overcome reading a letter Styron had written him. Mia Farrow read from the ending of "A Tidewater Morning." Ted Kennedy told an anecdote about Styron sailing home from Port Hyannis at night alone in a storm, and Carlos Fuentes told a magic realist anecdote about Styron signing a book for a girl in Paris just as the heavens opened, washing the autograph away. "But I knew," said Fuentes, "that the next morning, for that young Parisienne, when the page had dried out, Styron's signature had returned." Finally, Meryl Streep read from the ending of *Sophie's Choice.* Interspersed with all this, St. Bartholomew's echoed to Haydn and Mozart, as well as, to end with, "Amazing Grace." As the last chords subsided I glanced across the aisle, looked idly at a tall, dark-haired man in a long, gray coat, and caught the sad but steely eyes of Philip Roth. Had I still been young I might have accosted him after the service to discuss *The Ghost Writer,* or *Operation Shylock,* or *The Plot Against America.* But even as we exchanged glances—

with me knowing him instantly, and he seeing just another face in the crowd—I was under no illusion. Those days were gone.

When I look back now on the years that I knew Bill Styron—not as his family or close friends knew him, but at least far better than I ever imagined possible when I first read his work—I think of more lines from Emily Dickinson, whose words also end *Sophie's Choice.* "The Missing All—," she writes in Poem 985, "prevented Me from missing minor Things."[33] Since I yearned for something missing elsewhere, when the opportunity came to know this man and his world, I paid attention with peculiar intensity.

I had received my last letter from him in January 2003 and had buried it with the rest, like a time capsule, in my filing cabinet. It was about the British response to the opera, with a comment about a criticism of the novel. "Fortunately," wrote Styron, "I'm by now almost totally inured to such slanders."[34] The handwriting was smaller than the bold script of the holographs and earlier letters. Perhaps this was the result of his incapacitated hand, but it seemed to signal a distancing as Styron receded both from my life and from life itself. He was enduring that "epic, wretched descent" that Al Styron spoke of. Only on my return from the memorial service did I retrieve the bundle of letters, reread them, and begin to reflect on the books themselves. Naturally I reread the fiction. But I also reread the nonfiction and was struck by it in new ways. My sense of Styron is that whatever his faults in the eyes of others, he was toward me above all a kind, generous, compassionate man, just as he was to McGinniss, Mewshaw, Harington, and scores of other people who, in person or through letters, approached him with little to offer in return for his time and attention. I suppose one could argue that there were motives on his part beyond the instinct to be generous, but again the phrase that rings in my ear is Bob Loomis's that William Styron "was fully, intensely human." It struck me during the rereading of the nonfiction that if the personality we find in the novels is indeed the personality many of us encountered in life—"a long novel" being, as Styron writes to Leon Edwards in *Selected Letters,* "a perfect symbol of one's own strengths and weaknesses as a human" (234)—then the two sides of the person most obviously come together in the essays. This is one reason why I turn, in the next chapter, to these in advance of the fiction. They are the flipside of the same coin. The objections of Poe, Bakhtin et al. notwithstanding, they are the flesh-and-blood being writing directly, as "himself," onto the page.

CHAPTER 3

Self-Realization from *This Quiet Dust* to *Havanas in Camelot*

> I think there's a kind of ultimate vision that Camus had that helped
> form my own, a bleak, bleak view . . . he saw human destiny as being
> redeemed individually in terms of self-reliance, the only thing we've got.
> There's a desperate desire for self-identity.
>
> —STYRON, IN CONVERSATION, 1988

An author's thoughts on fellow writers clarify our sense of that author's
own artistic aims and values. In his *This Quiet Dust* essay on Malcolm
Cowley's *The Second Flowering*, Styron notes that the modernists possessed "a shared morality which viewed the husbanding of one's talent
as the highest possible goal" and so provided "a lesson in the art of
self-realization" (101–2). In Cowley's words, they displayed "such inner
qualities as energy, independence, rigor, and an original way of combining words (a style, a 'voice') and utter commitment to a dream." Cowley's
statement, writes Styron, "seems exemplary and true. Only two things
matter: talent and language" (102). His comments are characteristi-
cally forthright and generous. He spoke his mind in art as in life, which
is one reason why he made the occasional enemy, but he was always
sensitive to the qualities and achievements of other writers. He was
not combative or competitive and surely had no time for Hemingway's
notion that one must knock earlier writers out of the ring, or Mailer's
need to publicly disparage imagined rivals.[1] His public comments on
contemporaries are invariably generous. In letters, he was blunt rather
than bellicose and often responding to another's indignation at what a
writer or critic had said of Styron himself.[2] He had public exchanges, of

course, but it was not his nature to dismiss others' efforts out of animosity. Judging writing itself, however, was another matter. His assessments, while thoughtful, specific, and balanced by awareness of the imperfect nature of almost any creative achievement, can nevertheless be devastating. All this is apparent in his essays from *This Quiet Dust and Other Writings*, including the later, expanded version, through *Darkness Visible: A Memoir of Madness* to those selected for the posthumous *Havanas in Camelot: Personal Essays*. For Styron, "self-realization" as a writer included honoring the process in others (whether toward self-realization or, as he called it in conversation about Camus, "self-reliance" or "self-identity").[3] Moreover, his writings on fiction remind us that he himself sought the highest level of craftsmanship.

Following on from memories of the man, reviewing the nonfiction (bar the more clearly crafted *Darkness Visible*) reveals Styron at his least self-conscious. He is not trying to "transport" the reader, but simply offering asides to his main work. He introduces *This Quiet Dust* with the comment that he "always considered the writing of prose other than fiction something of a sideline" (xi). Indeed, since he was at heart a novelist, even his stories are mostly early work, novel excerpts, or sideshows to the major effort, and his essays might seem one step removed from even that. But actually his three nonfiction books are invaluable companions to the novels, not least because they reveal these same qualities of craft, compassion, and intimacy evident in the novel writing but in a less mediated form. With directness suggestive of the spoken word, they capture characteristic gestures, spontaneous responses, momentary postures, and incidental insights. They thus round out a personality always more refracted in the fiction. But just as the personality of the man helps elucidate the fiction, so it's misleading to posit too marked a distinction between the fiction and the nonfiction. Styron's combination of the crafted and the candid is especially characteristic of his essay writing and later fiction, which taken together constitute, more than any of his other work, his artistic statement.

I am not forgetting that self-realization through writing is a complex concept. All writing is performance; as Vladimir Nabokov writes in an essay on Flaubert, "All art is deception." Still, in his later writing Styron crafts a sense of direct address, so merging the art of the essay with that of the novel. Like Flaubert, he sought *le mot juste* in such a way that readers, far from being distracted by the overtly artful, might take the fluency for granted. Those who imagine elements to be extraneous are wrong. Despite the apparently languorous, improvisational voice, he molded his mature fiction entirely aware of the genre's possibilities and pitfalls. Indeed, not unlike Flaubert's shift from the limited scope of *Madame Bovary* to the larger sweep of *A Sentimental Education*, Styron's final novel (unlike the wholly novelistic voice of *Lie Down in Darkness*) combines dramatic, realist narrative with the essay form. His novels take on board the awkward nature of language but are never gratuitously self-referential. "The supremely necessary," as he wrote to Harington, "is the secret of art." The essays (along with the letters) provide evidence that if readers turn to the fiction in a spirit of trust it will reward them.[4]

"I have applied as much effort and have spent as much time, proportionately, to the crafting of these pieces as I have to the writing of the novels," Styron continues his "Note to the Reader" in *This Quiet Dust*. "It is just that the shorter, nonfiction works, perhaps because of their generally topical nature—seem to linger less reverberantly in one's own mind than the novels with their larger scope and multiplicity of elements" (xi). The art is in the essays just as in the fiction, then, but often with an eye on the moment rather than on sustained truths. Beyond that, though, as comparing *Sophie's Choice* with *A Sentimental Education* suggests, the two forms merge. Styron's essays contain powerful, descriptive writing, while *Sophie's Choice* contains both factual detail and essayistic prose. Each essay volume reveals, in his assessments of situations, individuals, and other literature, something of his qualities both as a human being and as a writer. Moreover, they clarify not merely whom he admired and sought to emulate—he cites many writers, after all, in *Sophie's Choice*—but also what aspects of their achievement most influenced him. Beyond this, they reflect his need to think in relation "to historical events."[5] Finally, Styron's essays naturally shed specific light on his own novels.

Self-realization naturally includes seeing your work in context, and *This Quiet Dust* is unique in Styron's oeuvre for containing extended assessments of other writers and critics. Above all, it shows his penchant for close attention. Moreover, his harsher judgments gain all the more authority from the fact that he is as generous as he is unfailingly exact. Despite his "mellow conviction" that critics are "totally irrelevant," much of *This Quiet Dust* is made up of social or literary criticism, and he's a master of the genre. The fact that the essays look beyond the self means that they reveal by default a sense of the man himself: his values, ideals, preoccupations, and the particular qualities that made him such an ambitious, engaging novelist.

His essay on *The Second Flowering* exemplifies this. Styron and his contemporaries differed from the modernists in important ways, even as they were influenced by them, so it's revealing to note what Styron felt he took from them and where he parts company. He admired their "shared morality" of viewing "the husbanding of one's talent as the highest possible goal" and their subsequent "lesson in the art of self-realization," as well as what Cowley refers to as their "energy, independence, rigor," originality of "style," and "voice." But in Styron's own fiction clearly more matters. Whereas the modernists sought (in Cowley's words) to be "the lords of language" (102), Styron, perhaps more profoundly influenced by the likes of Camus, Orwell, and Koestler, sought meaning as much from the wider world as from the self. His essays thus display "a lesson in the art of self-realization" quite different from that of the modernists. He acknowledges their attributes and incorporates their innovations, but overall his essays show that he moves into other territories.

By John Barth's terms of reference (even though he groups Styron with "the more traditionalist American writers"), Styron would seem to be the "ideal postmodernist author" in that he "neither merely repudiates nor merely imitates either his twentieth-century modernist parents or his nineteenth-century premodernist grandparents." Rather, "he has the first half of" the twentieth century "under his belt, but not on his back."[6] He recognizes the limitations inherent in admiration that is too acquiescent, including the academic tendency to smother the work of favored authors with an excess of analysis. He sees how easily criticism too doggedly applied can become pointless and irrelevant and cites the "thrice-told tales" and overanalysis of the generation that preceded his own. "Do we look forward to still more commentary on *The Bear* or Cummings' love lyric?" he asks. "Or another desolating inventory of the metaphors in *Gatsby*?" In contrast, he explains that he values Cowley's criticism because "the angle of vision seems new; that is, not only are his insights into these writers' works almost consistently arresting but so are his portraits of the men themselves" (96).

Cowley's assessments matter, for Styron, because he provides independent-minded observation of use to the reader in appreciating the work. *The Portable Faulkner* is "a jewel of exegesis" that "opened up Faulkner's world" to Styron as a young man "struggling to read a difficult writer who was then out of print, little known and less understood." He also values Cowley's sharp honesty. For instance, his succinct statement on the "sad bankruptcy" of Dos Passos's later fiction is, for Styron, an important comment on a stance that can devalue any writer's work. Dos Passos, says Cowley, broke rules that seem "to have been followed by great novelists," one of which is that "they can regard their characters with love or hate or anything in between, but cannot regard them with tired aversion." Cowley's "prevailing tone," writes Styron, "is not that of a dismantler of reputations, a type often so prompt to scuttle into sight with his little toolkit at the end of an era, but one of generosity and preoccupying concern" (97). Styron thus clarifies his thoughts on criticism at its best: serious, respectful, attentive, but focused only on artistic integrity.

His essay on Philip Rahv in *This Quiet Dust* provides another example of his critical values and their relationship to the self-realization that marks intellectual, emotional, and artistic maturity. On one level, his views might intimidate the (young) critic who sets out to assess a writer. But at least they provide a set of ideals to which criticism of that writer's work—if not all criticism—might aspire. He writes, for instance, of Rahv's "utter lack of parochialism, his refusal to be bamboozled by trends or fashionable currents and, most importantly, his ability to appreciate a work in terms of difficult and complex values which he had laid down for himself and which had nothing to do with anything so meretricious as race or region or competing vogues." He also commends Rahv's ability "to sniff out fools" and "the frauds and poseurs of literature" and his "unerring eye for the opportunists in his own critical profession," including the "trendy" and all who are "merely windy and inadequate, the pretentious academics who" lack "utterly the acquaintance with politics, philosophy and history" that is "essential to the critical faculty and a civilized perception of things" (287–88).

A cynic might read this in light of Rahv's description of *The Confessions of Nat Turner* in the *New York Times Review of Books* as "the best novel by an American writer that has appeared in some years." Nor was Styron above scoring points. Anyone acquainted with the negative comments on Styron by various critics offended by his attitude toward them can imagine whom he means by the "fools," "frauds and poseurs," and the rest. Nor would everyone agree with his definitions. "Civilized perception of things" sounds more like Orwell than any modernist. But that would seem to be the point. Styron admired Orwell's essays deeply, and Orwell, with a direct urgency to match his moral vision, wore his prejudices on his sleeve. Styron considered Orwell to be a writer who "tried to grab the issues" that Styron too thought mattered. He saw him as "one of the very important writers of the twentieth century," and not least because, of all writers, "who could have been less tied to a school, who could have been more spontaneous, who could have been more himself?" Such comments bespeak a belief once again in self-reliance that right or wrong at least pulses with honesty. What he values in others we can take to be the ideals he aspires to in his own writing, fiction or nonfiction.[7]

Styron's vision of artistic integrity informs his *This Quiet Dust* essays on two writers whose stars fell rapidly from their zenith. One is his friend James Jones, the other an early hero, Thomas Wolfe. He writes admiringly of Jones's best work, including *From Here to Eternity* and *The Thin Red Line*, regarding the latter as a novel of "rigorous integrity and disciplined art." But where criticism is needed he doesn't hold back. *Go to the Widow-Maker* is "a chaotic novel of immeasurable length, filled with plywood characters, implausible dialogue, and thick wedges of plain atrocious writing." Confronted with its lack of "grace and cohesion," he was plunged "into despondency" (295). What he therefore focuses on, as in discussing critics, is the product itself, and the extent to which it passes or fails the test of artistic integrity. His comments are harsh, but they are about the craft, not the person. Moreover, he acknowledges the likelihood of failure somewhere in the career of all artists. Hence *Go to the Widow-Maker* "represents one of those misshapen artefacts that virtually every good writer, in the sad and lonely misguidedness of his calling, comes up with sooner or later" (296). *Go to the Widow-Maker*, in other words, is the equivalent in Styron's oeuvre of *Set This House on Fire* or the never completed *Way of the Warrior*, at least when set against the cohesiveness of his best work.

In his essay on Wolfe, Styron again melds generosity with incisive criticism. His concern is with emotional, intellectual, and artistic maturity and the way this affects the shape of the work. In essence, Wolfe fails the test of self-realization in that while his writing has the energy to appeal to youth, it lacks the cohesion necessary to sustain the interest of more experienced readers. Styron acknowledges the huge effect "reading Wolfe had upon so many of us who were coming of age during or just after World War II" (75). He singles out *Look Homeward, Angel* for "its lyrical torrent and raw, ingenuous feeling, its precise and often exquisite rendition of place and mood, its buoyant humor and the vitality of its characters and, above all, the sense of youthful ache and promise and hunger and ecstasy which so corresponded to that of an eighteen-year-old reader." His description of experiencing such a work "at exactly the right moment" leaves even the older reader wanting to reread Wolfe—or maybe just be eighteen again (74). That Wolfe sometimes "went on for page after windy page about nothing, or with the most callow emotions" hardly mattered since Styron "was callow" himself. He "gobbled" up Wolfe's novels in under a fortnight, emerging "with a buoyant serenity of one whose life has been forever altered" (75). But as ever Styron is forthright. Having confirmed the context of Wolfe's influence, the rest of the essay discusses not just "the good Wolfe" but "the bad Wolfe" (77).

Wolfe's failure of self-realization, Styron argues, stemmed from a lack of self-awareness. His inability to reflect led to his anti-Semitism, but, beyond moral considerations, his failure to assess his own qualities and shortcomings diminished his art. It fed into his lack of discipline in crafting the novels. Again, Styron's judgments reveal his ideals. Wolfe's novels too often lack the "organic form" that arises "from the same drives and tensions that inspired the work in the beginning" (78). This led to "the awful contradiction in his books between this formlessness and those tremendous moments which still seem so touched with grandeur as to be imperishable" (79).

Styron's observations on Wolfe reveal his sense of the crucial importance in novel writing of form, or, in his grander term, *architecture*, but he equally shows that form is integral to the self-aware writer's vision. For Styron, whatever the attributes of Wolfe's work, it lacks these qualities. Much remains valuable. "Dated" he may be, but not in the sense of "insincere postures and attitudes: already a lot of Hemingway is dated in a way that Wolfe could never be." He was "a flawed but undeniable genius" because "of the clear glimpses he had at moments" about the human condition (86). Rather, he is dated in that "we now begin to realize how unpulled-together Wolfe's work really is." The "same shapelessness that mattered so little to us when we were younger" allows for "a lack of inner dramatic tension, without which no writer, not even Proust, can engage our mature attention for long." *Look Homeward, Angel* is Wolfe's best book because "here the powers of heart and mind most smoothly find their confluence" while a sense of place and time "lend to the book a genuine unity that Wolfe never recaptured in his later works" (79).

What Styron criticizes in Wolfe he patently avoided in his own mature work. Indeed, his attention to form produced complex novels the architecture of which is so unobtrusively seamless as to be virtually invisible on a first reading. (One thinks of Joan Didion's novelist husband, John Gregory Dunne, who "reread *Sophie's Choice* several times" in the summer of its publication, "trying to see how it worked.")[8] No doubt this search for cohesion caused Styron anguish, but it also produced his celebrated successes. The audaciousness of the artistically mature novels may be precisely what troubles some readers. But close readings of them are not least rewarding because they anticipate all manner of response.

The same first-rate criticism in the interests of self-realization can be found in an essay on Fitzgerald. Styron pinpoints the worst of Fitzgerald—"sloppy, hastily written fiction"—and the best: "the conscientious and coolly disciplined craftsman" who possessed a "stony, saving honesty and self-awareness" (89). Again, what he says of Fitzgerald amplifies what he aspired to in his own art and shows in his essays: "no writer ever had such appreciative and generous interest in his contemporaries, such an acute, unjealous response to excellence" (90). Such essays show Styron to have been an incisive critic, even as they provide insight for appreciating his novels. He values Wolfe over Hemingway for honesty, but Hemingway over Wolfe for craft. The best of Fitzgerald, as of Jones, is rigorous and disciplined. The worst is poorly organized and sloppy. But honesty and craft are ultimately linked by way of artistic integrity. Styron's novels aim at the same values. We can use the standards he himself sets to assess his work. We can expect from the contours of his criticism, for instance, a writer who will always seek felicitous phrasing and internal cohesion. He doesn't achieve these things in every work, but because he has set out his ideals we can see where he meets his own standards and where he falls short.

While he makes plenty of reference elsewhere to his other American literary heroes, *This Quiet Dust* contains an example of his admiration for that European exemplar of artistic integrity: Gustave Flaubert. The European novel massively informs Styron's art. He writes in other places of his admiration for Chateaubriand, Stendhal, Dostoevsky, and Tolstoy. But Flaubert's whole approach represented Styron's ideal, even though these other writers' less mercilessly disciplined stance appealed. In keeping with his tendency to merge fictional techniques with essayistic observations, Styron has his alter ego, Paul Whitehurst, in "Marriott, the Marine," speak of how "few others shared room with Flaubert" in his "private pantheon of writers" and how he'd memorized whole passages of *Madame Bovary* out of admiration for Flaubert's "painstaking regard for the nuances of language."[9]

In a *This Quiet Dust* essay on *Lie Down in Darkness* Styron spells out the French writer's influence on its composition. "Like Flaubert in *Madame Bovary*," he would "be able to anatomize bourgeois family life" (325). It was not a matter of imitation, but of learning the lesson of an art forged in solitude to exacting standards. Styron notes, for instance, that his own worst writing came when he was "indolent and imitative," false to his "true vision of reality," and "responsive to facile echoes rather than the inner voice" (326). The splendor of Flaubert's achievement, like that of some classic American writers, "derives from the very loneliness and obscurity out of which it flowered" (342). What mattered artistically to Flaubert mattered to Styron: the inner cohesion of the art, not the reputation or outer glory. ("There is no more crushingly contemptuous line in all of world fiction," he writes, "than the final sentence of *Madame Bovary*," in which the self-aggrandizing mediocrity, Homais, is awarded the Legion of Honor [341].) Styron delighted in accolades from his peers, but he kept his Pulitzer certificate for *The Confessions of Nat Turner* in what he refers to in *Selected Letters* as his "downstairs narcissistic bathroom"(431). With that first novel, he realized that "what had been lacking" was "a sense of architecture—a symmetry, perhaps unobtrusive but always there, without which a novel sprawls" (328). Once again, self-realization through artistic integrity is his literary ideal. Flaubert, as Styron said in conversation, tried "to wrench out of every scene its absolute substance."[10] Styron sought to do the same.

Beyond craft and literary context, self-realization for Styron meant regional and historical awareness. Not only in *This Quiet Dust* but also in *Havanas in Camelot,* in the essayistic elements of *Sophie's Choice,* and in conversation, he confirmed his curiosity about individuals caught up in "the course of human events." He was moved by "moments when human lives intersect with large historical events and become metaphors." Even those who "live in a backwater" are, he felt, "moved by the tides of history." Great writing can obviously "cross boundaries," but there is "an added dimension when it tries to grapple with these virtually incomprehensible things that go on in history."[11] The essays in *This Quiet Dust* remind us how strongly he himself identified with a region and era. A child of Newport News, Virginia, who had come of age late in World War II, Styron knew that his youth had intersected with a place of acute historical interest at one of its key moments. The James River was the "dominating physical presence of my childhood and early youth," he writes in "The James." Living right by it, he seemed to witness the river of history itself and immersed himself in it.

His very language—"backwater," "tides of history"—suggests the strength of that identification. "As I envision how a child growing up on the flanks of the Rockies or Sierras must ever afterward be enthralled to the memory of mountain peaks, or as I recollect how a writer like Willa Cather, brought up on the Nebraska prairies, was haunted for life by that majestically unending 'sea of grass,'" he writes, so the James was "so much a part of me that even now I wonder whether some of that salty-sweet water might not have entered my bloodstream." Much of this relates to the "spell of the river's prodigious history," but the past that the James represented "coexisted" with "a vital present" (315). Newport News life, he explains in introducing the "Service" section of *This Quiet Dust*, was "dominated by the biggest shipyard in America": he thus grew up in a "busy, deafening world" that was "revving up for the greatest clash of arms in history" (208). It would, moreover, be a war, he states in the *Tidewater Morning* tale "Love Day," that the son of an engineer "who helped build huge war machines" would be involved in "before he was old enough to vote" (27).

Styron would use this setting in different ways in his fiction, from the Port Warwick of *Lie Down in Darkness* to the dream that frames *The Confessions of Nat Turner* to Paul Whitehurst's paper route in "A Tidewater Morning." In seeking to understand the author more fully, it pays to remember this identification with the river as history and the river *of* history. "I loved the James," he writes, "and in memory its summertime shores are tangled with all that piercing delight of youthful romance; recollecting the moonlight in huge quicksilver oblongs on those dark waters, and the drugstore perfume of gardenia, and boys' and girls' voices, I no longer wonder why a river had such a lasting effect on my spirit, becoming almost in itself a metaphor for the painful sweetness of life and its mystery" (316).

It's therefore unsurprising that, in terms of the relationship between setting and history, Styron so identified with Mark Twain. In *Havanas in Camelot* he calls Twain his "most beloved literary forefather," not just out of affection for *Huckleberry Finn* but because of their "similar upbringings" amid "sullen racism." Both grew up "in villages on the banks of great rivers," in surroundings that "possessed a surface sweetness and innocence—under which lay a turmoil we were pleased to expose." Their subsequent novels both "gained indisputable success and a multitude of readers but, because they dealt with America's most profound dilemma—its racial anguish—in ways that were idiosyncratic and upsetting, and because they contained many ambiguities, they invited the wrath of critics, black and white, in controversies that have persisted to this day."[12] If the nostalgic vision of a riverside youth in "The James" is Twainesque, in another *This Quiet Dust* essay, "A Voice from the South," Styron reveals rather more of Twain's ambivalence about his environment. For all his love of the James's "murky expanse," he remained "uncharmed" by his birthplace. "Numberless factors shape one's needs and longings, and I may have been forced to escape any native environment," he admits. But a line he wrote in the Wanamaker diary he kept at age fourteen "became a prophecy: *I've got to get the hell away from here*" (57). In *Sophie's Choice,* Stingo's idealization of the South he hopes to take Sophie to, coupled with awareness of the reality, neatly captures this ambivalence.

Self-realization, therefore, involves not merely a "hyperintense sense of place" (57) but awareness of how place and history shape that self both in the individual and in the culture. For integral to this environment was not just the shipbuilding of the Tidewater but the legacy of slavery and the issue of race. On the one hand there was Styron's fascination with a people set apart. He would use, as he writes in the essay on *Lie Down in Darkness,* "the presence in the city of two messianic figures, Elder Solomon Lightfoot Michaux and his arch-rival Bishop Grace— known as Daddy Grace," combining them into Daddy Faith. Hungry to understand a spirituality so unlike his "pallid Presbyterianism," he was especially struck by its music, which "gave voice to such depths of anguish and highs of almost manic ecstasy" (58).[13] On the other hand, like Twain and indeed Orwell, Styron was a product of racist, class-ridden indoctrination and could not wholly "shake off" his "ambivalence" toward black Americans. "Bigotry, foolish and fangless but real nonetheless," was part of his makeup (58). For some commentators, none of these three writers shed their upbringing, but the very struggle toward self-realization, as opposed to the cultural identity plastered on each man in childhood, accounts for much of the dramatic conflict that makes up their worldview. Art for art's sake was never to be enough for one brought up to know the significance of the Tidewater region in terms of both slavery and World War II. Like Twain and Orwell, Styron was a product of his time and place.

For Styron, then, self-realization was entwined with the legacy of racism and atrocity. His fiction dealt with the weighty. The "frivolous, evasive," as he offhandedly called the post-Orwell "English spirit," was not his kind of writing.[14] In the "Victims" section of *This Quiet Dust,* indeed, such is his focus on real people that it's far from obvious that he's a novelist. This applies to his essays on the death-row inmate Benjamin Reid and on Lieutenant Calley, "principal executor" of the My Lai atrocity. Calley, for instance, "is not the first nobody whose brush with a large moment in history has personified that moment and helped to define it." Admitting that most "comparisons between America and Hitler's

Germany are strident and inept," Styron still feels that an analogy with Adolf Eichmann is appropriate. "The Nazi functionary and the loutish American officer" both sought "exculpation of their enormous crimes through insistence that they were merely cogs in a great machine" (237). This may signal the link between *Sophie's Choice* and the military fiction he sought to develop into *The Way of the Warrior,* but as with the discussion of Höss in *Sophie's Choice,* the mode is as much that of a journalist or historian as it is that of a novelist.

The historical contexts ultimately merge in Styron's awareness of the complex intermingling of race with warfare. In "A Farewell to Arms" he writes that "racism was as important, ideologically, to the conduct of the Pacific war" as "to the war in Vietnam," and perhaps even more so "since there was no such propagandistic cause as anti-Communism to impel those peach-cheeked youngsters to wage a war against an enemy caught in the thrall of a fanatical, even suicidal nationalism." He links this with the war in Europe, arguing that "racism in warfare had already been initiated by the Germans, who, imputing to them a subhuman status, had begun to exterminate hundreds of thousands of Russian prisoners of war (many gassed at Auschwitz) while in general treating their Anglo-Saxon foes with acceptable decency" (230). He also points out an unpalatable truth that associates German aggression with the military mind-set of any culture. Marines, he notes, train for "annihilation of the enemy" (231). Like young soldiers anywhere, they exist in a haze of "youthful machismo" (232) and a "seething lust for action" (233). The moral fiber of the individual does not differ as greatly as the context in which individuals find themselves. This is not to deny good and evil character or gradations of intelligence but to acknowledge that individuals and their actions are subject to the opportunities and traps of history. The more aware of this we are, the better we understand our own and others' behavior. For such awareness is what self-realization is surely about.

This Quiet Dust shows that Styron saw historical awareness as integral to his art. Perhaps this aspect of his writing seemed unfashionable to some. But as he said of Rahv, so one might say of him: his fiction, like his essays, are characterized by a "refusal to be bamboozled by trends or fashionable currents" and an ability to write "in terms of difficult and complex values which he had laid down for himself." *The Long March* may be a slight work by comparison with the major writing, but its central figure, the rebel marine Captain Mannix, exemplifies the Styronian ideal. "Beaten but indomitable," as he says of Mannix in *This Quiet Dust,* he is an "indefatigable man" (335). This is precisely the self-reliance that underpins Styron's admiration for the modernists, for the likes of Orwell and Camus, for critics like Cowley and Rahv, and for classic European authors such as Flaubert. It's also, therefore, what underpins *This Quiet Dust*, itself a hymn to "the art of self-realization."

In genesis and approach, *Darkness Visible*, Styron's immensely influential account of his experience of clinical depression, provides a very different example of his essay writing. It aids our understanding of this illness and sheds light on the themes and preoccupations of his fiction, but its compact, modulated voice exemplifies the masterful nature of the mature work. Reading *Lie Down in Darkness* beside *Darkness Visible*, Jeffrey Berman is struck by how Styron's characters "anticipate the symptoms of clinical depression" he would write about directly decades later. But Berman also notes that the young novelist could never have written such a work. At best, he "might have treated" the subject matter "satirically," whereas the mature writing is "more compassionate." *Darkness Visible* recognizably belongs to the author of *The Confessions of Nat Turner* and *Sophie's Choice* in that every paragraph is an orchestral blending of notes and tones, yet this memoir is also fresh and revealing. Standing aside and assessing the storm, Styron plays in a different key. He reviews his battles through the thicket of the writing life and, in Al Styron's phrase about her father in these years, beholds, sometimes with recoiling "horror," "his unreconstructed self."[15]

We need to be careful about directly linking the experiences Styron describes with his characters' dispositions. His own views on this in *Darkness Visible* are contradictory. He describes the memoir as the only time in his life when he has "felt it worthwhile" to make his "privacy public." He also claims that in the mid-eighties he was a near "ignoramus about depression." Yet he acknowledges that he now sees "how depression had clung close to the outer edges of" his life for years.[16] Rereading passages in his novels in which his "heroines have lurched down pathways toward doom," he's "stunned" by the accuracy with which he "created the landscape of depression in the minds of these young women." So the illness, when it finally came to him, was "no stranger, not even a visitor totally unannounced," but had tapped at his door "for decades" (78–79). *Darkness Visible* does suggest where a number of Styron's characters come from. It's impossible not to think of Stingo and Sophie, but also Milton and Peyton from *Lie Down in Darkness* and Peter and Cass from *Set This House on Fire*, when we read of Styron's "malaise and restlessness" (8), of "gloom crowding in," of "dread and alienation," "stifling anxiety" (12), and of a mind "dissolving" (13). In the early fiction especially, such emotions abound.[17]

Self-realization in *Darkness Visible* is about chiseling order from chaos. Such an activity might involve wishful thinking. One thinks not only of Styron's relapses but also of, say, John Berryman's sadly mistitled account of alcoholism, *Recovery* (1973), unfinished when he threw himself into the Mississippi in 1972. Indeed, Styron admits his own inclination to avert his eyes: "Most likely, as an incipient depressive, I had always subconsciously rejected or ignored the proper knowledge; it cut too close to the psychic bone, and I shoved it aside as an unwelcome addition to my store of information" (9). This alone should alert us to the possibility that the memoir blends forthrightness with necessary evasion. The creative act must barricade against despair. In a way, this is the case with Styron's writing from the outset. When he says in *Darkness Visible* that "one dreads the loss of all things, all people close and dear" (56), I think of Cass's anxiety about losing his family. When he writes of "fierce attachments" (57), I think of Milton's gathering of paraphernalia—a flag, a bottle—as if clinging to the wreckage of his life.

Since *Sophie's Choice* deals with Stingo's anxieties and Nathan's insanity, it's obvious that many aspects of the novel are autobiographical and likely that the illness helps explain some of them. When Styron in *Darkness Visible* writes of how, at "a later stage" of the disease, his "mind would be dominated by anarchic disconnections" (14), it's easy to think of Nathan's behavior but also to note that the novel, which in its juxtaposition of sex and the Holocaust caused such a stir, does indeed involve anarchic disconnections, even though one reading of this is that it parallels a common experience in contemplating the Holocaust.[18] Al Styron talks of her father's lows being punctuated by delusions and megalomania. Yet both she and he (in *Darkness Visible*) describe the depression, in Styron's words, as "not of the manic type—the one accompanied by euphoric highs" (38). It was, he says, "unipolar" (38), and she corroborates this (248). The truth, I suspect, is that Styron did experience "euphoric highs" but chose not to see this as part of the disease, as indeed it may not have been. Stingo may, as Bertram Wyatt-Brown notes, have "moments of deep and debilitating gloom and anxiety," but he also has difficulty managing his "euphoric high" when with Sophie and Nathan.[19] During the writing of that novel Styron, as he says in *Darkness Visible*, "used alcohol as the magical conduit to fantasy and euphoria, and the enhancement of the imagination," as well as "to calm the anxiety and incipient dread that I had hidden away for so long somewhere in the dungeons of my spirit" (40). The unanswerable question *Darkness Visible* poses is whether the memoir echoes the novels or the novels echo the experiences he illustrates in the memoir.

But quite beyond the light *Darkness Visible* shines on the fiction, the book reveals an invisible medical condition as felt from within. Even as Styron explains that depression is "so mysteriously painful and elusive in the way it becomes known to the self—to the mediating intellect—as to verge close to being beyond description" (7), he in fact vividly describes it. In turn he cites William James writing in *The Varieties of Religious Experience* of depression as "a positive and active anguish, a sort of psychical neuralgia wholly unknown to normal life" (17). This is not least interesting because both these writers are so good at describing something purportedly beyond description. Indeed, a powerful element of *Darkness Visible* is Styron's determination—he tries again and again; depression is a "trance," a "helpless stupor," "full time exhaustion" (17)— to use novelistic skills to describe the supposedly indescribable, just as *Sophie's Choice* makes use of the essay form to articulate the unspeakable.

Without the detail of *This Quiet Dust, Darkness Visible* still has something to say of other writers, and not least in terms of Styron's vision of self-realization. Of his triumvirate of engagé role models, he here singles out Camus, whose "unblinking vision" he thought "capable of frightening the soul to its marrow." This goes some way toward explaining the real angst and aims of *Set This House on Fire*: the determination to accept the existential truth. But Styron himself links it with *The Confessions of Nat Turner*. He likens Nat's predicament to "the cosmic loneliness" of the hero of *L'Etranger*, calling him Meursault's "rebel predecessor" who is "condemned and abandoned by man and God." Styron chiefly discusses Camus in terms of the French writer's own battles with depression, but because he so admired Camus's clarity of thought, the French writer comes across in the end not as a victim but as an inspiration: "a great cleanser" of Styron's intellect whose "unsettling pessimism" aroused him anew to "life's enigmatic promise" (21).

While the limits of self-realization are all too obvious in the face of mental illness, and Styron testifies to its horror, the humor and beauty of the prose defy the chaotic. We see humor in *This Quiet Dust* in, say, his description of the complacent jury who preside over the fate of Benjamin Reid. ("The jury was asked if it would like to retire and deliberate right away, or it if would like to have lunch first. It replied that it would like to have lunch. After it had fed itself it retired and came back with the verdict in a little over an hour" [127].) But the humor is more consistent and less sardonic in *Darkness Visible*, from the characterization of the psychiatrist, Dr. Gold, to the incidental description of the depressed self as "me, aged four and a half, tagging through a market after my long-suffering wife" (57). Therapy sessions, described as "organized infantilism," are seen through an ironic yet compassionate eye. The class is "run by a delirious young woman with a fixed, and indefatigable smile, who was plainly trained at a school offering courses in Teaching Art to the Mentally Ill." Told to take their "crayons and make drawings illustrative of themes" they themselves have chosen ("for example: My House"), Styron obeys "in humiliated rage," draws "a square, with a door and four cross-eyed windows, a chimney on top issuing forth a curlicue of smoke," and is showered with praise. As the weeks advance and his health improves, so does Styron's "sense of comedy."

> I began to dabble happily in colored modeling clay, sculpting at first a horrid little green skull with bared teeth, which our teacher pronounced a splendid replica of my depression. I then proceeded through intermediate stages of recuperation to a rosy and cherubic head with a "Have-A-Nice-Day" smile. Coinciding as it did with the day of my release, this creation truly overjoyed my instructress (whom I'd become fond of in spite of myself), since, as she told me, it was emblematic of my recovery, and therefore but one more example of the triumph over disease of Art Therapy. (74–75)

This wonderfully nuanced passage combines humor with modulated prose and an added fascination: is the patient really playing a game or merely believing this while actually being helped through the recovery process? At stake is the author's identity. On the one hand, he's in control of the material, molding the language like clay. *Les mots justes* are everywhere—"delirious," "fixed, and indefatigable," "humiliated rage," "dabbled happily," "pronounced"—each adding to the sense of his assured command of the situation and understanding of the teacher's character. On the other hand, there's room to doubt his claim that therapy has been useless. An outrage though it may be to the author's intellect, the therapist-patient interaction has produced a warmth (a fondness for her in spite of himself) that has accompanied his recovery, and perhaps aided it. We chuckle with Styron but suspect more.

All this goes into making *Darkness Visible* both masterly and moving.

As in *Sophie's Choice*, the chiaroscuro at times renders a dark subject unexpectedly light, so that we reflect on the darkness in context. The exhilaration of reading the work lies in the sense that we're being told painful truths within life's wider parameters. The overwhelming impression it leaves is of the paradox of the beautiful prose describing depression's messy reality. Styron purports to be recollecting in tranquility, but this is more projected desire than reality, a fact that makes the account all the braver. Self-realization can involve a stupendous effort to assert meaning in the face of overwhelming odds—a definition, of course, of existential defiance.

Havanas in Camelot, the last of the nonfiction I will look at before moving into the novels, is (*Selected Letter* aside) one of three books of Styron's writing published posthumously, the other two being *Letters to My Father*, which includes early stories, and *The Suicide Run*. A book of essays brought together at the end of a career might suggest marginality, but the apparently marginal can inform the bigger picture. Even the shortest statements, put down with care, and especially when self-motivated rather than commissioned, exist because the writer has felt them worthy of record. The "personal" essays of *Havanas in Camelot* are indeed very different from the more public essays of *This Quiet Dust* and lack the obvious public interest of *Darkness Visible*. But with regard to Styron's novels they are just as much expressions of his vision, and his commitment to self-realization within the cultural contexts that surrounded him and of which he was so learnedly aware.

A case in point is "Walking with Aquinnah," an essay about the need for, and joy of, solitude, albeit with the companionship of one of his series of beloved dogs. We see from the start that walking and writing share characteristics for Styron. "Our walks are for business and pleasure," he explains, "and also for survival—interlocking motives that have somehow acquired nearly equal importance in my mind." The brisk daily walk is designed "to force oneself into a contemplative mood" (151). The resistance at the start "is like a faint palpable ache, not in the feet or legs but somewhere around the rim of the cranium," and the opening minutes are thus "a splendid time to recollect old slights and disappointments and grudges." But "almost without fail there comes a transitional moment." He begins to contemplate his work. "Ideas, conceits, characters, even whole sentences and parts of paragraphs" pour into him, until he achieves "a state close to hypnosis" and is quite oblivious of his surroundings. Finally, he is "as heedless as the rhythmic motion" of his feet, as if he "were paddling through air like some great liberated goose or swan" (152–53). The description of walking becomes a description of working. All writers know the process. Tolstoy describes it in *Anna Karenina* when Levin, mowing with his serfs, becomes attuned to the rhythms of work. Joyce Carol Oates talks about it in terms of running, which, not unlike writing, felt for her "a little like dreaming: dreams in succession." William Stafford describes it as "like fishing": "I do not wait very long, for there is always a nibble—and this is where receptivity comes in." Mowing, running, fishing—all these are activity metaphors for much the same process.[20]

Styron's own analogy tells us some specific things about his personal creative process. He was no runner, flying through "dreams in succession," but a ponderous, ruminative novelist, requiring time and space to take flight. "I ain't no speedball," he wrote in an introductory letter to his first agent, Elizabeth McKee. "Do you just sharpen your pencils and sit?" I asked him in 1998. "Yes, and whine, 'the horror, the horror,'" he replied, "or follow that famous reflection of Conrad's" that he found writing "so difficult that almost never did he approach his writing desk without the urge to burst into tears."[21] Something in him resists the approaching effort. There is a physical but also a mental resistance, which might explain why the pain is in the head. But the act of walking, or working, transports him to another realm. The writer is in the Zone.

Once again, voice is important here. Like the *Darkness Visible* passage about "the triumph" of therapy, it illustrates how Styron's writing included enough expression of vulnerability to secure intimacy with his reader. For in truth, through the magic of writing, Styron is not without human company on this walk. The reader overhears his thoughts. So *Havanas in Camelot* provides insight into the writer's process, but also into the writer's nature. On rereading these essays I was struck, for instance, by how they show the openness of Styron's writing. Whereas in the "more French than American" engagé essays of *This Quiet Dust* he concentrates on the kinds of political issues that inform his mature fiction, here we see the emotional honesty—or attempt at such honesty—that draws us in the first place.[22] He doesn't pose, or retreat into irony, cynicism, or disdain. He may use strategies to enhance his fiction, but (notably in *Sophie's Choice*) he seeks not to trick you but to invite you on a journey that may involve emotional laceration but also enlightenment and catharsis. It's also the quality in his later fiction that blurs the lines between fiction and nonfiction. In these "personal essays," Styron, to use his comment on Orwell, comes across as "supremely himself."

At the same time, though, the word *personal* needs nuance. Our observant companion is not, in these essays any more than in *This Quiet Dust*, really interested in himself. We return, consequently, to a quality of self-realization that is awareness of oneself in the context of others. For instance, he writes of "personal" issues—the misery of prostate problems in "Too Late for Conversion or Prayer"; the terror of thinking one has a sexually transmitted disease in "A Case of the Great Pox"—but does so as informed observer even of his own emotions. This instinct to be the observer rather than the protagonist is constant throughout his career, and evident as early as *The Long March*, in which the narrator, Lieutenant Culver, watches Captain Mannix and Colonel Templeton. His narrators reveal much about themselves, but only because they focus on others. Even the superficially egotistical pronouncement "Call me Stingo," alluding to Melville's Ishmael, is really the narrator's ironic comment on Stingo's self-centeredness, and it also links Stingo to another observer rather than to a hero or antihero: a fellow traveler witnessing Ahab's self-destructive pursuit of Moby-Dick.

A pertinent essay in this regard is "Havanas in Camelot" itself, in which Styron effectively acts as Nick Carraway to John F. Kennedy's Jay Gatsby. Indeed, the essay reminds us that Styron himself was as capable as anybody else of being starstruck. His intimacy with the reader here arises from our joining him in witnessing the supposed glamor of celebrity, though the essay in fact pivots on Kennedy's vulnerability as a human being in an extraordinary situation. The most striking image of the doomed president is the final one Styron provides, which is (so he writes) the last he had. It captures Kennedy in a private moment of uncertainty at a New York party in November 1963. Hopeful "before going" that he and Rose "might get a brief glimpse of him and nothing more," on the way into dinner they find Kennedy "at the bottom of a flight of stairs looking momentarily lost and abandoned."

> As if arrested in an instant's solitude, he was talking to no one and pondering his cigar. He had a splendid Palm Beach tan. He threw his arms around us and uttered a line so cornily ingratiating that it gave blarney new meaning: "How did they get *you* to come here? They had a hard enough time getting me!" He asked me how the novel was coming, and once again he began to talk about race. Did I know any Negro writers? Could I suggest some Negro names for a meeting at the White House? And so on. Finally someone distracted him and he disappeared into the crowd.

> Sometime later, on his way out, he caught my eye and, smiling, said, "Take care."
>
> They were words I should have spoken to him, for exactly two weeks later, on another Friday, he was dead in Dallas. (16–17)

The onlooker, not the main act, Styron views the president with a compassionate eye as, if not exactly "an elegant young roughneck," then an ordinary man behind the public guise.[23] Again, too, the anecdote is beautifully crafted. The scenario is utterly believable in its incidental nature and the naturalness of the encounter. Styron wins over the reader by referring to the hope for a "glimpse," which is all that readers, at most, would be likely to have had of Kennedy. But the image of Kennedy at the bottom of a flight of stairs reveals the art. Perhaps Styron did meet Kennedy in this way, but how apt is the notion of the soon-to-die president, shorn of the trappings of worldly fame, in limbo, awaiting his call to ascend, whether to some imagined afterlife or merely the ether of history. In a *This Quiet Dust* essay on French president François Mitterrand's memoir *The Wheat and the Chaff*, Styron writes of "the good novelist's knack of looking past the obvious for the immanent, the particular, the revealing detail" (302). His vignette of Kennedy epitomizes this, capturing the individual as well as the image just prior to his apotheosis.

Havanas in Camelot touches on another important issue in Styron's fiction: his rejection of censorship. He wrote, as West puts it, "uncooperative novels" that brought "noisy criticism." Some readers were offended on racial grounds, some on cultural, some on religious, some on moral, some on professional. One can never be sure what will offend or who will be offended; rather as chemists grumbled at Flaubert's portrayal of Homais in *Madame Bovary*, so at least one librarian wrote to Styron complaining about his portrayal of Sholom Weiss ("a pallid dour thirtyish man with aggressive horn-rims and a green eyeshade" who reprimands Sophie for thinking there might be an American poet named Emil Dickens [103]).[24] But the fact is that Styron wrote about things others felt he shouldn't write about, and in ways that they felt compounded the offensiveness. On a "personal" level, "A Case of the Great Pox," which is in part about his relationship with his stepmother, Elizabeth, offers an intriguing insight into this impulse. "I thought her a prig," he writes. "She considered me a libertine." He characterizes the woman his father married for reasons Styron was "never able to fathom" as "ungainly, humorless," and "pleasure-shunning" (54–55). This is hardly compassionate, but beautifully modulates vocabulary and rhythm. The young man, who has already announced his "scepticism" and "fealty to Camus," is straightforward. He "thought" her a *prig*. The stepmother passes judgment down her nose at the youth, probably wordlessly, perhaps merely by dilating her well-blown nostrils. Styron's Latinate verbal expression tells us all we need to know about her facial expression. She "considered" him a *libertine*.

Moreover, this may well tell us a great deal about why, deep in his psyche, Styron felt justified in detailing Sophie and Stingo's consummation (as the stepmother might have put it). On the one hand, Styron was always out to detail the joys of life as well as, to use a phrase from *Sophie's Choice*, "the bitter bottom of things" (412). The artist must seek truth and need never answer to the censors, censurers, lobbyists, moralists, or the rest—who need not read the novels anyway. Asked about the sex scenes in *Sophie's Choice*, Styron said he celebrated the fact that, unlike Tolstoy, he could write about life in all its complex web of truths and in its combination of horror and beauty. Tolstoy, believing that "the aims of art" should be to have people "laugh and cry over it and love life," would have approved. But even Tolstoy could not show "life in all its countless, inexhaustible manifestations" when it came to sexuality. In *Anna Karenina* he resorted to describing erotic foreplay between Anna's lover, Vronsky, and his horse, Frou-Frou, as a substitute for Anna. Sex had to take place as a horse race, in the transition between chapters, and through death imagery ("He felt what a murderer must feel when looking at the body he has deprived of life"). In literary terms, Styron said, "I celebrated the fact that I had the choice, in our era, since World War II, which Tolstoy did not have." On the other hand, we can well imagine, and find evidence in *William Styron, A Life, Reading My Father,* and *Selected Letters,* that this strident rebellion stemmed on some level from the libertine's desire to shock the prig.[25]

So this collection of personal essays clarifies one of the most attractive things about Styron's writing. He combines commitment to his craft, and to addressing subject matter worthy of it, with a rebellious streak that champions the art of provocation. "If anything," he told me at one point, "I find I'm more rebellious the older I get." No wonder he kept Flaubert's dictum on a wall by the door of his study: "Be regular and orderly in your habits, like a good bourgeois, so that you may be violent and original in your work."[26] Again, the "personal" impulse is wedded to the historical. Meditating years after the fact, in "I'll Have to Ask Indianapolis," on the editorial interventions in *Lie Down in Darkness*, he notes that this does show you how, at mid-century, there still existed in certain quarters in America a point of view about free expression that was severely circumscribed, still profoundly in thrall to nineteenth-century standards and to prudery that now seems so quaint as to be almost touching. It could be said, of course, that we have gone over the edge; indeed, there have been some books published in recent years that I've found so scabrous and loathsome that I've yearned, at least for a moment, for a return to Victorian decorum and restraint. Yet my yearning is almost always short-lived. People, after all, are not *forced* to read garbage, which, even if it overwhelms us—or seems to at times—is preferable to censorship. (72–73)

Styron originally delivered these words in an address in 1994, when no one knew where the Internet would lead us, but even while they are prophetic of the dangers of a free-for-all, they stoutly defend free expression.[27]

Styron's final argument in "I'll Have to Ask Indianapolis" reminds us that, whatever else, the sex scenes in *Sophie's Choice* are not there to titillate but to further authenticate the psychology of the characters. "The present-day foes of sexually explicit writing," he points out, fail to understand that people are curious, and such foes "thus undermine their own cause." Nowadays, "the nearly universal availability of erotica" has, he suspects, left "the mass of people" discovering "an excruciating monotony" and so signing off for good. His advice, therefore, to "the censors who would re-establish the tyranny" of his youth is that they should accept "that it's the sordid absolutism of denial—not what is accessible—that turns people into cranks and makes them violent and mad" (78). This, he implies, is the context in which we assess Stingo's behavior. "The books in the Duke University library were the rocks and boulders to which I clung against my onrushing sense of doom and mortality," writes Styron in the essay (79). How interesting it is, then, that such a line is so close to the narrator's sense that Sophie's celebration of her sexuality is also forged, at least in part, from the same motivation— "a plunge into carnal oblivion and a flight from memory and grief" (496)—and that sex, or thoughts of sex, have "the capacity to obliterate the future, and the unspeakable dread of it" that besets Paul Whitehurst in the *Suicide Run* story "My Father's House" (147). Sex and death are as intertwined in Styron as in Tolstoy (or indeed Shakespeare), but Styron was uncensored, and he made the most of it.

So what shines through *Havanas in Camelot* is that "the art of self-realization" for Styron is deeply connected to his sense of responsibility to the written word even as he champions the right to freedom of expression against the yahoos, the censors, sections of academia, and, as noted, the prigs. Again and again in these essays, whether celebrating others, musing on his own trials, or writing of the joys and fears common to us all, he combines a determination to plough his own furrow with a thorough commitment to free, eloquent, and accurate expression. Once again, his assessment of the qualities of other writers tells us about the qualities he aspires to himself. In "Celebrating Capote," he concludes that "like all of us writers" Truman Capote "had his deficiencies and he made his mistakes, but I believe it to be beyond question that he never wrote a line that was not wrested from a true writer's anguished quest for the best that he can bring forth" (93). Similarly, writing of James Baldwin in "Jimmy in the House," he reveals his commitment to the writer as rebel. "A common conviction dominated our attitude toward the writing of fiction," he explains, "and this was that in the creation of novels and stories the writer should be free to demolish the barriers of color, to cross the forbidden line and write from the point of view of someone with a different skin." There were two Styrons, the observer and the protagonist—or at least the one who acted on conviction, who took the artistic risks. The first felt "reluctant to try to enter the mind of a slave," while the second "felt the necessity," and told Baldwin, whose "encouragement—so strong that it was as if he was daring me not to" won the day (98–100). A writer can break taboos, can forge paths, and can do so with dedication to the form. All lives are doomed, all ambition falters, even if sometimes only in the wake of success. But this is one of the positions we can take toward life, and the one that Styron chose. No less than *This Quiet Dust*, therefore, these essays are about "the art of self-realization."

I began with the penultimate essay, "Walking with Aquinnah," to show how even the most "personal" of essays reflects on Styron's overall craft and vision. The final, and slightest, essay in the collection is if anything even more personal, and easily the most moving. "In Vineyard Haven" was retrieved from his papers after his death. Bill is buried on Martha's Vineyard, as was surely his wish, beneath a pin oak in the graveyard near his Vineyard Haven home on High Hedge Lane, and the essay anticipates this. Like "Walking with Aquinnah," it's about solitude. For all the glamor of "Havanas in Camelot" and all the emphasis in his fiction on historical narratives, the great issues of the era and the nation, he took comfort in routine.

When I first read "In Vineyard Haven" I thought of Julien Sorel at the end of *The Red and the Black*. Julien is intensely ambitious but happiest in solitude even while such solitude is finally used to reflect upon community and his relations with others. In this sense Julien is the quintessential artist. Isolated in his prison cell, he is consoled by the fact that he "didn't *live in isolation* on earth." Rather, he "had a strong sense of *duty*," which he "had prescribed" to himself "for right or for wrong." "Like a solid tree-trunk," he's been "swayed" and "buffeted," but not "swept away."[28] For good or ill, Bill Styron the man shared with Julien—or with what Julien might have become had Stendhal allowed him to live into maturity—that sense of self-reliance, that drive, paradoxically most honed in solitude, even while its effect was public, to leave some monument to having lived. But it's not the glamor or praise that matters, day to day, if at all, it's life itself in commonplace manifestations: rolling the car off the ferry in the dock area each spring in anticipation of a summer on the Vineyard; "the homely façade of the A&P," Main Street's "unprepossessing ranks of mercantile emporiums" (159); Vineyard Haven's "forthright frowziness" (160).

> I like the small-town sidewalks and the kids on bikes and the trespassing gangs of dogs and the morning walk to the post-office past the Café du Port, with its warm smell of pastry and coffee. I like the whole barefoot, chattering mêlée of Main Street—even, God help me, the gawping tourists with their Instamatics and their avoirdupois. I like the preposterous gingerbread bank and the local lady shoppers with the Down East accents, discussing bahgins.
>
> Mostly I love the soft collision here of harbor and shore, the subtly haunting briny quality that all small towns have when they are situated on the sea. (161)

Clearly what attracted him to Vineyard Haven was on some level connected with the environment of his childhood. Newport News and Vineyard Haven become one in his description of the sounds of such environments, "sounds unknown to forlorn inland municipalities." For one accustomed to them, such sounds "lull the mind and soul" (161).

> The blast of the ferry horn—distant, melancholy—and the gentle thrumming of the ferry itself outward bound past the breakwater; the sizzling sound of sailboat hulls as they shear the waves; the luffing of sails and the muffled boom of the yacht club's gun; the

eerie wail of the breakwater siren in dense fog; the squabble and cry of gulls. And at night to fall gently asleep to the far-off moaning of the West Chop foghorn. And deep silence save for the faint *chink-chinking* of halyards against a single mast somewhere in the harbor's darkness.

Vineyard Haven. Sleep. Bliss. (161–62)

This is simultaneously a nostalgic passage and one about the contentment of growing older (Styron being sixty-five when this was first published). He started out with a novel about a community by a river and ended with a story about the same place. His novels in between involve the Amalfi coastline, a dream of "where the river meets the sea," and the beach at Coney Island.

One always has the feeling, in other words, that however historical in scope, Styron's art came out of something immensely personal and authentic that had to do with immediate environments and ordinary lives, even as it nods to the greatest of literature, from Stendhal to Melville to Tolstoy to Twain. For the artist engaged in the true "art of self-realization" the personal is always entwined with the historical. In making his statement, Styron sought to wed personal experience with the historical contexts that helped to create and shape it. His essays can be read in their own right as important elements of his writing career. They do provide insight into the novels, but they are very much part of who he was as a writer. More than this, they reveal aspects of the man himself—perhaps of his *ideal* self—his values, attitudes, beliefs, and explanations of the motivations behind his "uncooperative novels." They also reveal why his friends, family, and even readers who never met him in the flesh felt such loyalty to him. Few who read the essays sympathetically can return to the novels without a sense that this is a writer who has contemplated his craft and brought to it an innate generosity, a wealth of information, and a depth of insight that marks him out as a rare kind of writer. This is the spirit in which I now offer my personal rereading of the novels—returning first, appropriately enough, to his fictionalized vision of his childhood environment, a place that, no less than where he ended his days, echoed to the sound of water colliding softly with the land.

CHAPTER 4

The Significance of *Lie Down in Darkness*

> Her mind spanned forth, encompassing some small vision of the future.
> It was silly, and so easy: to think of a moment when time had run down
> like an old woman's heart, and the house on a sunny Sunday afternoon
> is full of grandchildren and, venerated, you rise to face the love of those
> who call you by name, being able to say then *accomplished, accomplished.*
> —*Lie Down in Darkness*, 1951

> I realize that you shouldn't look at your career as what you failed to do
> but as what you *did* do. I feel that to have written as painfully and labo-
> riously as I have—I'm not singing the blues, it's just true; there were
> extraordinary emotional, psychological difficulties involved in getting
> these works out—and to have produced what I have, is something I can
> celebrate.
> —STYRON, IN "LOOKING BACK," 1998

There are many remarkable things about *Lie Down in Darkness,* and one
of them is that Styron wrote such a novel in his mid-twenties and with
barely any publications to his name. But rereading it now, we can situate
it as part of the panorama of his career. Three particular books stand in
interesting relationship to this first novel. The best of his apprentice fiction is now available in *Letters to My Father,* together with letters written
at the time of the novel's composition. There is also *Sophie's Choice,* in
which Styron dramatizes both his youthful worldview and the writing
of his first novel under its original title, *Inheritance of Night.* Finally, we
can now reread *Lie Down in Darkness* in light of *Darkness Visible* and
Styron's battles with clinical depression. While this chapter focuses on
the significance of *Lie Down in Darkness* as a work of art, these later
publications form part of the discussion.

Before returning to the novel, for instance, it pays to ponder *Letters to My Father*. Not only the letters but also the apprentice fiction in the volume provides fresh context. On the one hand, the letters record the young Styron wrestling with its composition and intent upon emulating his heroes. Verifying his later memories in *This Quiet Dust*, the eighteen-year-old Styron tells his father that Thomas Wolfe "is the greatest writer of our time" (12). We also learn that he was reading, among others, Faulkner, Hemingway, Balzac, Maupassant, Joyce, Poe, and Dos Passos. On the other hand, the personality of the mature novelist is also evident. The young man has little to say about the stories, the novel, or the subject matter as such. There are just occasional comments; "The Long Dark Road" is "a story about a lynching, and the psychological effect of it on a young boy" (17). But he has plenty to say about the craft and effort of writing, and plenty, too, to say about society. In both cases, the mature writer and his views seem almost ready-formed.

To be sure, his description of "the *mechanics* of writing," of the need to wring "every possible drop of richness out of your mind and onto the page" (58), imitates the letters of Flaubert and Conrad. "The process of sitting down and writing is pure torture to me," he tells his father, "but at the same time I think about the book all the time and am in more or less a suspended state of worry and anxiety if I'm *not* writing" (64). Composition, he insists, is "a tedious and agonizing process and I loathe writing with almost a panic hatred" (69), to which one might respond with Henry James's thoughts on Flaubert: "His case was a doom because he felt of his vocation almost nothing but the difficulty." Whether or not this is conscious mimicking of Flaubert, or Conrad, or other literary figures who articulate their difficulties with their craft, the young man is very aware of their perspectives.

> I could have written a publishable novel by now, but if it's fifty years before I see print I'm going to make certain that what I submit to the public eye is as good as I can do, and not a shoddy substitute for the best. That perhaps sounds precious, but I believe it, and I'm going my solitary, painful way about it. In the meantime I'm paying homage to the masters—Flaubert, and now Tolstoy—and all the elements of this dreary period of indenture begin to settle gradually into their places—form, technique, style—like pegs in a cribbage board. (75)

But in truth, the mature writer fulfilled the prophesy he made at age twenty-four: he would bide his time and keep "writing with the same slow, identical painstakingness" that he expected to "be employing forty years from now" (97). "I have been reading the letters of Joseph Conrad, and really feel a kinship—if nothing but in spirit—with the late master," writes the young man, "for one discovers in the letters that writing, for Conrad, was the most despairing, painful job in the world" (61). In old age, Styron would still be citing Conrad's comment "that writing for him was so difficult that almost never did he approach his writing desk without the urge to burst into tears," even though he gained mature awareness, dramatized in *Sophie's Choice*, that such self-pity over one's art is indeed "precious" when set against real pain and despair.[1]

But he remained dedicated to his craft—almost tragically dedicated, one might think from *Reading My Father*—and just as this dedication never wavered, nor did some of his core beliefs. "The religion of the Church," he writes at age nineteen, "is a religion of hypocrisy. The good life is a life of *Good Will*," rather than "fanatical adherence to a Book, most of which is a gruesome melange of cruelty and pagan cosmology" (26). His goal in these letters too is essentially what preoccupies him in the later essays. He seeks and seems to find through the course of the letters "a measure of Emerson's self-reliance," and he defines this as a life goal (81). "The world situation is such that I—along, I suppose, with everyone else—really don't know whether a novel, or a symphony, or anything else, is worth the trouble or not," he writes aged eighteen. "But I suppose that if you relinquish your claim as an 'individual,' no matter what your endeavor might be, or in whatever state the world is in, you might as well cease living" (65).

Finally, these letters reveal attitudes that run smoothly into the older narrator's viewpoint in *Sophie's Choice*, so verifying the emotionally autobiographical element that so pulls us into that novel. "Even then," writes the narrator, "I was beginning to rue the lilac *fin de siècle* hours of my college days, with their total immersion in metaphysical poesy and Quality Lit., their yawning disdain of politics and the raw dirty world, and their quotidian homage to the *Kenyon Review*, to the New Criticism and the ectoplasmic Mr. Eliot" (193). In much the same vein, in a letter written when he was twenty-one, Styron insists that "for a person whose sole burning ambition is to write—like myself—college is useless beyond the Sophomore year. By that time he knows that further *wisdom* comes from reading men like Plato and Montaigne—*not* Cotton Mather—and from getting out in the world and *living*" (45). Similarly, his portrait of his boss, Edward Aswell, and of McGraw-Hill colleagues parallels his depiction of the Weasel and the drunken O'Farrell in *Sophie's Choice*, who, grieving the loss of his boy on Okinawa, tells Stingo to write his "*guts out*" (24). "I still bear a half-hearted resentment against the cold, pudgy little man who so abruptly dismissed me and I'm sure *he'll* never publish any of Styron's immortal and lucrative prose," writes the young Styron of the letters, while aware that Aswell may have done him a favor. "I would have for years, as I do now, wanted to write," he reflects, "but would have instead become more and more involved with *other people's work* until the actual *will* to write would have vanished and I would have nourished many regrets." O'Farrell clearly represents his friends at Whittlesey House who wished him "godspeed and were frankly and sincerely rather envious because they too," at his age, "wanted to write but got enmeshed in publishing" (57).

The path, then, is set. But one of the truly engaging elements of the letters is that the Styron we hear in them is not the "supercilious young man" the narrator calls Stingo (5–6). He is confident, yet modestly aware of his inexperience. Whereas James says that Flaubert's career was "singularly little marked by changes of scene, of fortune, of attitude, of occupation, of character, and, above all, as may be said, of mind," the young Styron knows that he is early in a journey and has much to learn.[2] His comments on his novel are markedly astute. Despite trying to write truthfully, he is aware, even during composition, that he doesn't "know enough yet about people to be writing a novel" (67). *Lie Down in Darkness* "naturally won't be the Great American Novel," but it will, he believes, be "about as good a first novel as you're likely to see. Besides, if it were my masterpiece, what would be the use of writing any more?" (94). The young Styron seems, then, to know his novel's imperfections. His art, he sees, "is far from maturity." Moreover, he notes "the maturation process taking place" even as the composition advances (69).

As one turns from these letters to the early stories in *Letters to My Father*, this fact of maturation is indisputable. The Styron who completed *Lie Down in Darkness* was light-years beyond the boy who wrote this apprentice work. Nevertheless, the stories suggest the preoccupations to come. All but "A Moment in Trieste" have mortality as a theme, whether in terms of violent death or of the onset of old age. "The Long Dark Road" and "A Moment in Trieste" testify to Styron's early interest in the intersection between individuals and the historical moment. What none of them even hint at is Styron's extraordinarily ambitious approach to the novel form. *Lie Down in Darkness* is saved from feeling like a first novel by an architecture that minimizes our sense of the author's personality, while the faulty design of *Set This House on Fire* sets in relief the brilliance of the structure of *Sophie's Choice*. Styron exhibits his concerns rather differently in *The Confessions of Nat Turner*, but all these novels can be seen to have grown from seeds found in these stories.

"A Moment in Trieste" is unremarkable in that it concerns young men's experiences with women. But, set in postwar Yugoslavia, it does refer to Tito's dictatorship, and to tensions between East and West, and so anticipate the significance of the historical moment in Styron's mature work. In this it anticipates, too, the postwar expatriate theme of *Set This House on Fire*. A drunken afternoon and evening spent by two American men and two Yugoslavian girls comes to an abrupt end as the mood turns ugly with anti-Americanism and the word "TITO" blazes on the hillside (210). Based on Styron's experience of traveling to Trieste soon after the war, it expresses a concern that might well have informed at least one potential manifestation of *The Way of the Warrior*. For Styron spoke of his interest in America's Cold War paranoia of the supposed Communist menace and at one point in the 1980s toyed with the idea of reprising the Trieste experience.[3]

"The Long Dark Road" provides fascinating evidence of just how early Styron wrestled with racial prejudice and our capacity for evil. It dawns on Dewey, a boy at an adult gathering, that he is witnessing a lynching party. Not unlike Huck Finn at the shooting of Boggs or the tarring and feathering of the King and Duke, Dewey is shocked but also potentially involved. He hears what is to happen and refers to the "nigger" but, faced with the actual victim and event, runs away into the woods. If the theme may derive from writings by Hardy, Orwell, or Twain, the context is of course thoroughly southern, and the name Dewey suggests Faulkner's influence. Dewey experiences a nightmarish recognition of what people are capable of and is running terrified from the culture he has been born into. The story ends with a distant train whistle "wailing up through the valley," and then all is quiet (182). Just as that whistle anticipates the locomotive that will begin and end *Lie Down in Darkness*, so the story itself foreshadows Styron's concerns in *The Confessions of Nat Turner* by showing southern whites demonizing the people they once enslaved. It also foreshadows his portrayal of the racism endemic to the Pacific war ("Everybody knows the fucking Jap cocksuckers are a bunch of suicidal apes," as Colonel Halloran puts it in "My Father's House" in *The Suicide Run* [152]). This preoccupation with racism haunted Styron's fiction from first to last.

"Sun on the River" is again about the shock of violent death as told from a boy's viewpoint but reads like an expression of Styron's own early knowledge of overwhelming grief. A young boy named Chris stands with friends watching the funeral motorcade of Jenny Pattison, the victim of a riding accident. He thinks of the few times he spoke with or saw her. "And now Jenny Pattison was dead," he reflects. "Gone. Just like that" (183). Her absence produces in him a similar sense of the "terrible loss" he recalls feeling when a storm toppled an oak he had known all his life, a feeling worsened when he sees Jenny's parents', and especially her father's, "inarticulate grief" (184). Later, he cycles to the river and thinks of how strange this ordinary Sunday afternoon is, how the familiar is rendered odd now that he realizes that the present "will go and never return" (185). As in "The Long Dark Road," what stands out is the sense of place, the raw emotions, and the boy's helplessness on experiencing finality. *Lie Down in Darkness* will address this theme of loss without consolation—the stark amazement at what is, what will go, and what has gone.

Lastly, three stories are about a third path to mortality: old age. "Autumn" and "The Ducks" are sensitive portrayals of the aging process. In "The Ducks," Thornton is an unfit fifty-five-year-old with heart trouble. His doctor has warned him not to be out in cold weather, but Thornton enjoys duck hunting, which gives him time to contemplate. When the ducks finally arrive, he shoots and misses. Thornton shouts at his dog, paddling among the decoys, but two more ducks arrive and veer off. He fumbles for cartridges, runs to get a good shot, and dies of a heart attack. "Autumn" concerns a day in the life of an aging schoolmaster, Weatherby, and tension between him and a youth named Calloway. Calloway's insolence and tardiness irritate Weatherby, but the boy is good at composition and writes a reasonable essay on sailing. Weatherby echoes Styron's own habits of the time in that he enjoys writing in a tavern, drinking beer in solitude, working on a manuscript, and watching the river's "flowing, somnolent beauty" as it runs out "like a man's life to the sea" (194). After a third bottle of beer, Weatherby returns to school to sleep, only to be awoken by the noise of Calloway and his friends. He confronts them, but a voice in the dark calls out, "You drunk old bastard" (196). Humiliated, he retreats to bed without resolving the situation. Overcome by "a rending pang of loneliness," he hears "a distant whistle" from the river, and his years sweep "down upon him like fallen leaves" (197).

The last story, "The Enormous Window," is also the tale of an older teacher's humiliation. Mr. Jones has a sickly wife and a stepdaughter but feels unrequited passion for a Margaret Temple. The insolent boy this time, Jeffries, is rumored to have been in possession of pornographic material. Mr. Jones tries to explain that sex is nothing to "snigger" about (219) but suspects that Jeffries's silence is designed to mock him. Margaret is going away to Ohio, where her father has had a stroke. After she and Mr. Jones have said farewell, he falls asleep by the river, misses chapel, and later goes out to where Margaret lives. He watches her through an enormous window, only to come crashing down from his perch. Believing that she's seen him, he wanders home, but encounters Jeffries, who later tells of Mr. Jones appearing like a "ghost out of the woods." "Sex!" Mr. Jones evidently cried, "Faith, boy!" And then he wandered off up the road muttering, "Love, love, love" (225).

These stories, then, focus on big themes rendered in terms of the author's limited experience but intense observation. Against the symbolic resonance of the James, they show an obsession with coming to terms with life in full awareness of death. ("It's what's *inside* the man that counts," Mr. Jones insists. "Self-discipline" [218].) So much narrower in scope and ambition than the work to come, they still foreshadow the seriousness of Styron's mature subject matter. But again, what they in no way foreshadow is that this young writer would compose a novel so structurally complex yet miraculously readable as *Lie Down in Darkness*. Interesting as the stories are, Styron's genius was in the novel form. To read them simply reminds us of this.

"Oh, Stingo," writes Styron in *Sophie's Choice*, "how I envy you in those faraway afternoons of first Novelhood (so long before middle age and the drowsy slack tides of inanition, gloomy boredom with fiction, and the pooping out of ego and ambition) when immortal longings impelled your every hyphen and semicolon and you had the faith of a child in the beauty you felt you were destined to bring forth" (112). *Lie Down in Darkness* is indeed ambitious. Maybe this "fine, rare, desperate" novel scares Joe McGinniss the older he gets because he can't "imagine how Styron could have written it at twenty-five."[4] Its significance as a novel, after all, lies not just in what Styron produced in artistic maturity but in a mastery of structure and language astonishing for one so young. But it may also scare McGinniss because of the only thing it shares with the early stories: death-hauntedness. For that formal ambition contrasts with its theme of helpless despair; it's not in the service of youthful exuberance, beginnings, or triumph, but of gloom, endings, and disaster. We barely hear Peyton Loftis, the young heroine, until her final monologue, and even then what is most striking is her lack of a sense of self or future. In looking at the significance of *Lie Down in Darkness*, therefore, I will concentrate on its harnessing of techniques old and new, but also on how its real power lies in the way this formal awareness holds together its emotional outpouring. Through this "composed energy"—to use Robert Fitzgerald's phrase quoted by Styron in *This Quiet Dust* (344)—the young author begins to assert his unique perspective in search of his ultimately very different literary voice.

The subject matter situates *Lie Down in Darkness* in a southern tradition, but the tension between bleak theme and ambitious, tightly orchestrated form is also a matter of authorial identity. The young author cannot afford the relaxed improvisation of *Sophie's Choice*. Structure and viewpoint allow creative and emotional control. "As we all know, first novels tend to be works by young people about young people's lives, and very introspective and subjective," said Styron in 1998. "As a consequence they have little that is fresh and new." Setting out to write *Lie Down in Darkness*, he "made a deliberate effort *not* to write that kind of book" but "to write about a fully-fledged, grown-up family situation."[5] Such discipline means that the novel more resembles *Madame Bovary* or *The Great Gatsby* than, say, *The Red and the Black* or *Anna Karenina*. But it's also far more claustrophobic, more brooding—more "desperate"—than either. The taut structure propels it toward denouement but also camouflages a young author who seems to have an uncanny ability to dramatize anxiety and depression even while he has less grasp of the psychology of middle age or parenthood. The resulting mixture of vivid scenes, mellifluous phrasing, and intriguing characterization makes it a remarkable and disturbing debut novel.

All critics see that it owes much to literary precursors, particularly modernists, and primarily Faulkner. "Almost any fool could detect an influence of Faulkner in *Lie Down in Darkness*," Styron himself said in 1965. But many also feel that it brings something new for the period. "As with the better Faulkner novels," writes Louis D. Rubin, it has "a sense of mattering." Tamsen Douglass Love points out in quoting Rubin that though critics recognize "this originality," few have explored its "specific elements." Rubin notes the portrayal of a new South, and Christopher Metress applies Harold Bloom's "anxiety of influence" theory with regard to *The Sound and the Fury*, but for Love "a larger dynamic" explains both readings. The differences in the two novels suggest those "between modernism and postmodernism." In consciously revising Faulkner, Styron achieves originality by realizing "the new world contexts in which his novel is grounded."[6]

I can hear Styron's spirit chortling at this. Arguments about "what modernism is, or postmodernism," seemed to him "ultimately of no importance." But Love does helpfully position *Lie Down in Darkness* as instrumental in taking the novel form into the realms of the postmodern without lapsing into the excessive introspection and self-reflection of the extreme metafiction fashionable in the 1960s and 1970s. It also helps to frame some less understood elements of Styron's later fiction. Certainly, he was concerned from the start to write freshly and relevantly about the world he knew. In 1954, he suggested that Faulkner's experiments with time in *The Sound and the Fury* were "justified" rather than wholly successful. "Faulkner doesn't give enough help to the reader," he said. "I'm all for the complexity of Faulkner, but not for the confusion. That goes for Joyce, too." Similarly, in 1968, he described as "healthy" the move "away from too much interior, private, Virginia Woolf–type writing—the novel of sensibility." His muted interest in the more introspective elements of modernism would also explain his indifference to the self-referential forms of postmodernism. "I'm not attracted to that kind of writing," he said in 1988. He recognized that "it has its own raison d'être," and that obviously "good writing" will "cross boundaries." But he also knew the kind of writing that moved him and felt "important." "More often than not" this didn't include postmodernism.[7]

The modernist approach, and perhaps postmodernist metafiction, makes sense if one believes, with Woolf in "Modern Fiction," that realist techniques are outmoded. Surely, too, Styron took on board Woolf's observation that "life is not a series of gig lamps symmetrically arranged," but "a luminous halo, a semi-transparent envelope surrounding us from the beginning of consciousness to the end." But, to reprise John Barth's description of his "ideal postmodernist author," Styron "has the first half of our century under his belt" rather than "on his back." He was no writer-as-follower. "I know only one thing," he said in 1977, "that I've gone my own way and I've never followed any trends. I've been trying to say what I wanted to say in the way I wanted to say it." In doing this he recognized the paradox that replacing gig lamps with halos and envelopes in fact led, in modernism, as much to opacity as to transparency, or in the case of some postmodernism, to the intellectual cul-de-sac of overt metafiction. "I believe in limited opacity," he said, "which is to say that once you have 'conned' the reader into reading you and getting engrossed in your work, then you can do all sorts of things. This is the time-honored tradition. Tolstoy did it."[8]

Not unconnected with this is the extent to which, from the start,

Styron needed both to immerse himself in literary composition—"The sacred Novel" Stingo worships in *Sophie's Choice* (112)—and to provide insight into sociohistorical problems. Writers "can be anything," he said, discussing a proposed 1988 visit to Chile to support the opposition to General Pinochet. They can choose "to be in an ivory tower and write *Ulysses*," or, "like Faulkner," they can "stay on the lot down there in Oxford and write." But if they want "to be engaged" they have "a perfect right, and even obligation, to do it that way." Without question, *Lie Down in Darkness* shows that Styron must have been tempted by the example of novelists from Henry James to Woolf to write books (in Joyce Carol Oates's phrase) "characterized by an extraordinary blocking out of vast areas of life and a minute, vivid, at times near hallucinatory obsession with psychic experience." But his work shifted from what he called the "ornate and complicated" element of *Lie Down in Darkness* toward an altogether "more direct and less self-conscious" style as his career progressed. While he conceded his "natural" urge to "retreat" into "a worship of intellectual endeavor" after World War II, he was also concerned to eschew the modernist tendency toward elitism through opacity. Evidently referred to by Faulkner as "the best first novel he had ever read" (so Styron was told by Faulkner's editor, Bob Linscott), *Lie Down in Darkness* thus uniquely blends realism and modernism, setting Styron up for the major work of *The Confessions of Nat Turner* and *Sophie's Choice*, which are, for Dawn Trouard, "postmodern novels that have the best of both worlds."[9]

In fact, for Love, Styron may have been forging postmodernism long before his readers became aware of what he was doing. Seeing *Lie Down in Darkness* as much more than a modernist-inspired early effort, she argues that the characterization of Helen, Milton, Peyton, and Maudie is a pioneering example of the late twentieth-century emphasis on appearance and interpretation over "ultimate truth" and "the fragmented multiplicity of the postmodern consciousness." Maudie's "textual silence," for instance (unlike Faulkner's dramatization of Benjy's consciousness), means that the second Loftis daughter "functions less as a character in her own right than a representation and/or projection of Helen's inner struggle." Equally, the portrayal of Daddy Faith, who wows their black servant Ella Swan, shows Styron, in contrast to Faulkner's portrayal of a preacher, "emphasizing representation" over substance. While Dilsey encounters "an absolute truth, which is infinitely greater than herself, Ella experiences only the truth she reads into her experience."

"Postmodern characters don't just fail to grasp central truths about the human experience," writes Love. "They imply that such central truths simply do not exist."[10]

Love's interpretation credits the young author with more sophistication than the evidence suggests. The many times that distinctive characterization gives way to, in Oates's phrase, a "near hallucinatory obsession with psychic experience" signals a lack of control over the emotional element of the material (as opposed to the structure and language) rather than a philosophical position on the fluidity of the "self." Had Styron abandoned the solid structure he steals from realism, he would surely have written the "introspective" first novel "about young people's lives" that he tried "*not* to write." But the angst-ridden Loftises are indeed, as Love shows, caught up in a maelstrom of misunderstandings born of their tendency to project their inner struggles onto one another, with the reader, too, caught up in a world of representation. This observation fits with the sense in Styron's later fiction that we're experiencing dramas about divided selves and the complexities of self-deception and self-representation. This very struggle to hold angst in place with disciplined structuring again helps account for the novel's originality as a statement about that immediate postwar era.

As Jeffrey Berman intimates, comparing *Lie Down in Darkness* with *Darkness Visible,* one other important aspect of the novel is its satire. It may appear to be primarily about middle-aged people, and only indirectly about a troubled young person, but we see these people with a degree of distortion. "It seems to me that only a great satirist can tackle the world's problems and articulate them," said Styron in 1954. But satire only takes you so far. It's a controlled tone, certainly when compared with the heart-laid-bare approach of his compassionate voice in artistic maturity. When the novelist John Gardner writes of the Styron of *Sophie's Choice* as an author whose capacity for "justice and compassion" is "almost awesome" and describes him as "the same old Styron," willing to bare "his chest to whatever knives it may possibly deserve," he doesn't mean the Styron of *Lie Down in Darkness,* but the mature author. There is no overt narrator in this first novel (beyond the young man taking the train in the opening pages, a remnant of the narrator of *Inheritance of Night*), so any thoughts or feelings are filtered through one character or another.[11] But Gardner is also noting the link between compassion and vulnerability, or openness to criticism. The Styron of *Lie Down in Darkness* is artistically defensive. Wielding the sword of satire, he wears the armor of careful structure and stylized lyricism. True empathy comes with maturity. The satire in *Lie Down in Darkness* goes hand in hand with the fact that otherwise diverse, middle-aged characters betray a self-obsession more likely in youth and not a little anticipatory of Stingo. Indeed, as Berman also notes, they exhibit "collectively" most of the characteristics of the "descent into sorrow and madness" that Styron documents in *Darkness Visible*. The young author disperses his state of mind across the narrative in an attempt to hide what is fairly visible.[12]

Finally, in terms of this tension between structure and theme, it remains instructive to recall not just how evidently threatening one acerbic contemporary and self-perceived rival, Norman Mailer, found *Lie Down in Darkness* but also what precisely he focused on. Near the height of his enmity against Styron and others, Mailer called it "the prettiest novel of our generation." It "has beauty at its best, is almost never sentimental, even has whispers of near-genius as the work of a twenty-three year old," he wrote. "It would have been the best novel of our generation if it had not lacked three qualities: Styron was not near to creating a man who could move on his feet, his mind was uncorrupted by a new idea, and his book was without evil. There was only Styron's sense of the tragic: misunderstanding—and that is too small a window to look upon the world we have known."[13] I say instructive because, all things considered, Mailer's criticisms are not in fact that harsh, while the implicit praise is revealing. He intends to goad Styron, but while "prettiest" is meant as an attack on authorial manhood, it's also an acknowledgment of structural complexity. "Almost never sentimental" suggests that in places it is just that, yet acknowledges that Styron mostly managed to curtail such tendencies. And while "the work of a twenty-three year old" undercuts the praise, "whispers of near-genius" is generous enough. Backhanded compliments are still compliments. Equally, once you prune the aggressive phrasing, Mailer's subsequent criticisms are mild and not inaccurate: Styron fails to create independent characters or say anything fresh about human existence, and he reduces the notion of evil to misunderstanding. Such comments merely underline Styron's own awareness—in that letter to his father—that he didn't "yet know enough about people to be writing a novel." As Love, Berman, and others point out, the characters' perspectives do merge into one another. Indeed, as Love suggests, perhaps this reveals the novel's significance as a statement on an emerging era. But even if the novel is an original expression of that world, few people at all, let alone in their twenties, are likely to have anything fresh to say about existence. The same goes for the nature of evil. Mailer's criticisms are hardly devastating, while his praise, however vituperatively expressed, is praise indeed.

The significance of *Lie Down in Darkness*, then, has to do not with what nineteenth-century Russian intellectuals called *proklatye voprosy*— "the accursed questions" of life's meaning or the nature of evil—nor with an especially profound understanding of human behavior.[14] It has to do with the originality and ambition of its design, and the tension between that design and the young author's expression of the world that his contemporaries faced. Here was a young man who had lost his mother when he was fourteen, participated in the buildup to the anticipated invasion of Japan in 1945—to be saved only by the Bomb ("20,000 tons, 100,000 lives")[15] that haunts Harry and Peyton—and been recalled, even as he completed the manuscript, as a reservist for Korea. He was caught between a youthful "sense of ineffable promise and certitude," to use a phrase from *Sophie's Choice* (67), and a horrifying awareness not just of mortality but of scales of destruction unimaginable before the twentieth century. The tension between form and sentiment equates to that balance between overarching ambition and almost all-pervasive gloom. When someone in their twenties imagines the thoughts of people in their fifties, it won't be all that accurate. Satire of a midcentury Tidewater community mingles with a sense that Milton, Helen, and Peyton are born of one youthful sensibility. But Styron counters this by combining realist scene-setting and chronology with modernist stream of consciousness and temporal experimentation, all nuanced by innovations that anticipate postmodernism.

Beyond structure and theme, there are further ways in which *Lie Down in Darkness* has proved its significance. These include its lyricism, which together with the structural sophistication and complex characterization leads to a unique blending of the formal and the fluid, as well as one further innovation that marks it as a pivotal novel: the deployment of what Edward Murray calls a "cinematic imagination."[16] This combination established Styron as an innovative novelist even before his versatility became apparent. The characterization is of interest whether seen as a depiction of fragmented selves, as versions of the author's own troubled psyche, or as something of both. As Berman has shown, it hints at the discussion of mental illness that Styron sets out in *Darkness Visible*, but, in literary terms, it also anticipates the emphasis on inner realism represented by notionally separate characters in *Set This House on Fire*; the merging of author and historical figure in *The Confessions of Nat Turner*; and the drama of self-presentation so important to *Sophie's Choice*.

The design of *Lie Down in Darkness* is perhaps its main triumph. It ensures narrative cohesion despite multiple viewpoints and approaches. The realist trajectory toward denouement, influenced by *Madame Bovary*, enables Styron to avoid opacity despite the dizzying time switches we experience while "the atoms," in one character or another, "fall upon the mind."[17] In this way he combines traditions that might in other novelists seem distinct. But perhaps, too, the success of *Lie Down in Darkness* in terms of its formal structure but fluid lyricism has to do with his deployment, consciously or not, of a relatively new depiction of time and space.

Mikhail Bakhtin describes the novel form's development in terms of just such innovations. His term *chronotope* stands for how a novelist arranges the time-space relationship. Hence Flaubert introduces "cyclical everyday time" into the novel form, while Dostoevsky uses crisis time and has a penchant for "the chronotope of the *threshold*," for instance, "the staircase, the front hall and corridor."[18] In turn, Styron helps develop a chronotope only available to writers in the twentieth century: the cinematic. This includes the freeze-frame, the zoom, and the splicing of diverse times and spaces. In other words, he builds complexity of chronology and viewpoint onto realist linearity and clear signaling of setting and character, interweaving two quite separate patterns of time and space in a way that novelists were perhaps only able to conceive of and readers able to handle in the wake of cinema. For example, whereas *Madame Bovary* follows the story of Emma from Charles Bovary's schooldays through to their marriage, then her disillusionment, adultery, and suicide, Styron follows Peyton's not dissimilar trajectory: childhood-marriage-affairs-suicide. In doing so he follows Flaubert in using social events to create a portrait of a society. But unlike Flaubert, he also (as in some modernist novels) follows an entirely different arrangement of space and time. Interspersing Peyton's life story is the dawn-to-dusk Port Warwick day of her funeral. This is further layered by flashbacks that capture Peyton's young life and tragic death, and eventually by Peyton's monologue of confused timescales and perspective.

Of course, the funeral ride comes from *As I Lay Dying*, and the novel begins with a train journey modeled on Robert Penn Warren's opening to his 1946 novel, *All The King's Men*.[19] But Styron melds such influences into something both vivid and lyrical. The Loftis tragedy then unfolds by way of seven lengthy chapters and concludes with a train clattering south into the dusk. In the meantime the reader experiences the day itself, and the essence of the three characters' lives, as well as those of their black servants, Ella and La Ruth Swan, Helen's confidant, Reverend Carey Carr, Milton's mistress, Dolly Bonner, and her husband, Sclater (nicknamed Pookie), Peyton's first lover, Dick Cartwright, and a family friend, Dr. Lawrence Holcomb. Moreover, the action occurs within a vivid geographic, cultural, and historical context by way of a family Sunday, football game, birthday party, Christmas, marriage, and funeral, as well as in the postwar New York Styron will depict again in *Sophie's Choice*. More remarkable still, given the timescales and viewpoints, the reader always knows what's happening, why it's happening, or who a given character is.[20]

An early flashback involving Milton awaiting Peyton's coffin in the heat and dust of the Port Warwick morning exemplifies the subtle time shifts. The characters perpetually seek to withdraw from the ghastly present into memories, if not necessarily of happier days, then of times when the tragedy was still far off. Here, for instance, Milton recalls his wedding to Helen.

> Heartsick, frightened, he turned away, watched the water, listening. *I do not propose to convince,* his father had said (in the feeble light of a March afternoon thirty years ago, before the house was finally condemned, but not long before; when even the lightest footstep on the stairs sent a plaintive wooden squeal through the joists and beams, reminder not only of the swiftly aging house but of the passing of a finer, more tranquil age). (14)

The subsequent scene foreshadows the fragility of their marriage and its tragic consequences. Young and in love, Milton must still contend with a world of snobbery epitomized by a general's wife telling Helen that Milton is "the pick of the Army" (18). In this way Styron constructs solid scenes of satiric observation through numerous time levels, yet with a relentless temporal advance taking place both in the hours of time present (the day) and in the years of time past (from the parental marriage to Peyton's death). While also jumping back and forth in time and space, he thus preserves a basic, realist linearity.

For all the rounded characterization that makes Milton, Helen, and Peyton memorable, a modernist-style lyricism merges these three distinct characters into phantoms of a single consciousness. The "luminous halo" of meandering minds interacts with the "gig lamps" of plot. Styron reserves the extended stream-of-consciousness monologue for the pen-ultimate section of the final chapter, where we enter Peyton's mind à la Molly Bloom in *Ulysses* and Quentin Compson in *The Sound and the Fury*. Yet, even in the limited third-person viewpoints that make up much of the novel, *Lie Down in Darkness* is striking for the way Styron shelves the pretense of objectivity evident from Stendhal to Tolstoy in favor of a lyricism that merges both character diction and viewpoints.

This unifying lyricism is everywhere. While Milton's perspective is mostly disorientated by drunkenness, his language seeps into or out of other viewpoints. He shares it with Helen in her neurotic lunacy and with Peyton in her suicidal depression. Because these viewpoints are distorted, respectively, by alcohol, painkillers, and depression, the overall effect is a strange mixture of social satire and delirium. Indeed, the author's general obsession with transience is apparent in all three characters, so that narration and characterization merge as often as they seem distinct. The emotional power of this intermingling of the structured and the fluid is beyond contention. What's less certain is whether it's a conscious attempt to develop the novel form or simply a young author's struggle to bind his narrative. For Love, the emphasis on interpretation over final "truth" suggests postmodernism's "fragmented multiplicity." But Styron attempts to provide objectivity through the viewpoints of characters such as the Reverend Carey Carr, Dick Cart-wright, and Dr. Holcomb.[21]

This is especially so with Carey. Because he is Helen's pastoral con-fidant, his judgments of her and of Milton are signaled as impartial, yet they demonstrably distort how things (within the realm of the story) really are. If readers doubt whose fault everything is—and Milton's behavior suggests we should—Carey's judgments are surely meant to sway us against Helen. We are told that "his initial pity" for her "had been tempered by a strong irritation" at a woman who had been "too selfish, too unwilling to make the usual compromises, to be happy. And although he didn't know her well, he would like to venture that she was also a complete prig" (126). (The word *prig* is unlikely to be lost on anyone aware of Styron's description of his stepmother in "A Case of the Great Pox.") Meanwhile that "poor fellow" Milton is "making a valiant try of it, and if he wasn't saving himself, he had gone a long way toward saving Helen" (247). The fact that such judgments invariably favor Mil-ton undercuts Love's idea that the novel champions appearance over grounded truth. Ultimately this is the writer's skillful attempt to disguise his youth. His mastery of technique cannot mask inexperience when it comes to understanding people with the impartiality and compassion that only maturity might bring.[22]

But it's the evidence of "cinematic" innovation in *Lie Down in Darkness* that most notably anticipates the audacious nature of Styron's mature work. The young Styron seems at least for a while to have been obsessed with film. In "Moviegoer" (1983), he explains how in the wake of his mother's death he and a cousin spent an indolent summer in which hardly a day went by without the boys attending a movie, including a ten-day period when they "viewed a total of sixteen." For Styron, his experience suggests how from the midcentury onward it was "virtually impossible for a writer of fiction to be immune to the influence of film on his work, or to fail to have movies impinge in an important way on his creative consciousness."[23] While film influenced writers from the modernists on, its impact on *Lie Down in Darkness* is profound. The novel not only employs cinematic techniques but also depicts time and space in cinematic ways. If the flashback technique is evident when Milton gazes at the water and recalls his wedding thirty years previously, elsewhere we find moving camera angles, zoom shots, freeze-frames, and unusual shot positioning.

At Peyton's sixteenth-birthday party, for instance, Helen is furious that Milton has given Peyton whiskey. Peyton tells Helen she despises her. We then follow Helen's eye as she takes in both close-up details and the party's panorama.

> Flushed, trembling, Helen returned to the terrace. Milton smiled at her gaily. She turned away. A cloud scudded over the lawn, darkening the day like a shuttered room. Wind shook in the trees around the terrace, rustling the young girls' hair, expiring with a tender sigh as the day returned in a rush of light: the shadow swept down the lawn, vaulted the swimming pool, vanished. Below, in a patch of sunlight, she saw a familiar figure.
>
> Oh, Maudie dear.
>
> Down the slope she hurried, holding her gown up. Maudie sat alone in a chair near the pool, eating an ice-cream cone, glittering braced leg outstretched before her as she gazed impassively out at the river and the approaching storm. Helen drew near her, bent down and looked into her face, saying. "Come on, dear. Come with me. We're going home now." (82–83)

Maudie takes Helen's hand. "Over the river thunder" breaks "with a crash." Bathers flee the pool. Drops fall amid "excited voices from the terrace." The musicians scurry indoors, "bearing aloft music stands and saxophones," while on the terrace Milton stands "talking with Peyton" (83).

Elsewhere in "Moviegoer," while sure that cinema caused his work "to be intensely visual," Styron describes himself as "not by nature a creature of the eye" but one who vibrates "instead to music" (105). This aural mind-set is true elsewhere in this first novel and in later work, but not here. Aurally the passage lacks distinction—it's not an example of the novel's *lyricism*. Nor does the writing have the rhythmic resonance of the mature work. Instead, its vibrancy is visual and its mode is cinematic. Perhaps a writer unexposed to film could have written it. After all, it has in abundance the quality Flaubert so valued in connecting description with action. Perhaps, too, in Helen's shift from idea to idea, it calls to mind Woolf. But from the moment she turns from Milton to the cloud, the passage is cinematic. Indeed, it's reminiscent of the scene in Fitzgerald's unfinished Hollywood novel, *The Last Tycoon* (1941), in which the director Monroe Starr explains what "making pictures" involves.[24] It's a series of images. Helen sees the wind in the trees, follows the shadow down the lawn to a patch of sunlight, and zooms in on the detail of Maudie's "glittering braced leg." Then, in a move like the swing of a camera, her eye sweeps back up to the terrace, the guests and musicians hurrying in from the rain, and Milton standing with Peyton.

Another example of the cinematic is Styron's deployment of the freeze-frame. In chapter 4 Helen (using projector imagery) tells Carey how, as she watched from a window as Milton prepared to drive Peyton to college, "something happened" and "it seemed that time itself had stopped":

nothing stirred, no leaf fell; beyond the shore the incoming waves lay without motion in piled-up billows, suspended one behind the other in endless, furrowed procession around the bay, as silent and unyielding as if they had been carved from glass. The evening wind had frozen in the trees. Below, Milton and Peyton sat like statues together, and Peyton had one hand raised to a place where sunlight had gathered in her hair. There was no sound or movement anywhere, except for the furious quick beating of Helen's heart.

Something happened. Wind rustled in the trees again, a leaf fell, children shouted far off, and as once more the waves began

> to wash against the sand, Peyton's arm went round his shoulder,
> he looked upward, they laughed and turned their heads down to
> read—all as if her mind had been a film projector in which the
> film had stopped to offer her motionless detail of the scene before
> her, and had just then, at that instant, begun to move again. (118)

On the face of it, Helen's vision here is no different from many scenes in
realist novels. One thinks of Raskolnikov's nightmares about the murder of the moneylender, or Anna Karenina on the train after meeting
Vronsky. Moreover, it dramatizes a poignancy of life—that we exist in
time and can never stop it—that was hardly news in 1951. But the particular manipulation of Helen's perspective is not of a kind to be found
in nineteenth-century realism, nor obviously stolen from modernism.
It's specifically influenced by the notion of time in frames. It draws attention to the constructed nature of language depicting thought, but
also to the artificiality of the moving image.

If Helen's moment is akin to Milton's desire (cited earlier) for time
to stop, he has his own freeze-frame moment in a scene that also shows
another cinematic strategy: shot positioning. In this scene, just as Helen
viewed Milton and Peyton through a window as if it were a cinema
screen, so Milton's position is akin to that of a moviegoer. "The only
observer," he has a "private view" of Harry kissing Peyton during a lull
in proceedings, and it brings a "visceral, drowsy hunger."

> Helen moved aside, a glass was lifted, there was the tinkle of
> laughter and the clatter of dishes; a lush fräulein voice sang
> "Tränen ins Auge" above the remote whine of strings, and through
> the sphere of his glass, iridescent as a rainbow, which he raised
> to his mouth, he saw their lips touch and their eyelids drift close,
> and flutter excitedly, their arms about each other in an anxious
> embrace. No one saw, no one noticed, except himself, and he
> was split up the middle with a violent, jealous tenderness such
> as he had rarely felt before. Only a moment had passed. Bubbles
> of champagne rose sour and sweet beneath his tongue, and he
> watched in a sort of enchantment: Harry, dark and Jewish, hand-
> some, blood gently pulsing at his brow, and Peyton, hair about
> her shoulders, eyelids so clear they might be transparent, drawn
> down, fluttering—her lips on his. (278)

This latest "ornate" set piece, constructed to capture the relationship between Milton and his daughter as she moves to the next stage of her life, is essentially realist but unlike anything in, say, Stendhal, Flaubert, Hardy, or Tolstoy. Particularly striking is the way Milton views the scene "through the sphere of his glass." I'm not aware of any similar kind of scene in Joyce or Faulkner, though perhaps there's something of Woolf about it. But I can well imagine such a scene in a film by Hitchcock or, perhaps more aptly, one about alcoholism, such as Billy Wilder's *The Lost Weekend* (1945).[25] What makes it feel cinematic is not merely its intensely visual nature but its use of a foreground prop through which the background is seen.

At the same time, the scene again illustrates that such approaches, remarkable as they are, don't quite disguise the author's youthful perspective. The sophisticated structure fails to mask a less convincing grasp of the psychology of adults in maturity. Milton is vivid and memorable; his personality is on display in every scene. His viewing of his daughter through a glass is symbolic of the fact that he sees everything through the glassy glaze—or glazy gaze—of his alcoholic stupor. But his perspective doesn't wholly ring true. Why does their kiss cause him "a visceral, drowsy hunger"? Why are the couple in an "anxious" embrace? Why is he "jealous"? Why do his eyes linger on "her lips on his"? These are not the emotions of a father, but of a suitor. While incest is a theme—albeit much toned down from early drafts—and no doubt a useful way for the author to express emotions he would know about, but under another guise, it comes across as a superficial remnant from the influence of Faulkner.[26]

Milton's cinematic moment highlights the novel's strengths, as well as its themes, even as it exemplifies the chinks in the structural armor that betray its author's youth. But the novel's significance, such scenes show, is about more than its novelistic acumen. Sophisticated as it is in its overall structure, in such examples we see the novel depicting time and space in ways fresh to the novel form. While *Lie Down in Darkness* was far from being a forerunner in using cinematic techniques per se, it was innovative for the era, and Styron would go on, specifically in *Sophie's Choice*, to exploit cinematic technique in more subtle and influential ways.

Lie Down in Darkness is significant not only in and of itself, and for its modernist-postmodernist contextual interest as part of the evolution of the novel form, but also, of course, with regard to his later work. Its tension between outer realism (a domestic tragedy) and inner realism (a drama of fragmented consciousness) anticipates *Set This House on Fire*, as well as, less obviously, the creation of what Carlos Fuentes calls "a meeting place" between Styron and Nat Turner.[27] It also hints at the complex rendering of time and memory in *Sophie's Choice* and is of general interest in terms of Styron's structural explorations and innovations from novel to novel. Equally, while the social critique is in the ironic vein Styron learned from the likes of Flaubert and Fitzgerald, there are also signs of how he would later critique human failings within larger historical contexts. These range from the trivial—self-pity, jealousy—to the more profound phenomenon of bigotry. Such concerns reappear tangentially in *Set This House on Fire* and directly in *The Confessions of Nat Turner*, while in *Sophie's Choice* Styron blends portrayal of the trivial with the profound, to devastating effect.

Lie Down in Darkness is as much a portrait of bigoted provincialism as of mental anguish. The obvious element of this is the portrayal of racial segregation, but Styron brings in other forms of bigotry, including class with Dolly and Pookie Bonner and anti-Semitism with Harry Miller. Black Americans are a constant presence, but only ever as Faulknerian stereotypes set up to contrast with the white community in terms of faith and endurance.[28] Ella, La Ruth, and Daddy Faith and his followers are perhaps bound to be presented as stereotypes, given the minds that view them. They are the subject of overt racism from the stupid (Dolly, Pookie, the La Farges), and even among more sophisticated characters— notably Milton—racism exists in passive form. We are left in little doubt that it's endemic to this society, whether fed by ignorance, malice, or evasiveness.

Just as Styron's portrayal of racism anticipates *The Confessions of Nat Turner* (in subject matter rather than approach), so his depiction of anti-Semitism anticipates his linking of Sophie's story with the history of the South. Chester La Farge makes an aside about "Zionist Wall Street" (91). Helen's prejudice is even more overt: Peyton's fiancé, Harry, is a "filthy little Jew" (312). More striking is the portrayal of Milton's anti-Semitism, which he tries to quell to Harry's face.

> He remembered at first his patronizing tone. He remembered saying something about Jews, how he liked them, something about a warm quality they had which Gentiles really didn't possess. He remembered Harry's eyebrows going up at this, remembered thinking *What the hell am I trying to convince him about?* But he also remembered that he couldn't stop talking about Jews, that

he felt compelled to go on making Harry think he was a grand
guy. (307)

Harry himself is one of the novel's few intelligent characters. An artist
living in New York, he is the author's mouthpiece. "I don't know what
good it'll do anyone but me, but I want to paint and paint and paint because I think that some agony is upon us," he says (377). Indeed, his final
rejection of Peyton reads rather like the author's expelling the character
from his imagination. When she accuses him of not trying to understand
her, he responds that he's "spent two years" trying to do so. "Get out,"
he tells her several times, and she does—out of his studio, into oblivion
(380–81).[29] But Harry is more than an author figure in that his presence
shows Styron already noting the seeds of evil in everyday attitudes and
being willing to place himself in a character of a background different
from his own. On this score, therefore, Mailer was demonstrably wrong.
There is plenty in Styron's first novel to suggest that he knew that evil
was not merely a question of misunderstanding, and not least in terms
of the bigotry that functions to relegate the Other to mere servitude or
to outright exclusion.

If *Lie Down in Darkness* anticipates Styron's later preoccupations in
general terms, it also does so specifically, and the links with *Sophie's
Choice* and *Darkness Visible* offer most food for thought. Read retrospec-
tively, *Lie Down in Darkness* (like *Set This House on Fire*, but in a very different way) is a companion to *Sophie's Choice*. They produce the effect of
a dialogue between the man starting his career and the man unwittingly
completing it. *Sophie's Choice* is made to mirror *Lie Down in Darkness*, so
that the novels seem reflected in one another. But they equally mirror
each other in the preoccupation with mental illness, and in this both, as
Berman shows, mirror *Darkness Visible*.[30] While I made some reference
to the memoir with regard to this first novel in the previous chapter,
before turning to *Sophie's Choice* I want to show how the novel can now
be read in light of the memoir in terms of the fluidity of characterization
in particular.

Styron acknowledged this concern with mental instability with regard to *Lie Down in Darkness* in interviews as well as in *Darkness Visible*.
"The book was a form of psychoanalysis which freed me from any need
to go to a shrink," he said. He began it "in a wildly unhappy state of
neurotic angst" but ended it "a relatively happy young man."[31] Hindsight
draws attention to such issues, but plainly all three main characters
suffer from "neurotic angst." As Berman notes, Loftis "finds himself

confronting depression whenever he dwells upon the losses in his life."
Meanwhile, Helen's deteriorating mental health produces "a cancerous
religiosity that sees sin and damnation everywhere." Peyton too "proves
to be beyond cure or redemption." "Her language" both in the letter
and in her "convoluted stream of consciousness interior monologue at
the end of the novel, evokes a symptomatology" similar to that found in
Darkness Visible: "sleeplessness, loss of mental clarity, panic and, most
striking of all, a sense of drowning." As Berman concludes, "It is now
clear that a central driving force" of Styron's writing "is the need to master psychic conflicts and heal himself."[32]

Berman's emphasis on the symptoms of depression thus provides a
further way of understanding the fluidity between supposedly disparate
characters beyond seeing it as the result of a consciously postmodern
perspective, or of a young author struggling to contain his vision within
a disciplined structure and ironic-satiric mode. From Christopher
Smart's eighteenth-century poem "Lines Written During a Period of Insanity," in which he describes himself as "buried above ground," to Sylvia
Plath's *The Bell Jar* or, more recently, Joyce Carol Oates's description of
standing on a debris-ridden shore unnoticed as a boat with "sparkling
lights, music, voices" pulls out to sea, images of depression abound in
motifs that suggest this sense of being cut off from the world.[33] Perhaps
the characterization in *Lie Down in Darkness* arose as a combination of
all three explanations, but the fact is that the monologues, no matter
which characters they belong to, return again and again to similar ideas
and refrains.

One basic image prevails: they feel that they are separated from the
world by a transparent barrier, usually glass or water. Milton's vision of
Peyton through glass is an apt example. Styron himself would in later
years (albeit after shock treatment) talk of this sense of a barrier—of
feeling "spacey"—and use his hands to simulate a helmet as he spoke of
it. But more striking still is the way Milton and Peyton become like two
versions of the same psyche. Both characters suffer from extreme nostalgia. Milton's reaction to seeing Peyton kiss Harry causes him "to recall a
note of music only half-heard, sunlight somewhere, something irretrievable" (278). Peyton talks of "a land lost from me, unvisited, irretrievable"
(385). Meanwhile, Milton anticipates Peyton's jumbled monologue in
reflecting on his drunkenness as like "trying to relive an experience in
time, with the minutes all scrambled." Just as Peyton's mind becomes delirious, so her father's thoughts are punctuated with words like *anxiety,*

disaster, sweat, and *fever,* and he feels a need "to drown himself utterly as in the sea or beneath sand" (306).

Indeed, the motif of drowning is particularly interesting. While Berman notes Peyton's "sense of drowning" (68), her monologue in fact continues Milton's ever more frequent references, as if his consciousness has seeped into his daughter's neurosis, as, for Styron in writing the novel, it surely had. From the moment that Milton sees her as if she were "a double image thrown back through the waters of an aquarium" (307), the novel is awash with submarine imagery. She tells Harry that she feels "as if she were walking undersea." She complains that the day is "filled with water" (330). Her monologue itself is then full of such imagery. Craving alcohol (like her father), she talks of thirst, yet this is bound up with a sense that to "drink" will lead to "drowning." She imagines being immersed "into the drowning day, like an octopus in a tank" (348). Further on she speaks of watching a friend of Harry's, Edmonia Lovett, as if "through water" and "in transparent aqueous light" (367). It seems plain that Styron remained preoccupied with this imagery even while ostensibly shifting to a different viewpoint, and so revealed symptoms of the affliction that would incapacitate him in later years and ultimately end his artistic life. One can at least point to passages in *Darkness Visible* to note such connections. Just as Milton and Peyton feel set apart from the world, so Styron describes depression as "a poisonous fogbank" (58). While he stresses that no description is really adequate, he also likens the sensation "to drowning or suffocation" (17). However much Quentin Compson's monologue may influence Peyton's, the portrayal of anguish has an authenticity whose value, as with *Darkness Visible,* goes beyond the literary.

Further parallels between Milton and Peyton include her state of mind being mistaken for drunkenness. A passerby comments that she is "drunk as she can be." What follows is a gruesome and distressing description of mental anguish. "I am not drunk—," Peyton tries to explain, her "mouth working" but no words coming out.

A train came by with that frightful noise; I put my hands over my ears, watching it in a blur of vanishing light, heading south, a forest of upthrust arms, all tilted as if by a gale. And I thought: it was not he who rejected me, but I him, and I had known all day that that must happen, by that rejection making the first part of my wished-for, yearned-for death-act, my head now glued to the executioner's block, the ax raised on high and I awaiting only the final, descending bloody chop: oh my God, why have I forsaken you? (382)

This description of anguish chimes all too well with Styron's explanation in the memoir that what he felt during depression was close to, if very different from, "actual pain" (16). Peyton is especially traumatized by noise, and not least by the sound of a train, which brings back that image of a train—borrowed also, one would think, from the motif that starts and ends Anna Karenina's tragedy in Tolstoy's suicide-based novel—hurtling into Port Warwick at dawn and out again at dusk.

Another symptom of mental illness that Berman notes in connection with *Darkness Visible* is that of the shadow self. Peyton, in Berman's words, "experiences in the final hours of her life the same wraithlike observer that her creator personally experienced thirty-five years later." "Did I have a companion?" she asks herself while climbing the stairs to the room where she will jump to her death. "I felt that someone was watching me, myself perhaps: at least I knew I was not alone." Whoever or whatever this "someone" is, she senses it "huddled in a corner of the cutting room," watching her "with mourning eyes" (385). Acknowledging the depression that periodically blighted his life from a young age, Styron forty years later writes of "the sense of being accompanied by a second self—a wraithlike observer who, not sharing the dementia of his double, is able to watch with dispassionate curiosity"—as "a phenomenon that a number of people have noted while in deep depression" (64–65). Such moments, in the slippage between characters' minds and between Styron's different works, provide an overall portrait of the "hunted and haunted" man that Al Styron describes her father as being.[34] On this level, *Lie Down in Darkness* would seem to be as much a portrait of depression as *Sophie's Choice*. This is so in terms of Helen as much as Milton or Peyton. But whereas Helen's behavior is seen in a more detached and less sympathetic way, Milton's "poisonous fogbank" merges with drowning imagery into Peyton's parallel sense of being cut off from the world. When Peyton says, "I can't pause to remember, for a guilt past memory or dreaming, much darker, impels me on" (386), she could as easily be mouthing words designed for Milton, or even the author's description of himself.[35]

To turn, finally, to *Sophie's Choice*, just as *Darkness Visible* sheds light on both novels, so their psychological mirroring of each other is multifaceted. "Mothers and fathers—they're at the core of one's own life somehow," suggests Sophie, and *Lie Down in Darkness* illustrates this observation too (462). For all the vast historical canvas of *Sophie's Choice*, each novel is about family. The dynamics have simply been turned around. In *Lie Down in Darkness* a potentially incestuous father views his daughter through the glass of alcoholism. In *Sophie's Choice* a mother tells a young man, through a whiskey haze, about the loss of her children, fully aware that she is both a mother figure to him and an object of desire. The first is the story of a father recalling the tragedy of his daughter. The last is the story of a son (and son figure) recalling the tragedy of a mother (and mother figure). The father who has lost a daughter becomes the son who has lost a mother, even while within that story there is a mother who has lost both a son and a daughter. In the first novel, Styron's dislike of his stepmother and guilt over his mother is turned into Peyton's ferocious war with Helen and guilt over Maudie. (Styron's cancer-ridden mother wore a leg brace after a fall.) In the last novel he speaks more directly of this by way of Stingo's description of his mother-guilt and mother-love as portrayed in his passion for Sophie. Only in "A Tidewater Morning" will he lay bare his searing childhood memory.

Equally, there are parallels between Peyton and Stingo in New York. Both defend the South. Both discover the joys of music. Yetta Zimmerman is a warmer portrait of the landlady, Mrs. Marsicano. Nathan's disappearances and Sophie's loyalty replicate the incident in which Harry disappears and Peyton promises that he will return to pay the rent. Morris Fink echoes Charles Marsicano. The chiropodist Dr. Blackstock and Nathan's brother, Larry, combine to resurrect the psychiatrist Dr. Strassman. Sophie's clock dream creates the illusion that Styron has somehow taken Peyton's clock dream from his memories of Sophie, and so on. An enlightening element of the New York scenes in *Lie Down in Darkness* is the sensitive portrayal of the violation Peyton suffers at the hands of the milkman, Terry. This is evidence enough that Styron deliberately constructed Stingo's insensitivity as to what sex actually constitutes from a woman's perspective. Styron's first novel would thus seem to counter the feminist critical tendency to tar him with Stingo's failings.

Sophie's Choice shows that *Lie Down in Darkness* holds the mature vision in embryonic form. From first to last Styron possessed huge artistic ambition set against a bleak vision. Life felt like a dark trap, but with beauty and sustenance as cracks of light. His response was to affirm it, through art as well as companionship, despite and against the intuition that no final meaning exists. "Who knows our last end," says Peyton, "thrown from the hub of the universe into the dark, into everlasting space: once he said we are small blind sea things pitched up wriggling on the rock of life to await the final engulfing wave." Harry's response—the artist's response—is that "it's time for belief" (378), and this remained Styron's basic position years later. "I have always thought," he said in his sixties, "that tragedy is so provisional."[36] Yet the preoccupation with guilt is always there, whether Peyton's and Milton's or Stingo's and Sophie's. Details are turned around, but that theme remains. Guilt is the root of the characters' impulse to double back, reexamine, reread. Both novels show Styron's unflinching engagement with the human psyche. They may have been written by sensibilities at different ends of life—one not three decades from birth, the other not three decades from death—but both combine craft and critique with experimentation and angst. Both reflect, moreover, a twentieth-century culture dominated by a sense that, in place of the myth of ultimate truth, we live by projections and representations.

Rereading *Lie Down in Darkness* therefore elicits admiration for Styron's technical skill together with awareness that this is a young man's novel in disguise. Styron knew this. *Selected Letters* shows him writing to Maxwell Geismar in 1957 that "though it was a fine job for a novice it was still more arty than art" (239). But its qualities converse with its flaws, and this tension between architecture, tone, and topic fascinates. The novel may betray his struggle to contain his desperate vision within a disciplined structure and tone. It may also reveal symptoms of the depression that would dog his later years. It may even anticipate a postmodern emphasis on fragmented selves and rejection of "ultimate truth." These ideas are not mutually exclusive. What lingers is the sense that its immense ambition anticipates the novelist who will dare to re-create Nat Turner and ponder the Holocaust through Sophie. Its "ornate," "arty" quality prevents us from caring about these characters in the way that we care about Sophie, Nathan, and Stingo. In particular, Maudie leaves us indifferent because, as West says, she's more a symbol than a character. But there's undeniable beauty in this lucid nightmare, beginning with a train arriving from New York and ending with one heading deeper south, with Daddy Faith pointing his finger at the reddening sky.[37]

Helen is no spokesperson for the young author, yet her "small vision of the future" does suggest his own. He too knew that there might come "a moment" when "the house on a sunny Sunday afternoon" would be "full of grandchildren," and he would "rise to face the love of those who call you by name, being able to say then, *accomplished, accomplished*" (122). For all Helen's vanity, the smallness of her vision, and the satiric thrust of this moment, I recall it in conjunction with a July afternoon on the lawn on Vineyard Haven in 1998. Styron, in his early seventies, sat watching the yachts bobbing in the bay. "You shouldn't look at your career as what you failed to do but as what you *did* do," he reflected, so he felt that for all the "extraordinary emotional, psychological difficulties involved in getting these works out," to have produced what he did was something to "celebrate." Rereading *Lie Down in Darkness*, it's clear that this first novel is indeed very much a part of that overall achievement.

CHAPTER 5

Two Readings of *Set This House on Fire*

> If they survive the storm itself, its fury almost always fades and then
> disappears.
>
> —*Darkness Visible,* 1990

It was always going to be hard for the young writer to swim triumphantly
through to a second major novel in the wake of his extraordinary debut.
Styron followed *Lie Down in Darkness* with the novella *The Long March*
and struggled to produce a second large novel to match or surpass his
first. But this is why *Set This House on Fire* is such a Rosetta Stone of his
work—a key to what he was up to. In it he tries to achieve a structural
sophistication and a manipulation of viewpoint unlike anything that had
been done before. This chapter provides two readings of *Set This House
on Fire.* The first assesses it as a novel of outer realism and, by comparing
it with *Sophie's Choice,* shows how and why it falls short on this score.
That in itself is a way of showing that had Styron not risked failure he
might never have discovered how to succeed. But the second reading assesses *Set This House on Fire* as a novel of inner or psychological realism
and, with reference to *The Brothers Karamazov,* suggests this to be a more
rewarding approach. These two readings follow on from the tension in
Lie Down in Darkness between the satiric impulse and the expression
of youthful angst. Judging from Styron's comments, he certainly meant
Set This House on Fire to be that social critique with a satirical edge. But
it's the underlying drama, with its debt to Dostoevsky in particular, that
gives the novel any lasting significance. Beyond structural ambition and
this tension between outer and inner realism, *Set This House on Fire* is
also interesting in terms of its theme of existential rebellion. A brief

critique of *The Long March* will help to bridge the gap from *Lie Down in Darkness.*

Simply because it was, for many years, one of Styron's relatively few book-length works, *The Long March* may have received, if only by comparison with the major novels, more critical attention than it merits. But it does show early signs of Styron's technique of integrating time shifts smoothly through the narrative. We witness Lieutenant Tom Culver's recollection of how Colonel Templeton ordered Culver and his fellow marine reservists on a long march in full pack through the night, and of Captain Al Mannix's inverse rebellion in attempting to carry out the absurd order to the letter. At the same time, we glimpse Culver's memories within memories. Important too is Styron's contemplation of the nature of authority. Caught between respect for it and for those who rebel against it, Culver anticipates Peter Leverett in *Set This House on Fire.* Not brave or foolhardy enough to rebel himself, Culver is fascinated by Mannix, whose rebellion against Templeton Styron means us to see as emblematic of humankind's plight in an indifferent universe. One of the novel's prevailing images is Mannix's memory of being held, paralytic, out of a window, not unlike a newborn child held upside down to cry: "upturned drunkenly above the abyss, blood rushing to his head, in terror clutching at the substanceless night."[1]

Mannix's supposed battle with Templeton results in, as Styron refers to the novella in *Sophie's Choice,* a "tragicomedy of the absurd" (450). Hampered by a nail in his boot, he becomes ever more frenzied and tortured in his quest. The irony, Culver knows, is that Templeton is oblivious. "Couldn't he see?" thinks Culver of Mannix. "That the Colonel didn't care and that was that?" The hike, for him, is not about "courage or sacrifice or suffering, but was only a task to be performed." He is "as far removed from the vulgar battle" that Mannix seeks as the "remotest stars" (111). Culver's description of the non-contest as a version of the human condition makes the novella top heavy. The struggle feels all too petty and inconsequential set against the language of mortality. But it does at least introduce the theme of authority, to which Styron will add nuance in later military works, as well as in his major novels. It also resurrects the theme of representation over substance, which Tamsen Douglass Love identifies in *Lie Down in Darkness* and which will remain significant in later work. The drama Culver articulates is Mannix's invention, just as humankind's vision of the world is a projection of our own inescapably language-shaped minds.

The Long March is also about status and the trappings of hierarchy. Templeton's demeanor, gestures, and possessions—specifically his silver pistol—all signal his sense of his status. He embodies a belief not merely in his own authority but in hierarchy. So the novella is not just about the ways that people, whether out of pragmatism or hero worship, accept authority but about an impulse that feeds authority: vanity. As in his later military fiction, Styron explores the ambivalence the powerless person can feel toward the empowered. The narrator of "Marriott, the Marine" in The Suicide Run, for instance, admits to "a residual respect—certainly fascination—which, demeaning as it may be," he finds "impossible to uproot" even years later (38). Meanwhile, Mannix has a bizarre love for Templeton, or for the battle engaged. He is a marine despite himself, proving his credentials even in the act of rebelling. Templeton's odd, tender, even mildly erotic holding of Mannix's injured foot at the end reveals the extent to which Mannix's attempt to complete the march has been a perverse love dance to woo a self-regarding man who is oblivious to Mannix's desire.

To this extent, The Long March is also about brainwashing. Both Culver and Mannix are drawn into the very ideology they try to avoid. Both fear they might not "make it." Moreover, Culver feels a mixture of "resentment or disgust" that his fear mingles with "fugitive pride" (70). The march is a structure imposed. Templeton is making a physical but also symbolic statement that he is in charge. But by taking up the challenge so vigorously, Mannix verifies this. He turns it into a struggle that both gives him purpose and challenges his own sense of meaning. This is something we do all the time with social structures. We make sense of life through symbolic acts. But to engage so fully is to legitimize the authority and to allow it its actual power. Mannix's tragedy, as Culver recognizes of himself as well, is his failure to assert autonomy. In the terms Styron provides in his essays, this is a failure of "self-realization." Both men surrender to a vision of the world created by others. Culver comes to see that he himself is "not man enough" to rebel, "far less simply a free man." Instead, he is "just another marine" as is "Mannix, and so many others" and they will "go on being marines forever" (102–3).

The paradox of military life as Styron portrays it, therefore, is that notions of heroic individualism exist amid a regimentation in which hierarchies are maintained and status conferred, rather than being the essence of the person. In the military, the aim is to train all soldiers to the same fighting level. The very lack of individualism among the participants, uniformed as they are to symbolize their position within the hierarchy, is part of the point. In this sense, Styron's version of the military becomes a microcosm for all society. "We are victims of ourselves," in Styron's words. "It's very hard to be an individual in this world."[2] In *The Long March*, the nature of the venture defeats the search for individualism from the start.

As the march continues, Culver and Mannix lose their sense of identity in a welter of disorientation. "During the first few miles" Culver is "at least in rough possession of his intellect, his mind lashing his spirit as pitilessly as his body." But later his brain, "long past cooperation," plays "hardly any part at all." Early on, Mannix becomes "superimposed upon Culver's own fantasies." Later, Mannix's actions seem "part of the general scheme, the nightmare." He's no longer Culver's "familiar friend, but something else—a shape, a ghost, a horror—a wild and threatful face reflected from the glass" (78). Culver comes to realize that all identity, all hierarchy, all order, is a fiction that provides meaning rather than reflecting any truth beyond our own minds. Mannix ends up, towel slipping, naked; he's both the newborn and the cadaver on the slab. In his own mind, and Culver's, he comes to epitomize existential defiance against the cold stars. But it's a dubious rebellion so far as the immediate world of military authority is concerned, since it merely reinforces his adherence to the system.

Styron takes up these themes in *Set This House on Fire*. "I'd rather be a failed ambitious writer than a mediocre writer who has tried nothing," he told Georgann Eubanks in 1984. This second novel verifies the sentiment. Ambitious it is, yet read as outer realism it's demonstrably less integrated than his other novels. Ironically, whereas *Lie Down in Darkness* triumphs in terms of a structure that helps disguise its author's youth, *Set This House on Fire* is usually seen as having a "structural flaw" (Louis Rubin's phrase). Indeed, it might seem hard to champion a novel that tells the same story twice for no evident reason. But sometimes we judge in terms of what we look for rather than what an author invites us to see.[3]

Given that *Set This House on Fire* provides two views of the same material and is thus a kind of double novel, it seems appropriate to offer two ways to read it. To begin with, I'll illustrate its failings as outer realism. But I'll then show how, by reading the novel as experimenting with viewpoint in order to challenge conventional representations, we can view it more rewardingly as inner realism. The novel registers a change, to use Styron's terms cited in the previous chapter, from the "ornate" mode of *Lie Down in Darkness*, by way of the straightforward third-person perspective of *The Long March*, toward the "direct" narrative voice of *The Confessions of Nat Turner* and *Sophie's Choice*. But this direct style is deceptive. It still deals with the kind of multifaceted, fragmented selves evident in *Lie Down in Darkness*. The changing style does, however, relate to the structural experimentation and to questions of identity, including authorial identity. As such, *Set This House on Fire* not only documents Styron's development toward his two classic novels but, as Georg Lukács recognized, has considerable literary merit in its own right in that its theme of "alienation" exemplifies what "links significant writing in our time with the great literature of the past."[4] My eventual reading of it in relation to *The Brothers Karamazov* should reinforce that view.

I

First, though, there is the question of how and why *Set This House on Fire* is Styron's least successful novel when seen in terms of outer realism and readers' expectations of how such novels work. The question is worth answering because Styron will adapt the experimental elements of *Set This House on Fire* more successfully for *Sophie's Choice*. The flaws shed light on the triumphs of the later novel and help show how that novel evolved. Where John Gregory Dunne reread *Sophie's Choice* several times "to see how it worked," *Set This House on Fire* can be reread to compare ambitious structuring that would seem to fail with ambitious structuring that clearly succeeds.

Lukács's praise notwithstanding, judged as outer realism *Set This House on Fire* compares poorly with Styron's other novels on fundamental levels. The extensive rejected material in the Library of Congress and his interventions in the galleys speak to the unusual trouble he had with its composition. But in terms of the finished product, the first issues in assessing its outer realism are (to use Styron's phrase from 1953 in *Letters to My Father*) the "problems of *Plot, Atmosphere,* and *Characterization*" (153). The plot is creaky, the atmosphere variable, and the characters cartoonish. As Judith Ruderman puts it, "The main events of this very long book" can "be quickly summarized."[5] The lawyer Peter Leverett is the recipient of the largesse of his old school friend, the dissolute playboy Mason Flagg. Mason is living in a villa in the fictional hilltop town of Sambuco (based on Ravello). Invited to visit, Peter drives from Rome and is put up in the Hotel Bella Vista because Mason is renting the downstairs apartment to the impoverished alcoholic painter Cass

Kinsolving, his wife, Poppy, and their several children. That night two people are murdered. One is a peasant girl, Francesca Ricci, who has also been raped. The other is Mason. It turns out that Mason raped Francesca, who, with Cass's help, was stealing medicine for her dying father, Michele. The village simpleton, Saverio, then stumbled across and killed her, and Cass then killed Mason, believing him to be the murderer. But it hardly matters. Few readers are likely to believe in or care for any of the characters or any of the violence or suffering they perpetrate or undergo. Peter really is what Stingo seeks not to be: a "hapless supernumerary" in a "tortured melodrama" (62).

To write melodrama is one thing, to tell such a story twice quite another. In part 1 we get Peter's viewpoint, and in part 2, largely Cass's, filtered through Peter. Hence Peter tells of Mason's invitation to Sambuco, of meeting the drunken Cass, and of learning of the murders the next day. He then retells the story as relayed to him by Cass two years after the event. The rationale for retelling the story is to match up Peter's partial ignorance with Cass's alcoholic amnesia and discover the sequence of events. The "structural flaw," therefore, is the use of a flimsy rationale to retell what is in any case an unconvincing story. Once again, the characters and the reader engage in the process of rereading, but the activity's results barely seem to warrant the time spent pursuing them. Worse still, this design fault leads to a flaw in terms of character interaction. Read as realism, *Set This House on Fire* commits the novelistic sin of containing interactions (between Peter and Cass, but also between Cass and Luigi Migliore, a local policeman) that lack dramatic conflict. Given their roles in the narrative—linked only by knowing Mason—no issue exists between Peter and Cass beyond their interest in discovering what happened. They are simply acquaintances in possession of half a story. Equally, Luigi merely cajoles Cass to give up booze. His role is to be a confessor, a bit like Porfiry Petrovich in *Crime and Punishment,* but unlike Porfiry he lacks apparent mischief and shows no interest in solving the crime. While Dostoevsky's scenes are masterful examples of suspense, the closest we get to conflict with Luigi is when Cass, irritated by the Italian's verbosity, utters one of the novel's truer comments: "Get on with your story" (349–40).

This structural weakness, however, highlights the structural strengths of *The Confessions of Nat Turner* and *Sophie's Choice.* Having a character listen to another's story is central to each novel, but in contrast to the lack of tension here, the white lawyer, Thomas Gray, needles Nat and Nat manipulates Gray, while Stingo is infatuated with Sophie as an older woman and Sophie perhaps sees in him something of what her own son might have become. Styron's galley cuts to Peter's and Cass's narrative explanations show that he tried to remedy this. It's true that he cut down on the dialogue between Nat and Gray too, but those cuts heighten the tension between what can or cannot be said. In *Set This House on Fire* the cuts simply shorten a meandering narrative.

Meanwhile, given that Peter and Cass are both in hock to Mason, a further weakness is that the three central characters are too alike. Cass may be poor, Peter middling, and Mason wealthy. Cass may have a vocation, Peter a job, and Mason an empty life bedecked with pretensions. But all three are thirty-something, white, male Americans frequenting Europe with varying degrees of purposelessness. Cass is supposedly a painter, Peter apparently a lawyer, and Mason evidently a playboy, but they're not convincingly portrayed any more than they're vivid as individuals. Whereas his successor, Nathan Landau, leaps from the page, Mason stays line-drawn flat. Indeed, in terms of *Set This House on Fire*, Norman Mailer's comment that Styron writes like "an angel about landscape, and an adolescent about people" seems exaggerated rather than inaccurate.[6]

For instance, while it's hard to show that Peter never really comes across as a lawyer, since lawyers might take any form, it's easier to say that Cass never speaks or sees like a painter. Compare Styron's depiction of a painter with, say, Patrick White's Hurtle Duffield in *The Vivisector* (1970) or Chaim Potok's eponymous hero in *My Name is Asher Lev* (1972), and the differences are quickly apparent. These protagonists see and think as painters; they observe people and ponder their art. This is never so with Cass. He never thinks or speaks about the craft and rarely looks with a painter's eye. His journal references to Cézanne, Turner, Delacroix, and others merely pay lip service. "Everything here like Cézanne's paintings of L'Estaque," he writes (291). "A kind of haze over all, too," he says further on, "like Turner's approach to Venice" (292), noting yet further on that Delacroix was "a fabulous painter" (293). None of this suggests that Cass knows much about the practice of painting, only that he knows painters' names and has seen their work. The most extensive comments he offers about his actual painting come when he tells Peter that the day Mason mistook him for a painter named Waldo Kasz and asked to see his work, "he didn't have a hell of a lot to show off," since he "hadn't done much in a long, long time." All he could produce was "five or six dreary figures and landscapes in oil, and some watercolors, and seven or eight ink and crayon sketches" (384). If it's hard to imagine him even doing this much, even less convincing is the idea that Cass can suddenly turn around and produce a painting for Mason. As Styron says in the *Paris Review* interview, "Style comes only after long, hard practice," but there is no evidence that Cass has ever had that dedication. Maybe part of the problem is that Cass is a painter who doesn't paint. But maybe he doesn't paint because he can't, and for one simple reason: he's merely a representation of a painter in a novel the surface realism of which is unconvincing.[7]

Other examples of the partial accuracy of Mailer's comment can be found in specific passages. For instance, chapter 9, in part 2, told from Cass's drunken viewpoint but narrated implicitly by Peter, involves a journey in which Mason drives Cass to the PX for supplies and, Cass hopes, for drugs for Michele. On the one hand, there are fabulous descriptions of the Amalfi landscape. On the road far above the sea, Cass recalls spring water "purling and splashing" from the cliffs "in whispery gush over the noise of the motor," while "far off, smoky Salerno" bakes "against the shore" (406). The summit achieved, the whole of Italy rolls "eastward, in haze, in blue, in a miracle of flux and change," and "steaming with noon far below, the Vesuvian plain" sweeps "toward the Apennines" (413). The very description, wonderful though it is, pinpoints the problem of characterization and viewpoint. Were the words Cass's, we might feel that he sees as a painter. But the words are Peter's. The blind-drunk Cass is unlikely to have seen the landscape in this kind of analytical, sensuous detail. We don't believe, in other words (and in contrast to the older narrator with Sophie), that Peter is accurately rendering Cass's drunken experience.

Indeed, "an angel about landscape and an adolescent about people" is also an apt critique of this episode in that the characters and plot, at least when viewed with expectations of outer realism, are just not worthy of the descriptions of landscape. The episode begins with Mason pronouncing that "Art is dead" (403) and proceeds with inconsequential conversation interspersed with descriptions of the drive, the landscape, and eventually Mason humiliating Cass at the PX. The dialogue reveals nothing much beyond Mason's adolescent outlook. They quarrel, for instance, about the pornographic painting that Cass has supposedly done for Mason and that Cass now wants back. Quite aside from the juvenile argument, we are asked to believe that the painting of a couple copulating is "pure realism" even though Cass painted it while "sickeningly plastered" and with "no model save his imagination" (405). Next Mason surmises that Francesca has been stealing from him, and he and

Cass engage in an excruciatingly puerile discussion about the filming in Sambuco, including Cass's query as to whether the actress, Alice Adair, might "put out" (410). By this time Cass is so drunk that he's semiconscious. Reaching the PX, he picks a fight and passes out. Mason rescues him and tells him what a "complete wreck" he has become (429). The relationship between these two thirty-something men perhaps lacks credibility because Mason in particular feels so unreal. "Begin with an individual, and before you know it you find that you have created a type," wrote F. Scott Fitzgerald. "Begin with a type and you find that you have created—nothing." Mason is nothing if not a type but, being only a type, becomes nothing. His opening remark that "Art is dead" is typical of his pretentious nonsense, and while Styron is satirizing literary poseurs, Mason—along with Francesca, Poppy, the film stars, and the rest—is too caricatured to draw any sort of emotional response from the reader.[8]

So it's not that *Set This House on Fire* lacks good writing but that flaws in structure, viewpoint, and characterization prevent the integration necessary for outer realism. The parts are better than the whole. Along with plot and characterization, Styron's comment to his father included "*Atmosphere.*" The lack of integration indeed seems partly tonal. Sometimes the novel aspires to tragedy. Sometimes its impulse is satiric. All too often it resorts to melodrama. Built in terms of the potentially comic and the potentially horrific, it contrasts the impoverished hamlet of Tramonti, forever in shadow, with the sunlit hilltop town of Sambuco. In doing so, it assembles a range of characters, from the tragic Riccis to the semicomic figures of Luigi and of Fausto Windgasser (a local who announces the murders by shouting that "It's twagic, like the Gweeks!" [220]). But the novel never settles into one mode. Perhaps the aim was to follow Flaubert again and combine satire with emotional engagement, but this requires a control of tone that Styron fails to achieve, so the reader is left with little confidence that the novelist knows what he is trying to do.

Also in terms of integration, I was struck on rereading by how many episodes I had completely forgotten. Many of these are in themselves interesting and powerful. The reason for my readerly amnesia, I realized, was not to do with the quality of the writing but with the fact that they are not essential to the novel's architecture. Styron is discursive in *The Confessions of Nat Turner* and *Sophie's Choice*. But in these novels everything is integral. *Nat Turner* is too different a novel, but specific passages from *Set This House on Fire* and *Sophie's Choice* are comparable. Peter in New York comes across as a Stingo figure, not least in that they share (along with Cass) a desire to protect vulnerable beauty from male aggression. As noted, Mason, the aggressor, is a prototype of Nathan. Rather than being mentally ill (which, if anything, is Cass's domain), Mason is simply a fraud, but like Nathan he is a wife beater, and his wife, Celia, a version of Sophie. In *Sophie's Choice*, however, the New York scenes and the relationship between Stingo, Sophie, and Nathan are crucial to how the interweaving of the characters' backgrounds, experiences, dispositions, and tensions all lead toward the horror of Sophie's actual choice, the fulfillment of Stingo's desires, and the tragedy of Sophie and Nathan's suicide. In *Set This House on Fire*, in contrast, Peter's earlier friendship with Mason and Celia has no bearing at all on Mason's relationship with Cass or the rape and murders at the core of the novel.

When Peter learns that Mason has beaten up Celia, we get, for instance, an interaction not unlike those between Stingo and Sophie. But the differences are hugely revealing, and not just because of the virtual irrelevance of the interaction between Peter and Celia to the novel as a whole. "That someone should do violence to this warm, gentle little lark of a girl" seems to the infatuated Peter "the foulest of all foul sins." "Where is he now?" he demands. "Where is the bastard? I'll lay him out."

> She had come around a bit and now, after easing herself up on her elbows, sat propped with her legs curled beneath her and with her head pillowed against the wall. In this pose—smeared hair, dirty bloodstained fingers, red-rimmed eyes and all—she looked both lovely and cruelly hurt, a flower upon which had been impressed the print of a dirty boot. For an instant I came very close to throwing my arms around her and telling her how madly and completely I adored her, but I was brought up short by her words, which mingled incredulity and desolation within me in equal parts.
>
> "Don't call him those names," she said gently. "I love him, Peter. I love him, you see. So you mustn't call him things like that. Please don't. I love him." (161–62)

The dynamics at the heart of *Sophie's Choice*, in which the narrator loves a woman in an abusive relationship, are in place here. But in the later novel that interaction is both central and rendered in more extreme terms, with a callow youth in love with a woman who has faced a parent's worst nightmares. Here, in contrast, we simply have a well-enough written but ultimately inconsequential episode. Its participants are the same age, and the young man's unrequited love is muted and prosaic. Celia is not a major character, and Peter will have little more to do with her. But nor will there be any truly important confrontation between Peter and Mason. Unlike Nathan, Mason is neither a danger nor a threat nor really much of an object of envy to Peter. The scene leads nowhere, and the novel moves on to other things.

Elsewhere in the New York scenes, Mason's excessive interest in sexuality foreshadows Nathan's and Stingo's. An aspect of this is his apparent bisexuality. At one point, he stages sex with Celia in such a way that Peter witnesses it. Not unlike Stingo, Peter finds himself in a "platonic ménage-a-trois" (157). But while in the later novel this makes psychological sense, with Sophie and Nathan as parental figures in an oedipal triangle, in *Set This House on Fire* it represents nothing other than adolescent notions of decadence. Styron ratchets up Mason's obsessions not through insight into his character but to build tension where none would otherwise exist. For instance, as with Mason and Peter, he suggests some sexual tension between Mason and Cass. Not content with showing his pornography to Peter, to whom he declares sex "the last frontier" (151), Mason seems to want Cass to be part of his sexual "circus" (414). Cass even claims that in raping Francesca "he was raping *me*" (443), an outburst that is both unconvincing and absurd.

Nor is Mason's supposed charisma any more believable than his sexual proclivities. Peter tells us of his "sorcerer's charm" (159), foreshadowing the *Sophie's Choice* description of Nathan as "utterly, fatally glamorous" (187). But whereas Stingo's naivety allows us to see Nathan's behavior in these terms, Peter has no such excuse and Mason never lives up to his billing. In some ways the narrative charts Peter's progression away from youthful adulation to adult skepticism. He admits that at school, for instance, he remained "beguiled by Mason while the other boys were losing interest" (75). But we still have to believe that Mason has some sort of hold on others beyond Peter. Celia, for instance, tells a skeptical Peter that Mason has an "enormous personality," that he is "an adventurer in the arts, a discoverer" (163). Although Mason-the-poseur is the point here, elsewhere he tells Peter that he is "sorry as hell" about his behavior, and it seems that we are meant to warm to him. ("Really I am. About last night, I mean," he says [169], much as Nathan will do.) Peter, however, is won over by a charm we never witness.

Like Nathan to Sophie, Mason is violent toward Celia and a fraud who must be exposed, but while Nathan's behavior is the result of his illness and so invites compassion, Mason's has no such explanation. Just as Stingo confronts Nathan, so Peter confronts Mason. In doing so he reveals Mason's true loneliness and vulnerability, and this directionless hedonist does, perhaps, with his twitching shoulder at times of stress, produce in the reader a sense of pity. Peter realizes that Mason's life is empty. "Future's darling," he has "one foot poised in thinnest air" (174). Such phrases might be used to describe Nathan, but even if a degree of sympathy for Mason is explicable, it's hard to see how Peter could be mesmerized. The best of Mason, as a character, is his tragic emptiness. The worst of Mason is that the empty personality adds up to an empty character, and there is nothing "enormous" about him at all.

Just as scrutinizing *Set This House on Fire* reveals its uncertainty of tone, while a close reading *Sophie's Choice* reveals Styron's art at its most powerful, so to juxtapose passages from the two novels is instructive. Set the last sentence of chapter 3 in the earlier novel against the last sentence of chapter 2 in the later novel, for instance, and it's clear that *Sophie's Choice* avoids the compositional errors of *Set This House on Fire*. A messy vision becomes high art. In the first example, Peter is embarking for Italy and is the beneficiary of Mason's generosity.

> With my cabinmates I got along very well: they were really gentle, accommodating fellows—somewhat hard to get next to, maybe, but far less depraved than Mason, it seemed to me, and a lot better adjusted. In Paris I got a letter from Mason, telling me that Celia had gone to Reno. I remember one characteristic phrase, which seemed—as with so much of Mason—to emerge from some insubstantial shadowland unacquainted either with sorrow or joy: "Weep, weep for Mason and Celia, Peter, we've gone to Splitsville." And it was not long after this that Mason faded from my mind. Yet I wish now I could recall the details of that shipboard dream I had, far out in mid-ocean, when I shot erect in my bunk and listened in a sweat to my fellow passengers snoring in the dark, and smelled the sweet scent of those blossoms, slowly dying, that he had given me, and was touched all over with the somehow-knowledge of Mason's certain doom. (174)

While remarkably similar in composition, the equivalent *Sophie's Choice* passage shows the difference between a novel in which the author is not yet secure in either his vision or his mature voice and a novel in which vision, voice, and overall effect all work toward the novel's ultimate impact. Here Stingo has just encountered Sophie and so embarked on his "voyage of discovery."

> Finally the music stopped and she stopped weeping too, while the restless creak of springs told me she had gone to bed. I lay there for a long time awake, listening to the soft night-sounds of Brooklyn—a far-off howling dog, a passing car, a burst of gentle laughter from a woman and a man on the edge of the park. I thought of Virginia, of home. I drifted off to sleep, but slept uneasily, indeed chaotically, once awakening in the unfamiliar darkness to find myself very close to some droll phallic penetration—through folds, or a hem, or a damp wrinkle—of my displaced pillow. Then again I fell asleep, only to wake with a start just before dawn, in the dead silence of that hour, with pounding heart and an icy chill staring straight up at my ceiling above which Sophie slept, understanding with a dreamer's fierce clarity that she was doomed. (53)

In both paragraphs the narrator awakens from uneasy sleep in unfamiliar darkness to recognize a key protagonist's doom. Although in the earlier novel it's only implicit ("shot erect"), both narrators might be said to awaken from a sexual dream to sudden revelation. But while in *Set This House on Fire* this is preceded by descriptions of Peter's cabinmates, who are irrelevant in having no further role to play, in *Sophie's Choice* the whole paragraph is integrated into the larger drama.

Attempts to closely read *Set This House on Fire* are fraught with this problem of a lack of integration—let alone saturation. For a start, here we have the unrealistic scenario of Mason bedecking the cabin with food and flowers in the first place (unlike in *Sophie's Choice*, where Nathan and Sophie's regard for food and flowers adds to the poignancy of their desperation to enchant and remain enchanted by life). In terms of the subsequent detail, the reader has no great interest in the fact that Peter "got along very well" with his cabinmates, or in who they are or how he interacts with them. Nor is it important to know what happened to Mason and his girlfriend or to be told Mason's ridiculous request that Peter "weep" because they've "gone to Splitsville." The description of the cabin and sweat and "dying" blossoms is well written, but since Mason already seems soon after this to have "faded" from Peter's mind, it's hard to feel anything beyond indifference.

Turn to the *Sophie's Choice* passage, and the contrast is immediate.

Stingo is just getting to know Sophie. He has witnessed her suffering at Nathan's hands. He's drawn to her in ways that we intuit but that he only has an inkling of. Space, time, and setting are all crucial. She is above him, beyond him, out of sight, yet he hears her weeping, hears her bedsprings. The effect is of simultaneous isolation and intimacy. The sounds of the Brooklyn night remind us of Stingo's intense loneliness, his desire for love (the "gentle laughter" of the couple in the park). He thinks of home, and we recall the loss of his mother. He and Sophie, two displaced beings, have met as strangers in this boardinghouse. She is effectively his cabinmate, to use the language of *Set This House on Fire,* on his "voyage of discovery," and she will be integral to his discoveries, both pleasurable and horrific. His uneasy, semidelirious sleep, evoked in "chaotically," has everything to do with his mingled thoughts of Sophie, whose predicament and bearing have so disturbed him, and of his mother-loss, homesickness, and sexual, spiritual, emotional, intellectual longing. Far from fading from his mind, his attraction to Sophie is already visceral and consuming. He awakens "staring straight up at" a ceiling above which she sleeps. His focus is absolutely on her, yet she's hidden above him, as is (one might say) his mother in heaven. Finally, in contrast to the awkward phrase "touched all over with the some-how knowledge of Mason's certain doom," Stingo understands "with a dreamer's fierce clarity that she was doomed." The former provokes questions in a way that the latter does not. What does "touched all over" mean? If it's implicitly sexual, it's hardly convincing. "Somehow-knowledge" is weak, and as for "certain doom," what would "uncertain doom" be? In the later passage we feel the horror of Stingo's "understanding." We don't need the details of the dream; the strength rests in our, and his, not knowing it. "Dreamer's fierce clarity" calls up the power of night thought. There is verisimilitude in the idea that Stingo's mind has worked something out while he slept, and explained to him why he is so troubled. Does he feel she's doomed partly because his mother was doomed? The layers are too dense to peel. But the scene is entirely appropriate, and integrated into all that will happen from then on.

So *Set This House on Fire*, if judged solely in terms of outer realism, fails. Its plot is melodramatic. The rationale for telling the story twice is unconvincing. The related structure produces dull character interaction instead of the tensions that propel realist fiction forward. The main characters are insufficiently different. Mason's supposed charisma is something we never experience. The unwieldy structure and lethargic character interaction are matched by a general problem of tone, and on the level of close reading, individual passages wilt under scrutiny. Often they fail to stay in the memory because they are not integrated into the overall structure, even while they anticipate scenes that are properly integrated and successfully executed in *Sophie's Choice*. The best that can be said about *Set This House on Fire* on this score is that it's an attempt to find a way forward after an extraordinary debut, so it at least sheds light on the sophisticated structures and successful innovations of later work.

II

But this twice-told novel deserves a second reading, from another perspective. What, for instance, might Lukács have meant when he wrote that its theme of "alienation" exemplifies the link between "significant writing in our time with the great literature of the past"? Suppose we view *Set This House on Fire* not in terms of its surface story but in terms of what is, after all, its stated subject? The title is from John Donne's letter "To the Earle of Carlile, and his Company, at Sion," a section of which forms the extensive epigraph. The "house" Donne refers to is "this body," and "the Master of the house" is the "soule." His concern is with being "secluded eternally" from God's sight. From the outset, therefore, Styron signals that it's not the outer drama that matters in *Set This House on Fire* but the inner drama, and that drama, as Lukács implies, is about, among other things, spiritual alienation. The novel's true subject, the title suggests, is the author's own struggle to progress as an artist and a human being. It's a psychological drama about selves and shadow selves, fraught with tension between inner and outer worlds, between, as it were, the shadowy valley of Tramonti and its suffering inhabitants, and the studio lights and sunshine of Sambuco, where the predominant tone is of art and artfulness—the moviemakers, the poseur, the painter, the lawyer. The lush, vivid landscape and conversational tone almost hoodwink us into seeing this as a novel of externalities. Granted, to view the novel as a dramatization of a single individual's psyche in search of meaning and a suitable artistic stance makes it sound rather inward-looking given the engaged novelist Styron would become. But such a view may provide insight into what he later referred to as the "psychological difficulties involved in getting these works out."[9] Moreover, the search for meaning does in fact lead directly to Cass's attempts to help the Ricci family and, beyond this novel, to the stories of Nat Turner and Sophie Zawistowska. The pattern of the personal and historical can already be glimpsed.

In rereading *Set This House on Fire* in terms of these preoccupations, the most obvious author to draw comparisons to is Dostoevsky, and the novel it most resembles is *The Brothers Karamazov.* So very different as these two writers and novels are, awareness of Dostoevsky's influence in terms of approach and subject matter helps explain what Styron was up to. A 1968 interview reveals that he "started reading the Russian novel" when he returned from Europe in 1953 and had been reading Dostoevsky "for the last fifteen years." There's nothing new in comparing Styron to Dostoevsky. Rhoda Sirlin implies it in her title *William Styron's "Sophie's Choice": Crime and Self-Punishment,* and Daniel Ross notes that critics particularly see Styron's "Dostoevskian element" in *Set This House on Fire.* European commentators too, including Robert Kanters and Radoslav Nenadál, ponder the connection. But the comparisons tend to be mere asides, when in fact the links are profound. Both writers are preoccupied with good and evil; both make use of the Gothic and especially the doppelgänger motif; and both were shaped by a troubled psychological vision not unconnected with the early loss of a parent. Like Dostoevsky, too, Styron was a family man yet haunted by demons he sought to excise through his work. Both writers' imaginations are such that they conceive the kernel of their dramas as (in Joyce Carol Oates's words on Dostoevsky) "a conflict within the parts of one self," and both are concerned (in Dostoevsky's case, for Oates, exclusively) "with psychological drama." I would add that in both writers the drama is inextricable from questions not just of moral behavior but of the existence of forms of enslavement and the desire for freedom, whether from poverty, imprisonment, or psychological captivity. For Dostoevsky is the quintessential writer of tensions between inner and outer worlds.[10]

Undoubtedly Dostoevsky was on Styron's mind. Cass's chaste love for Francesca echoes Raskolnikov's for Sonya Marmaladov in that both girls have impoverished parents the men seek to help. Cass's delirious dreams and hallucinations are also Raskolnikovian. Where Raskolnikov dreams of Mikolka beating a horse to death, Cass dreams of a crushed and dying dog and links it with the sight of peasant women burdened by huge bundles of sticks and peasants crushed by poverty and dying of tuberculosis (as happens to Michele). Moreover, Raskolnikov's "terrible dream" begins as a memory of loss (of his younger brother) and of being with his father, so at first we feel that we are being told of something real rather than imagined.[11] Only then does it transmute into the memory/dream of witnessing the horse's death. He in turn associates this with his acquaintance with the Marmaladovs—including Marmaladov himself, crushed beneath carriage wheels even as his wife is dying of tuberculosis—and his realization that he will kill the pawnbroker.

Similarly, Cass confuses reality and hallucination. He emerges "sober" from his alcoholic stupor the morning after killing Mason, yet the sea is "still boiling." Near the horizon turbulence seems "to jar the sea from its very depths," and geysers seem to spurt lava "toward a benign blue sky." But as the spray sinks "without a murmur," a boat sails "placidly upon the blue, untouched, unharmed" (479). Like Raskolnikov, Cass is a sick man who commits murder, and whose experience of events seems to have as much to do with a chemical imbalance as with anything else. Of course, the writers' visions differ. Styron lacked Christian faith, for one thing. Nor, it hardly needs saying, has *Set This House on Fire* remotely the power of *Crime and Punishment*. But out of Dostoevsky came existentialism, and out of existentialism came Styron. Alienation may therefore indeed be the link between *Set This House on Fire* and "great literature of the past."[12]

Dostoevsky's influence on Styron is formal as well as thematic. Like the Russian, he allows characters other than the narrator to speak at length. In *Crime and Punishment*, Marmaladov, Porfiry, Razhumkhin, and Svidrigailov all have monologues. Similar monologues occur in *The Brothers Karamazov*. Faced with Fyodor, their despicable father, the three brothers and a probable half-brother represent aspects of human potential. Mitka is dissolute; Ivan is an intellectual atheist; Alyosha is a simple (but not simplistic) spiritual brother. Then there's the epileptic Smerdyakov, whom Fyodor adopts amid rumors that he's his illegitimate son by way of a peasant, and who functions as Ivan's doppelgänger. After Fyodor's murder in book 1, the novel becomes an existential murder mystery. Suspicion falls on Ivan, but it turns out that the culprit was probably Smerdyakov. Like this later Dostoevsky novel of the inner life, *Set This House on Fire* renders viewpoint complex, fluid, and interchangeable. It involves a despicable Sugar Daddy in Mason, a conventional man in Peter, and a drunken artist in Cass. While it's Cass who kills the man who has taken him under his malevolent wing, in another echo of *The Brothers Karamazov*, Francesca is murdered by Saverio, an undeveloped version of Smerdyakov.

So awareness of *The Brothers Karamazov* informs a reading of *Set This House on Fire* as psychological drama, or inner realism, in two specific areas, both of which are easy targets for adverse criticism when the novel is viewed as outer realism. One is the disconcerting structure, the other is characterization. Ultimately doubleness connects the two areas. This is a twice-told tale about selves and shadow selves. Reflect on the genesis of the structure and it turns out that it grew from Styron's desire to write a novel in which a narrator begins "in the first person" and "ends up in the third person, the story so merging and mingling that one might accept without hesitation the fact that the narrator himself knew the uttermost nuances of another man's thought." What is unclear from this statement is quite why Styron would want to do this. But with hindsight, what appears to be a technical issue about viewpoint can now be read as a challenge not just to the conventions of outer realism but to notions of an individual's stable, singular identity. We can't know whether Styron acknowledged to himself the extent to which the novel was an inner drama, or whether he had sufficient distance from his subject matter to see how this affected the reading experience. In the years prior to its publication he seemed uncertain. In the 1954 *Paris Review* interview, for instance, he criticizes the trend toward "introspective" fiction. At the same time, though, he muses that his characters "all seem to end up, finally, closer to being like myself than like people I've actually observed" and that perhaps they were "not much more than sort of projected facets of myself." "Good writing," he comments, is always the product of "neurosis." In later years, he conceded that while he needed to follow *Lie Down in Darkness,* he "was trying to feel [his] way in certain directions" and didn't fully understand "what those directions were."[13]

Thus *Set This House on Fire* was very much an intellectual and psychological exploration one subject of which is its own construction. Styron would seem to have felt tension between writing of a world beyond the multifaceted self and needing to expurgate some of those facets so as to move to a position where he could write his two best novels. Given this, it's not surprising that the information we now have about Styron's battles with depression helps to clarify the way the novel unfolds. Styron needed to fight his own demons even as he sought to write beyond introspection. The notion of the shadow self, for instance, calls to mind Berman's discussion of how *Darkness Visible* draws attention to the symptoms of mental illness portrayed in *Lie Down in Darkness.* Like Dostoevsky, Styron pushed his psyche to the edge, just as the struggle between Cass and Mason ends with cliff-edge violence.

It would thus seem legitimate to see the raw awkwardness of Styron's twice-told narrative as a representation of an inner turmoil taking place against the backdrop of a lush and vibrant external landscape—a kind of vivid dream depicting the author's mind. On one level we might see the novel as a critique of American attitudes in the Eisenhower era. No doubt Styron conceived it as "a condemnation of postwar American culture," and maybe, for some readers, even in retrospect it is indeed "a probing critique of American society in the 1950s." But as Styron said in his acceptance speech for the 1970 Howells Medal, not only is "a novel speculative" and best when "magnificently unopinionated," but "almost by definition" fiction "is a kind of dream" that "often tells truths that are hard to bear" yet can "liberate the mind through the catharsis of fantasy, enigma, and terror." To reprise Christa Wolf's comment on the relationship between Dostoevsky and Raskolnikov, what we witness is a kind of "grisly mental experiment in the brain of the author."[14] The imperfection of the work thus testifies to the messiness of a struggle that makes the double structure of *Set This House on Fire* all the more interesting. It's as if the repeated process was necessary to Styron's exploration of perspective and identity.

In both *The Brothers Karamazov* and *Set This House on Fire* the doubleness may well come across on a first reading as amazingly awkward compared with the integrated nature of *Crime and Punishment* and *Sophie's Choice*. But both authors build doubleness, or the multifaceted self, into form and theme. Dostoevsky, who saw himself as a "realist in a higher sense," felt the need to provide a note to the reader to acknowledge the oddness of his two, connected novels and their relation to each other. It's a note that seems pertinent to *Set This House on Fire*.

> The trouble is that while I am dealing with one biography, I have two novels in my hands. The main novel is the second one—it deals with the activity of my hero in our own day, I mean, at this very moment. The action of the first novel, on the other hand, takes place thirteen years ago and is not really a novel but just a chapter out of my hero's adolescence. It is quite impossible for me to dispense with the first novel because without it a great deal in the second novel would be unintelligible. But this fact makes my original difficulty much more complicated: if I, the biographer, find that even one novel would be too much for such a modest and unheroic hero, then why on earth do I come out with two novels, and what is more: how do I explain such arrogance on my part?[15]

Styron's only personal note is his enigmatic epigraph, "L'ambizione del mio compito non mi impedì di fare molti sbagli" (the ambition of my task does not prevent me from making many mistakes). But this is at least a Dostoevskian admission that the novel's ambition and its rough-hewn nature are part of the same effort. Both are statements on the difficulties faced by the artist who tries to forge a new vision. Shadowing Dostoevsky, Styron offers two parallel narratives—one novel but two personalities—and there's a sense that he too can't dispense with the first narrative because much of the second narrative would then be unintelligible. Neither author answers the question why he structures the work as he does. Indeed, both concede that their novels are exploratory rather than dramas over which they have full control.

Set This House on Fire's doubleness is equally manifested in characterization, not least in terms of the doppelgänger motif. It contains numerous pairings as well as a triumvirate at its center. Peter's accident in knocking Luciano Di Lieto off his scooter at the start of the narrative and Di Lieto's subsequent recovery by its end once "the pressure upon his brain" has lifted (506) parallel Cass's murder of Mason and his awakening from his mental turmoil. Early on, too, Peter describes a recurring nightmare of the menacing approach of a dark "prowler" on a storm-lashed night, in which he phones his "dearest friend" for help, receives no answer, and turns to a tapping on the window to see the "murderous face of that selfsame friend" (6). The idea of different sides to a self is picked up, among other places, in Cass's comment that in Europe he "was *half* a person, trapped by terror, trapped by booze, trapped by self" (54). He describes his Parisian woes as "Kinsolving pitted against Kinsolving" (250). Meanwhile, both Peter and Luigi function as his shadow selves, rebuking and encouraging him; Mason comes to know Cass by mistaking him for that other painter, Waldo Kasz; and Cass's chaste relationship with Francesca seems bound up with his guilt over joining a man named Lonnie to ransack a sharecropper's hut when he was fifteen. In his mind, southern Italy doubles for the American South, and the Ricci family for the black family. Elsewhere Poppy mistakes Peter for Cass, thinking it's her husband in the spare room until Peter rolls over (235). At the same time, Cass's attitude toward Mason also seems to relate to Cass's sense of himself. He feels that he's perpetrated an "unnameable crime" (423) and dreams of watching himself die. Indeed, in crushing Mason's skull he seems to kill part of himself. He holds the body "close to his breast" as if they were one, before "hurling it into the void" (465).

The weaknesses of *Set This House on Fire* as outer realism thus make sense as inner realism. That Peter, Cass, and Mason are male American contemporaries seems apt when we think of them as one warring, authorial self trying to set his house on fire: to shake himself out of a booze-filled life (Cass), out of decadence (Mason), out of settling for mediocrity (Peter), and to alert himself to a richer awareness. The same goes for Peter and Luigi, who come to represent Cass's inner dialogue. Similarly, with Peter, *Set This House on Fire* is structured by way of a narrator who, while anxious and unhinged for his own reasons, is nevertheless—in line with Styron's description of depression in *Darkness Visible*—an observer, à la Harry Miller, Culver, and Stingo, of another's "oncoming disaster" (64). Since both Peter and Cass have had a sycophantic relationship with Mason, we really hear two versions of the same story. The novel as outer realism is damaged by the lack of conflict between Peter and Cass and the uncharismatic emptiness that is Mason. But see it as inner realism and Mason becomes a phenomenon of the mind that Peter/Cass must excise. In other words, rereading *Set This House on Fire* involves rethinking the nature of its subject and the rationale for Styron's technique and approach. This may well involve trusting the tale, not the teller, but the apparent sincerity of the teller's struggle to locate his subject matter holds the work together, on the psychological level, as art.

To contemplate Cass is to find further evidence that everything we witness is best viewed as the drama of a single consciousness. As West attests, the drafts of the novel show that Cass "is spun off from the original conception of Peter," and Styron developed them as distinct beings even as he eventually merged them "into one narrative consciousness."[16] He put much of his own neurosis into Cass. Well before killing Mason, Cass considers suicide: leaning over a gorge, he's "tormented by a horror of these gallant heights so ardent and so powerful that it was almost like love" (359). Sponging off Poppy, who has a small legacy from her father (335), he makes her "the scapegoat" for his "meanness" (253). Suffering from hallucinations and seizures, drinking to "kill the fear to which he was shackled like a fellow prisoner" (344), caught in an "endless circle of self-loathing" (254), and thinking of himself as "2 persons" (361), he shows signs of deep mental distress.

Given that Peter has some of these symptoms in milder form, it's plain that Cass remains a version of the same psyche. So far as the outer world is concerned, they are differentiated, but they only ring true when seen as versions of the author. Beyond their superficially different circumstances and diction, both are unhinged, uptight, and experience "dread" (Peter 204) and "the anxiety and the anguish" of existence (Cass 499). Both are from the South and nostalgic for it (266). Cass also shares with his author the experience of Paris, where he finds himself "paralyzed" as soon as he sits "in front of a sketch pad or a canvas" (250). The idea of painter's block is notably absent from the world beyond the novel; Styron, we can assume, is referring to writer's block. If we don't believe in Cass as a painter, we are at least convinced by his mental instability. His existential anxiety would seem to be the core truth about him. His desire for self-destruction is also a desire to destroy his family, not for lack of love but because mortality is too much to bear.

In this sense, to read *Set This House on Fire* as inner realism is to see it as an advance on *Lie Down in Darkness* in terms of philosophical maturity. Although it is about parental grief, nowhere in Styron's first novel do we find such passages of raw truth about the joy and anguish of parenthood when one juxtaposes love for one's children with life's fragility and one's own shortcomings. Styron will reprise this parental fear in *Sophie's Choice*. In both novels he has the courage to face what most of us avoid: the brutal truth that "unless all our intuitions are haywire," life on earth has no meaning—beyond, as Levin says at the end of *Anna Karenina*, that with which we "have the power to invest it."[17] "All my children are going to die," reflects Cass. The thought is "so desolating as to be beyond the realm of sorrow" (289–90). Like Milton, Sophie experiences precisely the parental nightmare that haunts Cass: the finality of a child's death in a world without religious comfort and on some level through one's own actions. But somehow in these two later works it feels more authentic.

Cass and Poppy, for instance, have an argument after a bout of sickness that goes to the core of Cass's—or Styron's—metaphysical anguish. Seeing the children "healthy & happy," he mentions to her that he'd "thought they were all goners." Poppy's response that she knew they'd get well because she "had FAITH" infuriates him.

> And then I blew my top—saying something on the order of Faith my ass, it was a *man* named Alexander Fleming who did it you idiot, and penicillin & 75,000 francs worth of medical care product not of faith in some dis-embodied gaseous vertebrate, and an hermaphrodite triply-damned incestuous one at that, but of mans own faith vain perhaps, but nonetheless faith in his hardwon decency & perfectability & his own compassionate concern with his mortal, agonizing plight on a half burnt out cinder that he didnt ask to be set down on in the first place. Not a SPOOK I told her. (294–95)

This is unremarkable writing, but thematically the passage is significant in terms of Styron's later work. Indeed, it's appropriate that Cass records this in a journal, because that's really what the novel amounts to: a setting down of ideas in pursuit of vision; a portrait of the artist at the drawing board, or, in Styron's words, "a novel less in search of completion than a creation in itself without a fully established metaphor."[18]

Lastly, the novel can be read as an example of Styron dredging up the silt from his own psyche in terms of Mason. For Mason seems to represent Styron's own bouts of self-loathing, or perhaps the final vestiges of immaturity. Certainly, he seems more interesting as a destructive phenomenon than as a human being. For Peter he's "hardly a man at all" and "committed to nothingness" (446). Perhaps he represents materialism, or alcohol ("I think you can see how dependent on me you've become," as he tells Cass [429]). He's the vile self that the suffering artist must confront, a self who will take advantage of Francesca whereas the empathic self would not. By this reading, the murder of Mason, as told to the passive recorder Peter, and as suggested earlier, is a symbolic suicide. Cass kills a part of himself, while Peter functions as the "second self" experienced by suicidal depressives, watching, with "curiosity," as Styron puts it in *Darkness Visible*, "as his companion struggles against the oncoming disaster, or decides to embrace it" (64–65). The parallels are not exact; Luigi is more the "dispassionate" observer than Peter. But still the novel becomes a psychological drama about one warring self setting the house of his soul on fire: shaking himself out of a booze-filled life, out of decadence, out of settling for mediocrity, in his quest to become a mature being and to adopt a position of responsibility toward one's own life and the lives of others "in the hope of being what I could be for a time" (500).

Set This House on Fire is thus two novels in one. As outer realism it barely works. But as inner realism it's the story of an author in search of structure, style, and subject matter. Its value and fascination lie in its rawness. It contains the ingredients of Styron's mature vision, even if he could not yet cook the recipe to perfection. In particular, it anticipates the way that his next two novels are dramas of how to reconcile our capacity for meanness, cruelty, egotism, self-obsession, and self-destruction with our capacity for generosity, compassion, selflessness, altruism, and self-reconstruction. Nat, Gray, Sophie, and Stingo all, to cite Styron's Malraux epigraph for *Sophie's Choice*, contain an "essential region of the soul" where these forms of good and evil meet. In both novels, altruism all too easily merges with egotism. Similarly, in *Set This House on Fire* Cass tries to atone for his youthful sins by helping Francesca, but in doing so he's also attracted to her and behaves egotistically and as "an intellectual bully" toward Poppy (295). Peter, the ineffectual observer, is painted with the same palate but without the extremes of color.

The most rewarding way to approach the novel is, then, to acknowledge what was implicit about *Lie Down in Darkness:* that the outer story camouflages an inner story, and all the voices and viewpoints are part of the same outpouring of internal angst. Throughout the novel implications abound that these characters resemble aspects of the same personality. Indeed, I am reminded again of Styron's comments in *Darkness Visible* about the "phenomenon that a number of people have noted while in deep depression" of "the sense of being accompanied by a second self" who watches with curiosity. "As I went about stolidly preparing for extinction," he writes, "I couldn't shake off a sense of melodrama—a melodrama in which I, the victim-to-be of self-murder, was both the solitary actor and lone member of the audience" (64–65). In *Darkness Visible,* Styron emphasizes the depressed person's "general feeling of worthlessness," "failure of self-esteem," "sense of self-hatred" (5), and "malaise and restlessness and sudden fits of anxiety" (8). While Cass drinks "to kill the fear to which he was shackled like a fellow prisoner," Styron admits in *Darkness Visible* that he used alcohol "as a shield against anxiety" (43). It's all too obvious, armed with this knowledge, that *Set This House on Fire* is a self-portrait. The sheer anguish of the novel and the desire, somehow, to escape this through "a presentiment of selflessness" (257) revealed in all their psychological authenticity.

The evidently flawed nature of *Set This House on Fire* is therefore both explicable and instructive. With *Lie Down in Darkness* Styron had shown mastery of some basic tenets of novel writing. He had shown that he could combine the realist and modernist modes, and whatever the limitations of his understanding of middle age, he had proved that he knew what the novel form could do. *Set This House on Fire* was his second apprenticeship. The novel represents the artist back in his workshop, his tools around him, and his huge, alarmingly unwieldy construction threatening to topple the minute he opens the doors and lets it out into the light of day. And perhaps it was only partly written for the light of day. Perhaps it was about the writer writing, about continuing until he found the form to express his vision. The epigraph to part 2, from Theodore Roethke's villanelle "The Waking," expresses this very well: Styron was learning by going where he had to go. Obsessed with mortality without hope of an afterlife, he was pouring himself into a creation whose shape mattered less than the process of creating. Jacob Kahn, the old artist to whom Asher Lev goes as an apprentice in Chaim Potok's *My Name is Asher Lev,* tells the would-be artist that "millions of people can draw. Art is whether or not there is a scream in him waiting to get out in a special way." "Or a laugh," responds Kahn's manager, Anna Shaeffer. "Picasso laughs too."[19] In *Set This House on Fire* Styron is in search of just such artistic expression. It only arrives in later work but probably would not have without the process that *Set This House on Fire* represents.

CHAPTER 6

The Confessions of Nat Turner
Carved of Air and Light

Not afraid of ghosts, are you?

—STYRON, IN CONVERSATION, 1990

Art by its nature is a transgressive act, and artists must accept being
punished for it. The more original and unsettling their art, the more
devastating the punishment.

—JOYCE CAROL OATES, *The Faith of a Writer*, 2003

The Confessions of Nat Turner is a ruminative novel, full of references to
the passing of time, the rotting away of material objects, and the disappearance of once vital, living beings. "Carved" (as Arthur Miller put it
of Styron's novels in general) with precision, the style and quality of
its writing invites us to contemplate not just an episode in American
history but the relationship of the past to the present. Typical of this
is Nat's description of a slaves' graveyard in "an abandoned corner of
a meadow," set off from it by "a plain pole fence" that has "long since
fallen into splintery ruin." Among the markers, many of which "have
toppled over to rot and mingle with the loamy earth," is a cedar head-
board with "letters which read: 'Tig' AET. 13." Nat's recollection of the
oddity of pondering, "age thirteen," the grave "of your own grandmother,
dead at thirteen herself," epitomizes the poignancy of one of the mysteries he tries to comprehend; it's not just that people can be cruel, can be
vicious, can enslave others, but that we exist and then are gone, that the
vibrant present, joyful or terrible in its immediacy, dissolves as if it had
been an illusion (131).

This mystery of time itself, at least as much as the story of race relations in America, is the novel's subject. Once upon a time, in "history," a slave named Nat Turner existed. Any truths about him must be glimpsed, only and inadequately, in historical records and in hearsay. Once upon a time, too, a man named William Styron existed. He wrote a novel that lit a controversy, now documented in books, essays, letters, and archives but beyond resolution. Some of its participants are now dust, and those still alive are old, or perhaps, when you read this, dead as well, just as the writer of these words will be, and you yourself, in time. *Ars longa, vita brevis.* The novel anticipates the demise of its own era, and the demise of all times in which one might, as "now," reread it, as surely as it meditates upon the lost era of Nat Turner.

In a novel full of disturbing episodes, none is more so than Nat's murder of Margaret Whitehead. Her attempt to flee perhaps the only man—young as she is—with whom she's felt sexual frisson combines the joy and terror of immediacy with a pondering of context. Their union has been tragically blocked by the social strictures of the antebellum South, and she flees him in the knowledge that, out of necessity rather than hatred, he intends to kill her. The incident traumatizes Nat and takes the momentum out of the insurrection. For Nat—the Nat conceived of by Styron—is a man of moral nobility, compassion, and empathy. Margaret's ghost appears to him soon after, vanishing "like an image carved of air and light" (415), but her presence haunts the final pages and goes with Nat himself, we must suppose, to his own, horrific death at the hands of a community that has imprisoned him from birth. But, irony on irony, the Nat whose mind we witness is himself a mere image carved of air and light by Styron through more than fifteen years of meditating upon the historical facts and imagining into being one of the most evocative, controversial, and influential novels in American literature. The image of Margaret as "carved of air and light," moreover, is the ghost of a ghost, for none of this *happened* as Styron makes us see it happen, and he keeps the alert reader constantly aware that this is a creative reconstruction, an imagining of events about which we know only a few facts.

But there is a further irony, not of Styron's making: the bulk of criticism accumulating on the novel treats it as something very different from the invitation to join in an imagined journey into a past we cannot in reality possibly revisit. It tends to view the novel not from within—not by way of immersion into this dreamlike realm of air and light—but from without. All commentators rightly set their own agendas, just as Styron chose his way of telling the story. But by and large they have chosen to read it as a conventional historical novel rather than "a meditation on history," or have placed it within the contexts of contemporary cultural debates. From *William Styron's Nat Turner: Ten Black Writers Respond* (1968) to Albert Stone's *The Return of Nat Turner* (1992), Mary Kemp Davis's *Nat Turner Before the Bar of Judgment* (1999), Scot French's *The Rebellious Slave* (2004), and Tim Ryan's *Calls and Responses* (2008), the interest has been in the treatment of history and race. The same is true of Charles Burnett, Frank Christopher, and Charles S. Greenberg's excellent documentary, *Nat Turner: A Troublesome Property* (2002). The novel's ostensible subject matter makes this tendency inevitable. The various commentaries show how indelible a mark *The Confessions of Nat Turner* has made on American cultural debate, and each commentary naturally adds to that impact.

Plainly, as French writes, the novel "remains the single most influential work" on Turner's insurrection, "overshadowing even the original 'Confessions' in public consciousness today." I agree, too, that "Styron did more to popularize the history and memory of Nat Turner's Rebellion than any other writer of the twentieth century," since "tens of thousands of Americans have come to know the event through the interpretive lens of Styron's novel or the critical responses to it." Because of this, the controversy has become more rather than less interesting as the decades have passed. It's had, as French notes, "a profound impact on scholarship as well, inspiring an outpouring of books, articles, and document collections that stress the multiplicity of perspectives on the event."[1] Equally, I agree with Davis that we should credit Styron "with being the first novelist" writing on Nat Turner "to explore the mystery of Turner's murder of Margaret Whitehead." Despite or because the novel "provoked a visceral response" in her, Davis provides an exceptionally sensitive reading of this relationship. She notes how, with Margaret "likely held captive by the prevailing sexual mores of her society" and Turner as "an ascetic" who "can think of nothing else," they "mirror each other in their sexual repression."[2]

But precisely because French, Davis, and others have so thoroughly explored the matter as part of that "outpouring," the way now seems open to take other avenues. No doubt, as French writes, "the political struggles of the sixties, including the controversy," did indeed profoundly transform "mainstream academic writing and popular culture by the mid-seventies," so that in place of "portrayals of black people as damaged by slavery" there came "a new wave of scholarship" highlighting "the vitality and autonomy of black community life under slavery."

No doubt, too, Styron was, as Davis argues, "shocked at the ferocity of the attacks upon his novel," if not necessarily because he "mistakenly assumed that Nat's 'heroic' deeds had been erased from African Americans' historical memory." But all this is still to view the novel primarily in terms of race, and so to emphasize racial difference. Similarly, Davis notes that as a result of the impact of Styron's novel the historian Henry Irving Tragle brought to light documents that "were not readily accessible" until he "transcribed and published them in 1971," in his compilation of original materials *The Southampton Slave Revolt of 1831*. For Davis, "their previous absence from the historical record necessarily problematizes those novels whose claims to authenticity are based on pre-1971 historical sources." True as that may be, Styron was not claiming historical "authenticity"; he merely wrote a novel, and the authenticity of an artistic reconstruction doesn't survive or perish by its sources. If it did, we'd have to downgrade *Richard III*, *Macbeth*, and the rest. Naturally, Styron was interested in actual lives, but actuality, even when it can be verified, is merely a novelist's starting point. More important is what the novel does seek to do, which, as Henry Louis Gates Jr. puts it, is to "challenge easy essentialist distinctions between black and white." Given that, it would be ironic indeed not to contemplate the novel beyond the race question. My intention is therefore to enter the novel much as Styron himself enters the world of Nat Turner, with sympathy for its evident aims (as these later critics do too) but without the emphasis on race at the forefront. My quixotic quest, perhaps deeply ironic in that the author is now placed in the position of the historical figure he wrote about, is to suggest a rereading that might mirror how Styron saw the novel himself.[3]

Approaching *The Confessions of Nat Turner* on its own terms, it's intriguing to reread the 1965 title essay of *This Quiet Dust and Other Writings*. In the latter part, Styron describes a day in Southampton County in the spring of 1961 and his surprise during the morning that there seems so little to see. The live oak from which Nat was hanged in Courtland (Jerusalem's post–Civil War name) has long gone, and his guide, the local sheriff, knows of no other landmarks. Styron begins to wonder what kind of monument he expected to find. An afternoon visit to the vicinity of the rebellion at least brings with it the possibility that, with Drewry's map, he can "pick up the trail" and get some "sense of the light and shadow that played over that scene of slaughter and retribution" so long ago. But he begins to feel that this man he's imagined for so long is "a phantom no more real than some half recollected image from a fairy tale" (26). Then, on the way back to Courtland, "against the sun-splashed woods" he sees the silhouette of a familiar house (27).

"This Quiet Dust" is not least fascinating in that Styron was unlikely to have envisaged the controversy that would later surround his novel. The voice of the essay is virtually the same one he gives Nat Turner, while the mood is not political but mystical, and never more so than when he enters this house. Early on, the essay contains sentences he'll revise in his author's note. "The relativity of time allows us elastic definitions," he writes, "1831 was yesterday. Yet the year 1831, in the presidency of Andrew Jackson, lay in the very dawn of our modern history" (15). But as the title, taken from Emily Dickinson, signals, his focus is merely on the wonderment of time. It later transpired that the house was not the Whiteheads', as Styron thinks in the essay, but the Vaughans', where the last murders occurred. As West notes, the mistake "was symbolic of his approach." While he's wrong about the house, his instincts are right and push him "toward what was arguably the central event of the rebellion, the murder after which the enterprise fell into disarray."[4] Filled at the time of Styron's visit with corn to feed pigs, the house is "sheltered by an enormous oak," as if the hanging tree has reappeared like the ghost of Nat protecting his would-have-been lover, Margaret. Pondering the murder, Styron climbs over the crumbling sill, leans against the rotting doorframe, and, amid the "scrabbling" and "squeaking of mice," imagines a "rustle of taffeta, and rushing feet, and a shrill girlish piping of terror." Past and present seem momentarily "indistinguishable" (30). Like Nat in the novel, Styron imagines Margaret's ghost. Author and protagonist merge as if Styron, home to a landscape from his past, is no less a ghost than Nat Turner.

And where is Nat Turner? In what sense did he and Margaret exist and in what sense has Styron invented them? "White Americans live with the nigger they've invented," said James Baldwin. But Nietzsche reminded us long before this that we always "invent and make up the person with whom we associate—and immediately forget it." To be human is to invent. We tend to assess others in ways that justify personal needs. Nat Turner is inevitably Styron's shadow self, just as Styron is our projection, in the twenty-first century, as we envisage him standing in that ruined home in 1961 ruminating on events 130 years earlier. In returning to antebellum Southampton County he was confronting that fact, and that past, and intent upon merging identities across the decades and the supposed racial boundary. In this sense *The Confessions of*

Nat Turner is a story of time travel, a ghost story, a merging of two orders of time.[5]

Twenty-nine years later, in the summer of 1990, I was walking up the path to Styron's guest cottage when he called through the twilight, "Not afraid of ghosts, are you? A lot of people have lived in that cottage. A lot of time has passed." With that, he disappeared into the shadows and a door clinked shut down at the main house. I trudged up the steps, pushed through the screen door, and edged down the musty passageway to switch on a light. Dominating the gloomy, cavernous central room hung that large etching of a fearsome Nat Turner. Up the staircase lay the study where Styron had written parts of the novel during the winter months between 1961 and the end of 1966; where Baldwin spent the winter of 1960–61, beginning *The Fire Next Time;* and where others— Carlos Fuentes, Romain Gary, Jean Seberg—spent moments of their, in the latter two cases tragic, lives. Moreover, the cottage had its own history before the Styrons renovated it. If ghosts exist, I thought, they'll be here. It was during my weeks in that cottage that I began to see how *The Confessions of Nat Turner,* along with *Sophie's Choice,* was born of a fascination with passing time quite at odds with the stridently sociopolitical rhetoric of many of Styron's commentators. While he was not at all indifferent to such concerns, the fury of intellectual and emotional debate all too easily drowns out the extent to which these novels were born of a sense of solitude and contemplation, or as he put it, "meditation."

Of course, had the novel not also been a transgression, in entering forbidden territory to confront difficult truths in American history and culture, it would not have had such impact. So before I enter the novel itself, my second epigraph equally needs a fuller context. This is not least because, in the passage it's from, Joyce Carol Oates combines the idea of art as transgression with that of ghostly selves, all in a scenario that spookily echoes Styron's encounter with that house in Southampton County. Oates recalls that in childhood she "tirelessly 'explored' the countryside; neighboring farms, a treasure trove of old barns, abandoned houses and forbidden properties of all kinds, some of them presumably dangerous," and that these activities are "bound up with storytelling" in that "there's a ghost-self, a 'fictitious' self, in such settings."

> For this reason I believe that any form of art is a species of exploration and transgression. (I never saw a NO TRESPASSING sign that wasn't a summons to my rebellious blood. Such signs, dutifully posted on trees and fence railings, might as well cry

COME RIGHT IN!) To write is to invade another's space, if only to memorialize it; to write is to invite angry censure from those who don't write, or don't write in quite the way you do, for whom you may seem a threat. Art by its nature is a transgressive act, and artists must accept being punished for it. The more original and unsettling their art, the more devastating the punishment.[6]

The Confessions of Nat Turner is not merely art as "exploration and transgression," it's a double transgression. It presumes to depict a contentious historical event, and a white writer presumes, for the first time in American literature, "to take on the persona of a black man."[7] With regard to the mores of its time, it transgresses historically, politically, and ethnically. It merges the ghost story—the crossing over from one time to another—with the story of racial transgression, the previously untried idea of a symbolic merging of races by way of a single being made up of a first-person "black" narrator and a "white" author. Styron's clamber through the window of the Vaughan house echoes Nat Turner's clandestine entrance during the insurrection. He is breaking into another's space, but in doing so he is both the author and his ghost-self version of Nat Turner.

This symbolic merging of selves exists throughout the novel. But, as Oates warns, even if the motive is to memorialize, such an act invites "angry censure": the greater the transgression, and "the more original and unsettling" the art, the greater the punishment. Styron trespasses. Ergo: Styron is punished. His sin is to usurp the voice of a black historical figure in order to claim a common humanity for Americans, and to opt for complexity over simplicity. Three eminent black Americans favorable to his cause have put it eloquently. For Baldwin, he began "the common history—*ours*." For Toni Morrison, "he had every right to write the book." "He went into territory that *is* his territory," and for her this was "admirable." For Gates, he was "a brilliant writer" who, as noted earlier, challenged "easy essentialist distinctions between black and white."[8] In other words, he dared to move beyond race (and invite readers to move beyond an author's race) to better understand what it means to be human. Not everybody sees it that way, but this at least seems to have been the author's motive. This is therefore what I mean by reading the novel on its own terms, or from within.

Read on its own terms it's an imagining of a historical figure and era in full awareness that such attempts only ever reproduce the author's projection of a past that's beyond knowing. The commentary that best

shows this is *Nat Turner: A Troublesome Property*, which ends with Burnett pointing out that even his documentary, which seeks to be objective and factual, is a representation of representations. Like *Lie Down in
Darkness* and *Set This House on Fire*, *The Confessions of Nat Turner* shows
Styron's acute awareness of the inherent creativity involved in all human
relations. No doubt, too, my own reading is a representation, but one
that I hope complements the spirit in which the novel was written. A
number of passages imply that this meditation goes far deeper than its
ostensible subject matter and suggest that it's a meditation on, among
other things, rereading. In pondering the life of Nat Turner, Styron
imagines Nat himself contemplating the past in terms of his own life. In
turn, the author invites the reader to witness him imagining Nat reliving
his past, in an echo on echo of that most basic human desire, to understand our lives and the lives of others through memory. The reading
experience thus becomes a meditation not just on Nat Turner and the
antebellum South but on history itself, and on the human condition.
That this was part of what Styron hoped to achieve is apparent from his
1968 comment that the novel dramatizes our "quest for faith and certitude in a pandemonious world" and that he thought the book would one
day be read "more in this light than as a strict rendition of the history
of slavery in this country."[9] The fact that so far this hasn't happened is
precisely why, rather than add yet more words to the discussion of the
novel as history or in terms of the controversy, I will read it this way
now.

Beyond the question of motive is the choice of voice. I have already
noted that the voice Styron uses for Nat Turner is barely distinguish-
able from the one he uses in "This Quiet Dust." At best it's a hybrid. It
hints at the orotund inflections of Frederick Douglass or W. E. B. Du
Bois and renders Nat's thoughts within the limitations of what he could
have known as a slave in 1831 but is also akin to the direct, first-person
voice Styron uses in *Set This House on Fire*. The author's viewpoint is
thus always implicit. In Dawn Trouard's words, this "self-reflexive document" draws attention to the relationship between "history, language,
and truth." It's not Nat Turner's actual account of life as a slave in the
antebellum South but Styron's meditation on the man and his historical
moment. Styron, as he put it, was trying subtly to establish that a black
slave was clearly "not going to think and feel" in this way. "It was a kind
of transcription" or "illusion." "A writer has to at some point assume that
readers are either going to accept it or not," he went on. "You have a

contract with a reader," and those who, the controversy aside, "objected to *The Confessions of Nat Turner* on literary grounds just didn't accept the contract." To read the novel on its own terms involves accepting that Nat's narrative voice is self-evidently an illusion. The style reinforces the fact that Styron was doing no more than trying to imagine Nat Turner's world and life as if from within and that he knew going in that he'd fail.[10]

In a way, the direct, first-person voice is also what makes it contentious. For one of the novel's obvious yet least noted qualities is that it's highly readable. Had it been told in a superficially more complex way—let's say, stream-of-consciousness or multiperspective—it might not have brought Nat Turner's world so vividly to life. The problem, for hostile readers, seems to have been in part the fear that the very vividness of the novel made it seem to represent the truth. Moreover, the immediacy and intimacy of the authorial voice belies its subtlety. Styron places no structural or stylistic hindrances in the reader's way and so invites us to respond in light of our own interests and concerns. This makes it easy enough to forgo reading the novel as meditation. The easier the essential issues are to grasp, the harder it is to respond to their subtleties. Step back from the readability and the subject matter for a moment, view it as a novel designed to move beyond race, and an author's race, and those complexities emerge.

Beyond motive and voice, there is this theme of time. Implicit in the narrative voice is the merging of past and present. "The relativity of time allows us elastic definitions: the year 1831 was, simultaneously, a long time ago and only yesterday," runs the author's note. "Perhaps the reader will wish to draw a moral from this narrative, but it has been my own intention to try to re-create a man and his era, and to produce a work that is less an 'historical novel' in conventional terms than a meditation on history." To read these lines in 1967 would be to see them in light of the civil rights unrest. But we know from "This Quiet Dust" that Styron had the phrasing in mind several years before that, and the words read differently when viewed over a broader timescale. Styron is suggesting that this is a novel about time on several levels. It's about the antebellum South, but more broadly it's about how history interacts with memory and imagination. It's about how we re-create the past. He distances himself from any impulse to compare the two eras. The novel, he emphasizes, is not a morality tale. Readers may "wish to draw a moral from this narrative," but if so, that is their doing, not the author's.

To draw a moral is to judge, and the question of judgment is paramount given the multitude of judgments on the novel itself. Just as

Styron explained in the 1970 Howells Medal speech that the best novels are "magnificently unopinionated," so judgment as a concept is deeply ironized in *The Confessions of Nat Turner*, just as it is in *Sophie's Choice*. This is not least because judgment is a key concept in religious institutions, for which Styron had little sympathy. *Sophie's Choice* ends not with "judgment day—only morning. Morning: excellent and fair" (515). We cannot judge the "victim and accomplice, accessory" Sophie, whose moment of greatest horror comes when Von Niemand forces on her the most grotesque imaginable version of the grotesque-enough notion of judgment day (219). "Judgment Day," meanwhile, is the title of the first section of *The Confessions of Nat Turner*, although it's all too clear that Judge Cobb is detached from his role as upholder of his society's racist laws. As for the complexity of judging Nat on any level of metaphysical morality, such a task would keep celestial attorneys occupied far beyond kingdom come. In our conversations, Styron avoided judging the events in the novel. I asked him to consider a question he had himself put in an essay: did Nat gain or lose his humanity by killing Margaret? "I think it's unresolved," he responded. "I don't know whether you gain or lose your humanity by killing someone else." "Is he a hero?" I asked. "I don't think the question is necessarily answerable," he replied.[11]

In his treatment of time, therefore, Styron's concern is not to judge the 1960s by way of the antebellum 1800s but to contemplate the past in the present in more general terms. While the narrative is deceptively linear, time in the novel shimmies, sometimes in time present, mostly in time past, but with a constant sense of a third time frame: that of the decades that separate Nat Turner from William Styron. Intensely immediate on one level, on another level it implies a merging of timescales. As with the time frames of all Styron's novels, a detailed breakdown of the complex arrangement of time through memory in Nat's story can be found in John Kenny Crane's *The Root of All Evil*.[12] But even Crane's detailed analysis only partly reveals the novel's seamless temporal patterns. Part 2, for instance, opens with Nat's recollection of living with his mother "in the big house at Turner's Mill," at age "twelve or thereabouts" (119). One night, we learn, a salesman stops by and Nat becomes the center of attention when Miss Nell makes him demonstrate his spelling ability, so filling him with a sense of promise and joy. Styron then cuts to Nat in prison describing how "memories like this" punctuate his last days (129). This allows Styron to cut next to what Nat knows of his grandmother, her death at thirteen and the result that his orphaned mother is taken into the house and Nat is born to "become

a house nigger" rather than "a field or timber hand" (130). This then
leads to a description of the slave graveyard and cuts back again to Nat's
memories of his mother (132). Part 2 now remains linear, ending with
Nat in his twenties. The scenes are linked by suggestion, as well as by
years that pass in a paragraph.

The time present, around which all the other scenes revolve—Nat in
his cell awaiting hanging, talking with his lawyer and confessor, Thomas
Ruffin Gray, or reflecting—allows Styron to interweave past and present
in Nat's own life. He does this through two types of scene: those that are
contemplative and those dealing with immediacy. The former are meditations on time itself; they evoke memories, the imagination, even the
ghostly. The latter deal with moments of humor, sexual tension, and violence. Examples of contemplative scenes are Nat's recurring dream; his
reflections on the graveyard; his thoughts about a Saturday in October;
his evocations of the South; and his time alone in Turner's house as he
awaits collection by Thomas Moore. Examples of scenes of immediate,
intense experience include his humorous times with Hark; Travis's rape
of Nat's mother; Nat's moments of sexual frisson with Margaret; and the
carnage of the insurrection itself. The first kind of scene reminds us that
this is a meditation on the part of an author creating the illusion of the
past. But the sense of immediacy that he achieves through the second
kind of scene ensures that we are never left entirely with the impression
of the novel as meditation. The physical and psychological realism of
key scenes shocks the reader away from too conscious awareness of the
manipulation of time or the dialogue between past and present. Then,
at crucial moments, there are scenes that combine action with contemplation to haunting effect, the most powerful of these being Margaret's
murder.

To take the contemplative scenes first, the novel opens with Nat's
recurring dream. The day in his dream is not wholly timeless. We know
that it's afternoon. But the scene contains strange negations. The sun
"seems to cast no shadow anywhere." "It may be the commencement of
spring or perhaps the end of summer." "The air is almost seasonless—
benign and neutral, windless, devoid of heat or cold." Even Nat's boat is
"a skiff or maybe a canoe." He has "no sense of discomfort nor even of
exertion." Beyond the estuary is "the boundless sea." The shores are "unpeopled, silent; no deer run through the forests" and there's "an effect
of great silence and of an even greater solitude, as if life here had not
so much perished as simply disappeared," leaving everything "to exist
forever unchanged like this beneath the light of a motionless afternoon

sun" (3). But this enigmatic scene becomes explicable when we read the novel as being about the ghosts we summon up to explain the past and ourselves. On one level, Nat is simply dreaming of freedom, but it's also as if he exists outside time, coming into consciousness through the imagination of the author: born, as well as borne, to relive his destiny. Nat, as always, sees a building on a promontory, "stark white and serene against a blue and cloudless sky." "Formed of marble, like a temple," and possessing recesses but "no columns or windows" and no visible door, this building "seems to have no purpose." If it's a temple, it's one "in which no one worships, or a sarcophagus in which no one lies buried, or a monument to something mysterious, ineffable, and without name" (4). Readers have interpreted this temple in the tradition of the great American symbols of *Moby-Dick* and *The Scarlet Letter*. For Toni Morrison it's the white world—"the sealed white structure" that defeats any attempt at dialogue between the races.[13] Nat himself can find no meaning in it, but there is at least the implication that beyond the "physical world" that Nat's voice creates so vividly there is a supernatural world, and this proves to be so.

Such contemplative scenes in the novel are often about the passing of time itself and the activity of imagining the past. This emphasis on the disappearance of almost all trace of the past is everywhere to be found, from the recurring dream to the description of the graveyard, to which Nat is constantly drawn "as if seeking among all those toppled and crumbling wood markers" an "early lesson in mortality" (131–32). For instance, Nat's encounter with Judge Cobb is not merely a dramatic interaction between two intelligent men peering at each other through the transparent barrier of institutional racism. Through Cobb's description of the "blighted domain" of Virginia, Styron also contextualizes Nat's fate. Cobb bemoans the "wrecked and ravaged" soil "turned to useless dust by that abominable weed" (68). What has Virginia "now become?" he asks Nat rhetorically. "A *nursery* for Mississippi, Alabama, Arkansas. A monstrous breeding farm to supply the sinew to gratify the maw of Eli Whitney's infernal machine" (69). In this and other passages Styron's meditation on history provides succinct summaries of the economic context of Nat's rebellion.

The novel contains many such scenes with this quality of contemplation, whether of the past or of the lived moment. Recalling turning eighteen, for instance, Nat describes "one of those dusty, ocherous autumnal days whose vivid weather never again seems so sweet and inviting after that youthful time of discovery: woodsmoke and maple leaves blazing in the trees, an odor of apples everywhere like a winy haze, squirrels scampering for chinquapins at the edge of the woods, a constant stridor of crickets among the withering grass, and over all a ripe sunny heat edged with feathery gusts of wind smelling of charred oak and winter" (183–84). In such moments, Styron transports the reader into this long past era. We are not simply told about Nat; we are with him in the autumn woods, just as we will be with him in the violence of the insurrection.

To see this is to see what Gates might mean when he describes Styron as "a brilliant writer." He wears his research lightly and combines it with what he knows. Hence the evocation of southern weather is no less a part of the novel than is any other aspect. When Nat contemplates the "great boiling clouds" that hang "on the far horizon," we know that this is a narrative born of intimacy with the southern climate. "It was hot and muggy and a moist haze with a hint of storm about it blurred the greenish sky," he tells us. "By late morning the sun burned down through murky waves of heat, so oppressive that even the birds retreated, silent, to the leafy blue sanctuary of the woods" (228). In this and other ways Styron evokes not merely an era but a landscape and region. As his fellow southern writer Barry Hannah put it in a 1994 letter to Styron about *A Tidewater Morning,* "Among working writers, I feel you and [Cormac] McCarthy put the physical world on page the very best. So solid that a spiritual resonance results—rare, rare."[14]

Indeed, one of the most evocative of these contemplative scenes is Nat's description of Turner's deserted house, a scene that employs a notably powerful use of silence, the silence both of the moment and of the past in the present. "The stillness of the plantation" seems to Nat "so oppressive and strange" that he suddenly thinks, "jittery with a vague terror," that he's "been stricken by deafness" (230).

> Dismantled of everything that could be moved—of crystal chandeliers and grandfather's clock, carpets and piano and sideboards and chairs—the cavernous room echoed with a tomblike roar to my sudden sneeze. The reverberation smashed from wall to wall with the sound of waterfalls, cataracts, then became silent. Only a lofty mirror, webbed with minute cracklings and bluish with age, embedded immovably between two upright columns against the wall, remained as sure proof of past habitation: its blurred and liquid depths reflected the far side of the hall, and there four immaculate rectangles marked the vanished portraits of Turner forebears; two stern gentlemen in white wigs and cocked hats,

two serene ladies with modest bosoms bedecked in ribbons and flounces of pink satin, they had been nameless to me yet over the years as familiar as kin: their absence was suddenly shocking, like swift multiple deaths. (230–31)

Such passages reinforce the novel as a meditation on history, on time. Nat's reference to "swift multiple deaths" reminds us, moreover, that the insurrection is already behind him. He has turned to violence and is recalling his journey toward that fact. The emphasis on silence, here and elsewhere, signals this as a representation both of Nat remembering in solitude and of Styron himself imagining and writing in solitude, by hand, in a state of virtual meditation.

Such silence links to the opening and Nat's dream, which is also the author's dream, a kind of floating back, in the manner of a time traveler, into the past or, for Nat, forward into the future, a time before humanity and a time when humanity has disappeared.

There was no wind, the trees in the surrounding woods were quiet; yet because of this very stillness they seemed a solid mass stretching out on all sides of me in perfect circumference to the last boundaries of the world, an all-pervading triumphant mass of greenery. Nothing but this still and ruined plantation existed; it was the very heart of the universe and I was the master not alone of its being at the present instant but of all its past and hence all its memories. Solitary and sovereign as I gazed down upon this wrecked backwater of time, I suddenly felt myself its possessor; in a twinkling I became white—white as clabber cheese, white, stark white, white as a marble Episcopalian. (232)

As in a symphony, motifs echo, loudly, quietly, implicitly. This particular scene builds into a storm. Lightning cracks a magnolia in two. The scene thus stands as a microcosm of Nat's life, "suspended" as he is "between two existences" (299). Once again, the author, as his shadow self Nat Turner, is the contemplator of ruined time. It's he, we understand, who is standing in the decayed mansion in his own time ("white as clabber cheese" indeed) imagining Nat there in *his* time. The author, no less than Nat, is "between two existences," for "the relativity of time allows us elastic definitions."

Styron uses these contemplative scenes to reprise the theme of time passing and of characters' sense of their own helpless position as ephemeral beings in the river of history. There is, for instance, Samuel Turner's nearly inaudible warning, long before leaving Nat in the empty house, that "all this we see here will be gone too, and the mill wheel will crumble away and the wind will whistle at night through these deserted halls" (220). This feels like, not just Samuel's awareness of the economic plight he faces, but his glimpse into history, as if momentarily aware that he is part of a continuum and therefore in a way already past. And indeed, Nat, or Styron, goes on to describe the disintegration of Turner's Mill and the death of a culture.

> Slowly these sounds diminished, faded, became still altogether, and the fields and rutted roadways lay as starkly deserted as a place ravaged by the plague: weeds and brambles invaded the cornfields and the meadows; sills, frames, and doors fell apart in the empty outbuildings. At night, where once glowing hearths lit each cabin down the slope, now all lay in suffocating dark like the departure of the campfires of some army on the plains of Israel. (225)

Nat is aware of the Bible and so of ancient history, but his voice is also Styron's in that, while Nat looks forward to the future, Styron is looking back to the past and pondering a culture that vanished as surely as our own world will dissolve into history, to be found only in ancient structures and artifacts and in the imaginations of future generations. This is literature in the river of history, meditating on its own moment even as it meditates on time past. For we are all, no less than Nat at the juncture between saying good-bye to Turner and awaiting Eppes, "adrift between that which was past and those things yet to come" (228).

Set against these contemplative scenes, which create the novel's meditative mood, are scenes of action. Some are darkly comic: the description of, say, Hark running to escape his master and nearly being decapitated by the washing line, or Nat as a boy going to the privy and Willis burning him from beneath. In their oblique references to hanging and burning, such episodes contain the implication of actual violence perpetrated against slaves. Other scenes, such as the one in which Moore whips Nat, are direct and violent. Rather oddly, there are very few—perhaps too few—scenes of physical violence against slaves, at least of the extreme kind we find in Frederick Douglass. But there is plenty of implicit, unseen, and mental brutality, and the power of scenes that do include violence, including the insurrection, is often in the descriptions of its effect on those who perpetrate or witness it. One example is the young Nat seeing his mother deal with McBride's rape of her. Another is Nat's botched attempt to kill Travis. His first attempt misses altogether, and Travis escapes from bed "with a terrified bellow" and tries to escape "through the wall" (388). On Nat's second attempt the blade twists from his hands, so Will steps in and decapitates the couple. But the horror is as much in the victims' animal panic as in the bounce of Travis's head on the floor, "the unimaginable blood," or the hatchet's "final *chunk-chunk*" (390–91). What conjoins these two scenes is not just the horror of what Nat witnesses but also our awareness of Nat's own horror at what rape and killing involve.

The novel's eruption into violence is all the more powerful for the brooding quality of the scenes that lead up to it. In this sense it manipulates time not only in terms of memory and history but in terms of anticipation. When the insurrection explodes into action, the demonic Will performs the main acts of violence and challenges Nat to lead by example. Will, as Davis notes, is Nat's "shadow self." He symbolizes Nat's "repressed will and the repressed will of the generic slave."[15] Like a Dostoevskian double, he threatens to "seize control" of events (403). While Nat is feeling unwell and noticing that the morning mist is "the color of pearl" (404), Will is riding a "great foaming stallion" and carrying a "Satanic mirror" that, when the horse rears, snares "the sun blindingly," throwing back "a shimmering vista of sky, leaves, and a blur of black and brown faces" that whirl "in a glassy void" (407). If there are shades of Karamazov and Smerdyakov here, there is also that added sense of the cinematic: all that silence; all those episodes of comedy, of recognition, of change; all those murmurs, events, intimacies, and then this violent denouement. For the deaths are far more real here than in *Set This House on Fire*, as real in their way as the moneylender's or Lisaveta's in *Crime and Punishment*. In terms of Styron's own work, the scene of Cass murdering Mason is not even worthy of comparison with that of the ultimate scene: Nat murdering Margaret.

Styron dramatizes Nat's relationship with Margaret as a series of compelling encounters between two people who, mirroring one another not only, as Davis puts in, "in their sexual repression" but also in sensitivity and intellect, could easily fall in love, and not just because their society forbids it. We are not privy to Margaret's mind, but we are aware that Nat cannot articulate how he feels. Their deeply disturbing final encounter is a synthesis and culmination of the contemplative and action scenes. The novel builds up to it in various ways, but not least through earlier present-moment scenes between the two that make the denouement all the more devastating.

In one of these Nat and Margaret are riding in a buggy to the Vaughan house. Nat has witnessed Margaret's "grimace of disgust" at her brother Richard and his friends setting out to hunt down Will, who has run off after breaking Nathaniel Francis's arm. She looks straight at Nat and challenges him to admit that if treated badly he too would strike back. The more she reveals her sympathy for the plight of blacks, and her view that slavery should be abolished, the more her presence stifles him. He becomes acutely conscious that, "elbow kissing elbow," he cannot "avoid touching her" (367). Although he tells himself that he feels only "boredom and lust," there's obvious affinity between them (368). She gets him to stop to end the suffering of a crushed turtle and to drink from a brook. Catching his eye again, her gaze is "insistent, inviting, daring"—"the longest encounter" Nat can recall "ever having with a white person's eyes." Rising from the brook, she stumbles against him. Decorum is restored, but he continually attempts to qualify his responses and to interpret them in terms of "desire and hatred." His heart swells in his throat "unaccountably" (372). His emptiness is "without reason" (374). But what he's really feeling is neither "lust" nor "hatred"; it's "desire," yes, but the kind experienced in mutual, burgeoning love. In truth they're both entangled in the moment, intensely aware of each other and of the "incandescence" of their physical responses (372). He can't help but glimpse her body, her clothes, "the saucy tilt of a dimpled chin" (364). But her emotions are as apparent as Nat's and signaled by her unflinching, "insistent" gaze (372) and by the way she seems to "relax" against him and perceptibly tremble at the intimacy (374). Both of them are suppressing emotions too dangerous to acknowledge.

Pitch-perfect as this scene is, the final encounter more than matches it. When it arrives, we're again in a powerful present moment but also in the world of ghosts, and of personal and historical memory. As with so much in the novel, its drama involves the relativity of time. Read it closely and a great many of the novel's elements fall into place. "Soundless, uttering not a word," Margaret scrambles from her hiding place to flee Nat "like the wind." Nat races round the house. He thinks she's slipped away, but she's "merely fallen down in the waist-high grass." She rises again, "a small and slender figure in the distance," resuming "her flight toward a crooked far-off fence." In a quiet broken only by his own exertion and the noise of grasshoppers, he reaches her as she tries "to clamber over the rotted pole fence" (413). To the sound only of "her hurtful, ragged breathing" he plunges "the sword into her side, just below and behind her breast" (413–14). She screams on the first thrust but not on the second. "Pulsing blood" encrimsons "the taffeta's blue." The scream echoes "like a far angelic cry." She calls to him to kill her in "not so much voice as memory," and attempted murder becomes mercy killing (414). Nat circles her body. He finds himself "seated on a log" and thinking of memories that seem "centuries before." Then he resumes his "meaningless and ordained circuit of her body, not near it yet ever within sight as if that crumpled blue were the center of an orbit around whose path" he must make his "ceaseless pilgrimage" (415).

A close reading clarifies several things. It returns us back to the inaccessible white temple, for Nat is the moon and Margaret the earth, or perhaps the white world he can never be part of. He circles her body, but his "orbit" calls to mind something else. He is recognizing what it is to be an empathic human being. His circling in turn brings us back to the novel as ghost story; the author at the Vaughan house in 1961; and the "This Quiet Dust" essay with which we began. Styron himself has, as it were, joined Nat to contemplate this killing. For Margaret and Nat are like ghosts before the author's eyes as he imagines this event, or Nat recalling it. This crucial scene, which haunted Styron from early in the writing, is the aesthetic reason why Nat Turner as depicted could not have had a wife. The scene shows him to be a tragic hero. After it he admits that he spares a girl he sees running away. This is the beginning of the end not just because she will raise the alarm but because he implicitly acknowledges the horror and futility of the killing. He thus reveals his essential compassion and humanity. Literally, Margaret becomes a ghost for Nat before the end of this scene. He thinks he hears "again her whispery voice" and sees her "rise from the blazing field with arms outstretched as if to a legion of invisible onlookers, her brown hair and innocent school gown teased by the wind" before she vanishes "like an image carved of air and light" (415). He and the author thus effectively become one.

To ponder this scene is to meditate on "history." For what is Margaret, what is Nat, but "an image carved of air and light"? She and Nat are remembered beings from long ago, resurrected by Styron's attempt to wed the past with the present and to reconstruct this tragic episode. She tries to escape by clambering over that "rotted pole fence," but one of the poles gives way "in crunching powdery collapse" (413). The fence would seem to be more than a hundred years old, as if the author were standing in the field where the dreadful confrontation took place, witnessing the ghosts of these two beings, superimposed upon his present as they forever reenact their final encounter. All is virtually silent. In cinema, the events would be silent, certainly, perhaps slowed down, for these are ephemeral beings. Where in the not dissimilar encounter between Cass and Mason Styron produced only melodrama, here he gets it painfully right.

Nat's beginning and ending wrap themselves around each other. The dream of the sea he has never seen and of a way to a homeland he has never known has a terrible poignancy. But it's also a dream we all share, as Wallace Stevens puts it in "The Idea of Order at Key West," about "the obscurity of ourselves and of our origins / in deeper demarcations, keener sounds." Styron's novel is above all (as Morrison says of all literature) about "being human in the world." When Bill Clinton, at Styron's memorial service, noted that we are 99 percent genetically identical, he made the same point. We exist on this spinning planet and had better try to get along. Maybe in a postnational, postethnic world (in which America has now had a postethnic president, or at least one beyond ethnic essentialism) the book can be read in that spirit.[16] "The white inscrutable paradigm of mystery" may, as Morrison surmises, be the white world but is also the privileged strangeness of existence. Nat "cannot dwell on that place too long," for "to try to explore the mystery would be only to throw open portals on even deeper mysteries, on and on everlastingly, into the remotest corridors of thought and time" (422). The novel thus comes to be about the relationship between the mind and reality. Nat is suspended between his imagination and the physical world—between his emotions and his imprisonment. But then so are we all. What a slave faces in extremis, we all face to one degree or another. We are all tied to life, unasked for opportunity though it is, and destined to be expelled from it as we die and the molecules that have clung together in physicality and consciousness disperse and in all likelihood again render us not even oblivious but nonexistent.

So we come to the other feature of the novel's time present: the dialogue between Nat Turner and Thomas Gray. As Trouard notes, Styron foregrounds "Nat's own meditation" by way of this dialogue and the record Nat knows Gray is "artistically" constructing. Nat's description of Gray amplifies the fact that this sleazy manipulator is, in Daniel Fabricant's words, keen to maintain "the Southern social order," to promote his own role in events, and to shape "history itself as a literary construction."

But, just as the personality of Nat Turner as Styron presents him is self-consciously a "meeting place" (in Fuentes's phrase) between the novelist and what one might know or imagine of the figure "buried under a 100 years of history," as Gates puts it, so it's implicit that Gray too is merely Styron's imaginative rendering of the man behind the document. To this extent, the interaction between them is a symbolic meeting, not only between Styron and Gray and two sides of Styron's imagination—the rebel slave and the racist lawyer—but also between Nat and Styron.[17]

There is, Trouard points out, a distinctly self-conscious element to a "frame story" that involves "the flawed construction of a confession of a black revolutionist by 'a white racist,' and each man's view of his role in history."[18] If we keep in mind the ghost theme, along with the "the relativity of time" and the novel as "a meditation on history," details stand out. Like *Set This House on Fire* and *Sophie's Choice*, *The Confessions of Nat Turner* is built on dialogue, with one character's story filtered through another's. But unlike in *Set This House on Fire*, the dialogue both is central to the novel's structure and contains tension, in fact a double tension, since the interaction between Nat and Gray is not only between black and white or slave and master but between past and present. Nat tells his own story *despite* his recorder. Gray's version of events, which he checks with Nat during their dialogue, exists as a historical document, but Nat's version, told only, as Judith Ruderman notes, "to the reader," exists beyond Gray's awareness.[19] This structure provides Nat Turner, or at least Styron's version of him, with a belated triumph over history and over Gray. But Gray is also the conduit between Styron and Nat Turner. Meditating on history, Styron encounters Nat through Gray even as Nat meditates on his personal past. But it's equally implicit that, through Gray, Nat Turner meets Styron and has his portal into the future. For while Gray is an antebellum lawyer, wedded to the institutional racism of his society, we could be forgiven for thinking that he is also a self-demeaning, self-deprecating version of Styron himself, or of how Styron might have been circa 1831: a brandy-sodden, tobacco-chewing skeptic with a gift for the gab.

We receive numerous invitations to imagine Gray as Styron's imagined counterpart, or even as Styron "himself." Early on, Nat feels that he may have made Gray up. He has "the impression dim and fleeting, of hallucination, of talk buried deep in dreams" (35). It's as if Nat is somehow aware of the metafictional truth: that Gray is indeed the author's distorted self-image beamed back in time for this encounter. Again, toward the end, when Gray gives Nat the Bible, Nat has a momentary sense that Gray is "another man" whom he's never recognized before. One might see this as another moment of metafictional insight: Nat's hazy awareness that he's a character in a novel. Moreover, the Bible gesture seems more in line with an encounter between the historical figure and the author than between Nat and Gray. Gray's explanation for it—"you've been pretty fair and square with me, all in all" (425)—is unconvincing. His motivation is negligible and there's scant earlier suggestion that he's simply a compassionate man. Gray has been absent while Styron and the reader have heard Nat's story. So it's not so much Gray who hands Nat the Bible and shakes his hand, as Styron himself—a man with certain similarities to Gray, perhaps, in demeanor, in erudition, in worldly skepticism, in his interest in understanding Nat, and even, perhaps, in some residue of prejudice on racial matters formed by his cultural upbringing. Styron means to publish, as Gray did, and means to assume Nat's voice, as Gray did. It's the author who reaches through the bars of the centuries and now bids his character farewell. It's the author, too, who has given Nat a book in the sense that he's written *The Confessions of Nat Turner,* which is also the gift of years of his life. Those of the ten black writers, therefore, who claimed that these were the confessions of William Styron far more than they were those of Nat Turner weren't wrong. Careful reading suggests that this notion is built into the novel.

Styron doesn't step forward and state that *The Confessions of Nat Turner* is a self-conscious act of meditation. He allows us to read it as historical realism. As Trouard argues, he avoids the "sterile trickery" of overtly self-referential postmodernist writing but combines the best of both worlds, revisioning "the vitality of the great tradition" that involves "story and character" "through a self-conscious premise" (490). We have already seen, both in "This Quiet Dust" and in Styron's other novels, that he moves beyond traditional realism in his depiction of human experience and that like Dostoevsky he's something of a psychological realist. When one begins to view *The Confessions of Nat Turner* (and later *Sophie's Choice*) in these terms, too, a great many other elements come into focus. The encounter between Nat and Gray is reminiscent, for instance, of Ivan Karamazov's encounter with the devil. Both Dostoevsky and Styron use the ambiguous status of these meetings—physical, spiritual, or merely imagined—to express ideas fundamental to their work. This allows the meditation to go far beyond reflections on racism, slavery, and American history. Not unlike Karamazov's with the devil, Nat's encounter with Gray is in part a debate about faith and the nature of good and evil. With access to books and ideas that Nat knows nothing of, Gray effectively comes from another world. He has the perspective of an educated white southerner of the time, but he also has a distinctly Styronian sensibility when it comes to matters of religious faith.

Specifically, the encounter between Nat and Gray is a debate between faith and science. Gray tells Nat about William Herschel and that the sun is one of "not millions, but *billions* of stars all revolvin' around in a great big kind of cartwheel that he calls a galaxy. And this sun of our'n is just a piddlin' little third-rate star swimmin' around amongst millions of other stars on the edge of the galaxy." He leans toward "Reverend" Nat and offers the challenge to believers that philosophers and scientists from Emmanuel Kant to Richard Dawkins have echoed down through the centuries: "How do you square that with God?" But Gray is not content to dismiss religion as "hogwash." He wants Nat to see the "*evil*" of his "dad-burned Bible" (111). Whether Nat ever finds redemption as opposed to spiritual comfort is a moot point, but part 1 ends with Nat asking aloud, "*Then what I done was wrong, Lord?*" and wondering, if that be the case, whether there's "*no redemption*" (115). The irony is clear enough. Having spoken to an apparently physical being who, for the reader, is implicitly a ghost from the future and so a figment of Nat's imagination, he is left speaking aloud to another being whose status may equally be nothing more than imaginary.

To borrow Dawkins's title, Gray (or Styron) challenges Nat over what he sees as Nat's "God Delusion."[20] This is one example of the novel's being much more a meditation on history than a conventional historical novel. It dramatizes a dialogue that has long shaped history and human actions—religious faith versus existential awareness—and that again has literary links with Dostoevsky. Much is made of Nat's "apartness from God" (23), his sense of an "awful silence" (78) but, unlike with Dostoevsky, there's little sense that spiritual redemption would be other than illusory. Gray is satirized on several levels. His bombastic eloquence is littered with errors and self-revealing bigotry. But when it comes to the science, he is Styron's mouthpiece.

The novel thus expresses a Camusian, existential acceptance of the strangeness of reality and the bleakness of our plight, together with an equally Camusian assertion of what Styron elsewhere refers to as self-realization. "Even when what the artist creates is a denial," *Selected Letters* shows Styron citing Camus in 1957, "it still affirms something and pays homage to the miserable, magnificent life we live" (238). We know *The Confessions of Nat Turner* was partly inspired by *L'Etranger*, and in 1987 Styron cited Camus's influence as "a writer who had abandoned almost but not all hope." Styron's characters are invariably hostile to institutional religion, which he considered "hollow." Even Nat Turner's religious sensibility is self-fashioned from biblical study. But the phrase "almost but not all" is interesting. The *desire* for meaning is everywhere apparent as a Camusian paradox of rebellion against a mindless universe. It's there in Milton's and Cass's drunken misery, in Peyton's suicidal despair, in Nat's one-sided dialogues with what, in all three of the other novels, Styron refers to as a "gaseous vertebrate." It was part of his makeup. "Taking the broadest philosophical view of human destiny," he said, "you realize you're a speck of dust" and that the earth will surely "be turned into a cinder." But his writing nevertheless always contains a nod toward the provisional nature of knowledge. We can only strongly suspect that religion entirely stems from a need for meaning, yet for Styron the "worst fate" is to be unable "to assert oneself." Art is affirmation, the unacceptable alternative being to "lay down your tools and do nothing."[21]

This is the context in which Styron invites us to assess his version of Nat Turner. Trezevant calls Nat "a fiend beyond parallel" (80). The prosecutor sees Meursault as "a monster."[22] Camus speaks of Meursault (in his 1955 preface to *L'Etranger*) as "the only Christ we deserve," and the same might be said of Nat. But they are very different. Camus's hero has given up hope of anything beyond life or any meaning in it. Nat has not. He is a noble man reluctantly engaged in warfare. Meursault's rage only manifests itself in prison, against the priest. Nat's anger has by then extinguished itself. He never flares up at Gray, and Gray is not a priest but a lawyer. The reverend confesses to the lawyer—a notably secular confession, and a nicely ironic reversal. Perhaps, too, just as Nat has taught Gray something of what it means to be a slave, so Gray has introduced new contexts to Nat. His "orbit" of Margaret, like a "pilgrimage" beneath the blazing sun, recalls Gray's reference to Herschel and to what Gray sees as the lie of the Bible. Those two words juxtapose science and religion. "All madness, illusion, error, dream, and strife" diminishes to nothing, whether in the face of Margaret's Christian vision of "an eternity of love" or of the blunt truth of eternity that science suggests (415). As in *L'Etranger*, murder beneath a blazing sun places human activity within the timescale of the indifferent universe. Nat must face the possibility of futility. His redemption is not Christian but humanist. It recognizes meaning between individuals rather than beyond this world. The areligious nature of this redemption, indeed, exists in the final phrasing, which implies that he reaches it not through transcendence but through the very physicality of life—orgasm. Notable too is the fact that Gray is more intelligent and empathic, his dubious conversion to outright compassion at the end notwithstanding, than the novel's clergymen or than Camus's priest. Among Styron's departures from Gray's version of events are the facts that Nat never raises his voice or fist to Gray and the latter never assesses Nat as any sort of monster or devil. As Styron's alter ego, he treats Nat with the respect due to a fellow human whose rebellion against total odds has come to nothing, as it surely will for us all.

To end this chapter, I'll turn briefly to the Marine Corps fiction that Styron wrote before and after *Sophie's Choice*. The best of this is available in *The Suicide Run*, while another tale, "Love Day," appears in *A Tidewater Morning*. These potential excerpts from *The Way of the Warrior* are marginal to Styron's overall achievement. He may, in *Set This House on Fire*, have produced one comparatively inferior effort, but he never wrote a run-of-the-mill novel. His nature was to immerse himself emotionally and intellectually in subjects serious enough to be "worth risking a word,"[23] so his forte was in the architectural grandeur and subtlety of the truly ambitious narrative. The mature short fiction about the Marine Corps constitutes no more than a range of unassembled parts of a project that failed to materialize. All we have are suggestions of what might have been had he managed to sustain his remarkable ability to construct a complex novel. But while we cannot assess these extracts within the dynamics of a complicated whole, they still shed light on issues of interest to his work in general. These include the notion of self-realization and his portrayal of masculinity.

We can only speculate on why Styron never managed to bring this material to fruition. Perhaps, initially, it was the pressure of expectation in the wake of *The Confessions of Nat Turner*. Perhaps he was then merely, and fortunately, waylaid by *Sophie's Choice*. Perhaps, beyond that, it had to do with failing health, or maybe, as Al Styron speculates, the depressive episodes of his later years were in part the result of his struggles with the novel. But his obsession with writing about his military experience may also have been fundamentally problematic in terms of the kind of impact he hoped *The Way of the Warrior* would have. In *Reading My Father*, Al puts into words what I, too, feel: that, at least as Styron seemed to be approaching it, it just isn't subject matter with broad appeal. Moreover, to the extent that portrayals of American military life of that era do appeal, it's hard to see how Styron's treatment of it would have differed from other novels in the genre. What she knew of the manuscript was that "as always, it was to be a 'Big Book,' about the skeins of troubled history running through the American South in which he was raised. It was about War and Race. And, at its heart, it was to be a love story." She recalls thinking "how much more" she would have enjoyed "a tale of romance than the war story Daddy seemed forever bent on."[24] Perhaps she meant that "a war story" is okay if it's to be just another novel. But Styron wasn't interested in producing just another novel. He would have needed to depict peace as well as war. His worlds are multidimensional statements about individuals in the contexts of society and history. I suspect, therefore, that the paradoxical parochialism of military life, in terms of creating his kind of panoramic drama, was at least one, profound obstacle to creating a novel with the sustained impact of *Lie Down in Darkness, The Confessions of Nat Turner,* and *Sophie's Choice.*

At any rate, it's evident from the material we have that the subject matter as Styron tends to approach it lacks the dimension for portraying life in the round. The Marine Corps he experienced was an all-male world. Obviously an all-male world can provide subject matter for great literature, and not just about the military (*Moby-Dick* being the obvious example), but the scenario still, to my mind, reduced Styron's options for exercising his own strengths, not least his ability to write convincingly both about women and from a female viewpoint. The subtitle of *The Suicide Run, Five Tales of the Marine Corps,* immediately signals a potential limiting of scope and circle of readers, as indeed does the phrase "The Way of the Warrior" (a translation, as has often been noted, from the Japanese word for the Samurai way, *Bushidō*). Male camaraderie is all very well, but it is not a theme of immediate and obvious universal appeal. To a large extent, indeed, the tales deal with a male world in which women, however much they remain the focus of intense male interest, are socially sidelined. A younger, fitter Styron might have found ways round this through a complex series of flashbacks, narrative switches, stories within stories, and reflections on reflections, but unless he came up with a novel whose dynamic was beyond rather than within military life, the fact would still remain that, unlike with Nat and Margaret and Sophie and Stingo, the time present of the main action would have lacked any such male-female frisson. (Indeed, this is one of the things lacking in *Set This House on Fire,* in which female characters, whether Poppy, Celia, or Francesca, are largely reactive participants in a male drama.) While there's some evidence in the published writing that Styron sought complexity on this level, the difficulties of this task are also apparent in the manuscript material that he "constructed, deconstructed, and constructed again and again over the course of years."[25] That Styron may have recognized the difficulty perhaps explains why the book he planned never materialized, even as the writing on the military that we do have reminds us just how miraculous the architecture of his best novels really is.

That said, the fact that he's writing largely about an all-male environment does provide broader insight into his critique of maleness. One point of attack on *The Confessions of Nat Turner* was that Styron emasculated Nat, while one form of attack on *Sophie's Choice* was that the narrator is a chauvinist with an unreflectively masculine view of women.[26] The Marine Corps tales offer further evidence that the truth is much more complicated. Moreover, Styron's depiction of maleness takes place in the context of a broader and abiding preoccupation with the simultaneous urge toward conformity and rebellion that characterizes all his fiction. In these and other ways his writing on the military contains themes that transcend their ostensible subject matter and are worthy of comment. They may revolve around Styron's marine experiences, but all these stories can be read in terms of the struggle of the individual to forge a path through life—always here threatened by imminent destruction—in light of the mixture of tyranny and temptation to conform that characterizes (male) society. All deal with the existence of hierarchies and of the relations between different forms and degrees of power. They are about men's quiet agreements to adhere to or rebel against these hierarchies and about the web of relationships that exist between careerists, sycophants, rebels, loners, and all the more subtle individual social identities that mingle within and around us. The stories gain their interest from the narrowness and intensity of the system that Styron found himself a part of but also from the universality of the theme of implementation of, acceptance of, or resistance to power. While the military world as Styron presents it becomes a microcosm of the world men in particular tend to live in—especially in all-male environments— it also represents a version of that world set in relief. For the business of the military is to attack or defend a society to the point of death.

Styron also sees the world of the marines as he experienced it in the forties as an environment that reveals life in the raw but at the same time blatantly feeds vanity, highlighting advancement and fueling a constant tension between those individuals who bolster their identity by rising in the hierarchy and those who rebel. To some extent, Styron's narrators are evenhanded in depicting these tussles. They have a capacity for hero worship and often admire the aura that can accompany status. But they are also sharp-eyed about pomposity, façades, and inflated egos. Equally, they memorialize those who rebel against the odds. In the end, they critique conformity and promote the quest for self-realization against the threat of imminent oblivion.

To this extent Styron's writing on the military helps to clarify his emotional and intellectual vision. For what these stories really turn on is the relative price—all along the scale from petty concerns to issues of survival—of choosing between rebellion and conformity during our brief, fragile existence. In this sense they share subject matter with *Set This House on Fire, The Confessions of Nat Turner,* and *Sophie's Choice.* Does an individual accept enslavement or rebel? Do we choose to follow orders, keep our heads down, avoid confrontation, or assert our individuality? What price do we pay for the choices we make? What is the price of self-realization? We should keep in mind, too, in reading these tales, that rebels can take many forms. The purest rebel is the criminal, or the subordinate who refuses to be cowed. Most people have a streak of rebellion mingled with a need for conformity. This is by and large the makeup of Milton, Culver, Peter, Stingo, even Nat. But another class of rebel stakes all on making a personal statement. In other words, in the broadest sense, there's the self-maker, or self-realizer, or artist, who, to use Styron's favorite Flaubert dictum, is "orderly" in his habits "like a good bourgeois, so that [he] may be violent and original" in his work. To this extent, these tales are statements about the significance of art. They reflect Styron's own admiration for Camus, for Orwell, but really for all who choose self-reliance over the seductions of living on others' terms: the "Kilroy was here" statement, as Styron put it in our 1988 conversation, but done "with a sense of nobility and dignity."[27]

If all this does indeed seem some distance from the ostensible subject matter of the military, a run through the stories provides ample illustration that this is what, at core, they are about. Rereading them calls to mind comments Styron made about this issue of self-realization and about the individual within the river of history. For such works are further illustrations that he felt that human beings' relationship to history was at the heart of the most significant literature of any era. "I know what grabs me, what moves me, what I find central and important," he said in 1988, "and it is the course of human events. I am moved by moments when human lives intersect with large historical events and become metaphors." He felt that "all writing is important when it's good, but there's an added dimension when it tries to grapple with these virtually incomprehensible things that go on in history." Contrasting such writing with "frivolous and evasive" fiction, he believed that "there are moments in history which allow for the creation of certain works." Such a perspective illustrates the connection between all his novels. *Lie Down in Darkness* is structured around the war years, and Milton and Peyton's mutual angst is not unconnected with that terrifying era and the emergence of the atomic age. *Set This House on Fire* is set during postwar European reconstruction and the rise of American consumerist culture. Nat Turner's personal story becomes emblematic of both the human cost of the institution of slavery and the racial conflicts that still characterize American society. Sophie's story is inextricably bound up with World War II and the Holocaust, just as Stingo is very much a young man of his era and place. A novel about the military would have fit this pattern of lives intersecting "with large historical events."[28]

We can also see the theme of (male) self-realization in the first tale in *The Suicide Run*. Dating from the early 1950s, "Blankenship" is the start of a novel begun after *The Long March*. Charles Blankenship is in charge of a guardhouse. Two prisoners have just escaped on his watch. He is confronted with McFee, a rebel marine who has provoked a guard, Mulcahy, into hitting him. Blankenship learns about McFee's history. The winner of two Purple Hearts, he has been court-martialed and imprisoned for desertion. He received this sentence "not because his admirable record had been ignored" but for resisting arrest "with such homicidal fury" that, out of bullets, he'd resorted "to cups, ketchup bottles, and, in a final spasm, even his own wristwatch as 'missiles.'" McFee is a man of total defiance, and Blankenship sees him, within the realms of military law, as a sinner "being justly punished" (32). McFee's continued defiance, however, provokes Blankenship into hitting him with Mulcahy's club. Blankenship's regret is that "it should have been a lesser, meaner man than McFee who had impelled him to do it." But his actions stem from the fact that McFee gives the lie to his worldview. "The whole Marine Corps is one big jail," McFee has told him. Even as Blankenship hits him, McFee's response—"You're the yardbird, you son of a bitch" (33)—is defiant. McFee, then, is in some ways a version of Captain Mannix but in other ways more interesting. Again it's a drama of authority and rebellion, and of the recognition on the part of the man in authority that true bravery comes from standing outside the system. Whether McFee's stance is wise with regard to personal cost is another matter. But such a question is not just for an incident but for a lifetime: self-realization and rebellion both have a price. McFee antagonizes authority into revealing the brutality at its core. Blankenship is an example of one who, without being himself evil, is an adherer to someone else's system rather than a self-realizer.

"Marriott, the Marine" (1971) picks up on this theme. The narrator feels alienated from the Marine Corps he has had to rejoin and "the whole humiliating baggage of a caste system calculated to bring out in men their basest vanities" (38). He is mad at himself for being "dumb enough" to accept the offer of a promotion to first lieutenant if he stayed on as a reserve (39). The tale underlines not just that like any individual he's at the mercy of his historical moment but also that he hasn't the stomach truly to go it alone. Membership brings him recognition. But amid this uncertainty, he encounters Lieutenant Colonel Paul Marriott, who, in his older-brother charisma and even in individual scenes, anticipates Nathan Landau. Amid the narrator's fear of war, and surrounded by regulars "wrapped up in their training manuals and tables of organization and their dreams of advancement" (55), the narrator at least has his "southern gothic romance" to consider, and he allows his friend Lacy to read it (56). When Lacy tells him that Marriott would like to read it too, the narrator is doubtful, but Marriott's reaction suggests to him that maybe the military is not without its intellectuals. In a scene that foreshadows Stingo's false moment of euphoria with Sophie and Nathan, the narrator finds himself at a buffet at which "a liquor-warm mood of felicity" lulls him "into a deceptive feeling of peace." For the first time since arriving at camp, he feels "buoyed by alcohol" instead of having "it feed and aggravate" his "discontent."

> Beyond any doubt it was Colonel Marriott who was responsible for this gentle euphoria: that the Marine Corps contained one regular officer capable of such enlightened, original conversation was enough to make me want to revise entirely my jaundiced estimate of military life. And although I recollect our talk being "literary" (at twenty-six I doted on such earnest discourse), I found the Colonel unpretentiously knowledgeable—astonishing me all the more since pretentiousness in matters they know little about is a common trait among career officers, especially those above the rank of captain. But even before this I was taken with him; he displayed a sympathy for my predicament that was quite out of the ordinary. (61–62)

"What about this book of yours?" asks Marriott à la Sophie, Nathan, and John F. Kennedy as portrayed in "Havanas in Camelot." "Lacy's very excited about what he's read. He says it's bound to cause a big stir when it comes out" (63). Reworking the scene for *Sophie's Choice*, Styron will even recycle phrases.[29]

Marriott then engages the narrator in an unexpected discussion of *Madame Bovary*. The Colonel's refined interest in literature turns out, however, as does Nathan's, to hide a harsher truth. When the conversation is interrupted, the narrator is brought "quickly back to earth." Something causes his "wonderful mood to snap in two," and he sees that Marriott, "like the prince transformed into baser stuff at one stroke of the wand," is "once again a mere lieutenant-colonel" (65). Some days later he meets Marriott again, but in between he has had to put up with his roommate, Dee Jeeter, having his father to stay. Dee's father is "an old time marine," says Dee, with an impressive combat record. Now, though, he's a sick old man often laid low by "a paroxysm of coughing," the noise of which tries the narrator's patience through the night (75). The Gunner, as he's referred to, subsequently dies in the hospital. When the narrator meets Marriott again, he confides his feelings about a relatively poor review of his novel. Marriott duly reassures him that the review is by someone young or jealous or both. But when the narrator also confesses his guilt about the old man beginning to die in his room, Marriott's initial observation that the narrator is not responsible is overtaken by his sense of awe at hearing who the old man was.

Marriott's eulogy of the old man's record reveals his intense identification with the Marine Corps. Disappointed though he is, the narrator realizes how foolish it is "to feel that way." Marriott is "above all, first and foremost, *always* a marine," and "it had been the dreamiest wishful thinking, goofy as a schoolgirl's, to see him as truly 'literary' or 'artistic' when these were merely components of an enlightened and superior dilettantism" (90). The narrator suddenly sees that Marriott, despite his vivid anecdotal style, is somehow false. This revelation has nothing of the force of Stingo's recognition that his mentor, Nathan, is insane, but it does reveal the story's core theme in line with Styron's preoccupations in the other stories. Marriott, like Mannix and Blankenship, is a conformist. Each reveals the potential to achieve individual self-realization, but each fails the test. The story ends with the narrator understanding that Marriott's "ties to the small elite fellowship to which he belonged" are ultimately as strong as those "which bind other men to a vocation in science or the arts or a political belief or—to be more nearly precise—

a church" (91). The potential male role model reveals himself to have abdicated personal autonomy in favor of a group mind-set. The notion of the marine, therefore, stands for the notion of membership of any kind: it's a basic social and religious impulse that rejects the search for self-realization in favor of adherence to a group. Such a stance may be entirely natural, but it compromises the unflinching individualism the narrator seems to seek. His disappointment in Marriott is set within the context of existential awareness that heroic individualism is the purest stance against the void. Group effort is not ignoble as such, but to lose one's identity in any group in the way that Marriott does is to forgo responsibility by working within the rules of the collective. The heroism of the artist (which manifests itself beyond the more obvious forms of art) is the struggle to achieve self-realization.

The remaining tales—"The Suicide Run," "My Father's House," and "Elobey, Annobón, and Corisco"—again reflect Styron's preoccupation with self-realization and deepen his depiction of masculinity, not least in terms of a candid exploration of awareness of imminent death. "The Suicide Run" involves a reckless drive to meet a wife and a girlfriend and the nearness of a fatal accident, after which the two friends renegotiate their values. As so often in Styron's work, the story juxtaposes sex and death, with the former used as a way to forget about the latter. If the core of this story is bravado, the men in the latter two stories reflect implicitly or directly on the nature of courage and fear. In an ironic twist on Franklin Roosevelt's statement that Americans had "nothing to fear but fear itself," they fear precisely that at the crucial time they will lack courage. "My Father's House," while again about something other than the military in its framing story about Paul Whitehurst and his stepmother, includes a lengthy flashback about military experience that details the nature of fear. Paul, in particular, suffers an ever-present fear of sudden death. "It didn't take long for the instruments of modern warfare to turn a human body into just such a repulsive emulsion," he reflects on witnessing squashed snails. "One of the riflemen of my pla-toon, a big muscular farm boy from South Dakota, had seen, strewn on the Tarawa beachhead, a string of guts twelve feet long belonging to the marine who, only seconds before the mortar blast, had been his best buddy." Would he too, Paul wonders, "be immolated in one foul form or another, consumed by fire or rent apart by steel or crushed like a snail?" (145).

Paul admits to fear but only implicitly addresses fear of fear—that his courage will fail him. Styron, however, articulates this in the vignette

"Elobey, Annobón, and Corisco." "I found myself in a conflict I had never anticipated," says the narrator, "afraid of going into battle, yet even more afraid of betraying my fear, which would be an ugly prelude to the most harrowing fear of all—that when forced to the test in combat I would demonstrate my absolute terror, fall apart, and fail my fellow marines" (192). To combat this "terror," he retreats to his tent, lies gazing up at the canvas, and tries to "exorcise the dread," whispering the names of three islands off the west coast of Africa that had adorned a stamp he owned during a stamp-collecting period of childhood—Elobey, Annobón, and Corisco (192). The search for self-realization occurs amid a fear of oblivion and desperation not to bow to this cowardice. These are stories of men, and of male camaraderie, to be sure, but their subject matter includes the vulnerability beneath male bravado.

In the end the tales in *The Suicide Run* are all about eager youths, who happen to be marines near the end of World War II or against the background of the Korean War, facing early on the smallness of the individual and the horror of our common fate. In the *Tidewater Morning* story "Love Day," too, Styron weaves a version of all war, or at least preparation for war, from training to awaiting combat. "Love Day" is uneven, and particularly weak in terms of the supposedly charismatic figure of Happy Halloran, who also appears in "Marriott, the Marine" and "My Father's House." It's not just that Halloran is contrived (he has a handlebar moustache and a tendency to lapse into Scottish and Irish brogues) but that Styron uses Halloran's tedious yarns as a clunky device for allowing Paul Whitehurst to daydream. Nevertheless, the story does contain vivid descriptions of life aboard ship awaiting combat and enters the territory Styron would portray masterfully in "A Tidewater Morning." In a poignant scene, during Paul's reminiscences while Halloran holds court, we see the young boy with his mother dying and his father enraged by his inability to fix their broken-down car. More generally, the father's frustration is at his impotence in the face of his wife's illness. The story perhaps provides insight into the source of the breakdown of the hearse in *Lie Down in Darkness*. But more profoundly, it joins "My Father's House" in courageously addressing in detail the nature of dread.

What we learn from all this is the extent to which Styron again sought to wed his personal story to historical events. Central as this is to *Sophie's Choice*, it would surely have been so to *The Way of the Warrior*. In "Love Day," he writes of "the power of history to utterly victimize humanity, composed of forgettable ciphers like myself."[30] Critics of *Sophie's Choice* misread Stingo's egotism for Styron's. But Stingo's egotism, these tales confirm, is in any case bravado. Most interesting about this military writing is not the machismo world one might expect but a sensitive portrayal of the fear and dread behind the macho stance, which is not just that of the young marine, but of the strident male. The narrator of "Marriott, the Marine" vainly seeks in his potential hero a genuine sensitivity to and comprehension of human feeling. Paradoxically, had this novel materialized as a whole rather than merely in parts, it would have spoken eloquently of maleness in a way quite at odds with the more superficial criticism of *The Confessions of Nat Turner* as portraying an emasculated Nat Turner and *Sophie's Choice* as being itself chauvinistic. Styron's male characters may express a range of supposedly masculine traits, but they are no strangers to vulnerability, sensitivity, and fear. These Marine Corps tales thus renew the sense that in terms of his portrayal of human complexity Styron has at times been one of the least understood of writers.

CHAPTER 7

Reflections

Terror and Tenderness in *Sophie's Choice*

> In all important transactions of life we have to take a leap in the dark.
> . . . If we decide to leave the riddles unanswered, that is a choice. If we
> waver in our answer, that too is a choice; but whatever choice we make,
> we make it at our peril.
> —JAMES FITZJAMES STEPHEN, *Liberty, Equality, Fraternity,* 1873

Rereading *Sophie's Choice* for this book coincided with my first visit
to Auschwitz and my discovery that the Auschwitz of my mind only
vaguely resembled the physical sites. Perhaps like many first-time visitors, I felt I already knew the place. Yet I hadn't fully taken in that what
we call "Auschwitz" (the German name) consists of three main sites
near the town of Oświęcim. Auschwitz I is the original, compact "parent" camp with the ARBEIT MACHT FREI sign. This is the place many
people think of as Auschwitz, although they may also have in mind
Auschwitz-Birkenau, or Auschwitz II, the vast, sprawling site with its
train track running in beneath the entrance tower, a camp built specifically for killing. Finally, Monowitz-Buna, or Auschwitz III, was where
prisoners were put to work in the site factories.

Tadeusz Borowski's *This Way for the Gas, Ladies and Gentlemen* is
largely about Auschwitz I, although his fiancée, writes Jan Kott, "was in
the F.K.L. *(Frauen Konzentration Lager),* the women's barracks, at Birkenau."[1] Olga Lengyel's *Five Chimneys* and Shlomo Venezia's *Inside the Gas
Chambers* are primarily about Birkenau, and an image of the Birkenau
entrance punctuates Claude Lanzmann's documentary, *Shoah*. Primo
Levi's *If This is a Man* testifies to his time at Monowitz-Buna, though

he also had experience of Auschwitz I. Of his returns in 1965 and 1982, Levi wrote about Auschwitz I (or "Auschwitz central," as he calls it, one "of some forty camps") that he "didn't feel anything much." For all the "pitiful relics" on display, he felt that it was "just a museum—something static, rearranged, contrived." Monowitz itself "no longer exists" in that "the rubber factory to which it was annexed" now "occupies the whole area." Whatever is there is closed to the public, but as you near Oświęcim on a clear day from Kraków—or Cracow, as Styron spells the city in *Sophie's Choice* and as I therefore refer to it—you see two gigantic factory chimneys to your left, gray against the rural skyline. Only Birkenau, which Levi had never seen as a prisoner and which had not "been prettied up," produced in him "a feeling of violent anguish."[2]

Rereading such testimonies after visiting Auschwitz I and Birkenau, you think about what happened where. *Sophie's Choice* involves artistic license, yet while many of the events Styron describes never happened, the real and the fictional do coincide. "In April of 1943," Sophie tells Stingo, "I was sent to the concentration camp in the south of Poland called Auschwitz-Birkenau" (143). She is actually sent to Birkenau from Warsaw, having left Cracow to find work in 1940, not long after learning that her father and his colleagues have been shot at Sachsenhausen on New Year's Day (86).[3] The train south takes not the usual "six or seven hours" but "two complete days and a night" (144). It's at Birkenau that she must make her Choice. She's then sent to Auschwitz I and remains there twenty months, including a spell in Höss's villa.

The gateway to Auschwitz I seems too small. But then so does Auschwitz I, even though more than twenty thousand prisoners inhabited it. Once a barracks for the Sixth Polish Cavalry Battalion, it comprises about thirty blocks, each perhaps the length of a basketball court, two storeys high with a cellar. The most memorable one you enter is Block 4. Here you find a glass case half the length of the block and taking up the wall of a long room. Behind the glass at a 40-degree angle lies the disintegrating hair of forty thousand women and children. ("I was given scissors and had to cut off the women's hair," explains Venezia in the only extensive firsthand account by a Sonderkommando survivor. "Especially useful were the long tresses, easy to cut off and transport.")[4]

Responses to this room are invariably complex. One member of our group, who had been before, chose not to go in. On my own first visit I felt a horrified disengagement, a stepping back from full human response. Later, I recorded my thoughts. "The room," I wrote, "has a palpable smell. The source of this, even though it's behind glass, is the hair. It is utterly repellent." During a second visit, knowing what to expect, I felt I could be more objective, so I entered determined to find words to describe the smell. I thought it would be of decay, of life turning to dust. The room turned out to have no smell at all. There was nothing to describe. I suppose my first response had to do with being confronted with what Julia Kristeva terms the *abject*. ("What is *abject*," she writes in *Powers of Horror*, "the jettisoned object, is radically excluded, and draws me toward the place where meaning collapses. . . . There I am, at the border of my condition as a living being. My body extricates itself, as being alive, from that border.")[5]

You are looking at death. "The corpse, seen without God, and outside of science, is the utmost abjection. It is death infecting life," writes Kristeva. "It beckons to us and ends up engulfing us."[6] You baulk at the mountain of anonymity and so seek something to help you imagine those whose hair this was. Hair in life being a source of attraction, you look for the remnants of beauty. There is no dark hair, it's all long faded, but this straggle of lighter hair must have belonged to a very blonde girl, this dullish red plait to an astonishing redhead. This glass case stays with you. You never look at hair the same way again. Walking the corridors, you become aware of the hair of those around you. Back home, you remove hair blocking the vacuum cleaner. You get your hair cut. It lies in clumps. You comb your children's hair, or find a lock from childhood. And so on.

At Auschwitz you next encounter a small, glassed-in space containing a roll of canvas 20 percent of whose content is human hair. Another section, the length of a squash or racquetball court, is deep in pots and pans enameled in blue, green, or red. A small case holds rusted cans that contained the Zyklon B gas pellets. A standing case holds turquoise pellets the size of pills. "Twenty minutes," the guide is saying, "two thousand people . . . suffocation . . . no need for heating . . . twenty degrees plus . . . body heat enough." To find out what this gas did to people, you read Venezia.

In Block 5 you see thousands of adults' shoes. You notice a green sandal. Then you see children's shoes. "In the dark halls of the museum that is now what remains of Auschwitz, I see a heap of children's shoes," writes Kristeva. "The abjection of Nazi crime reaches its apex when death . . . interferes with what, in my living universe, is supposed to save me from death: childhood, science. . . ."[7] Your eye lingers on a small blue suede boot. You imagine that it belonged to a girl of eight. The boots were her special footwear. Her mother agreed that she could wear them as the family were ordered to assemble. "In total," says the guide, "the Allies found between fifteen and sixteen million pairs of shoes." You see a pair of black lace-ups tied together. "After a time," Venezia explains, "they also added an instruction to use the laces to tie shoes in pairs. In fact this was to facilitate the process of sorting out when the things arrived at *Kanadakommando*."[8] The owner of these shoes tied them together for eternity.

On it goes. Prosthetics of all shapes and sizes: false legs, braces, contraptions for hip and back support, crutches, a tangle of metal and leather—all designed to help people. Then there are the suitcases, many emblazoned with identification: *Jnes Meyer Köln J 05377, Klement Hedwig 8.10.1898, M. Frank. 12.4.15. HOLLAND.* A tangle of wire spectacles, some in surprising shapes, some with colored rims or lenses; hairbrushes, utensils, ladles, sieves, toys, a broken doll—"pitiful relics." While there are similar items in the United States Holocaust Memorial Museum in Washington, DC, the shock here is the volume of material, part of a vast store making up only a fraction of that collected by "the German Nazis" (to use our guide's phrase). Auschwitz today, I learned from a clutch of *sprawozdania*, the dual-language annual reports, handed me by a young man in the small bookshop, holds and protects a horrendous number of objects that the Germans failed "to ship into the depths of the Reich." These include "more than 110,000 shoes; approximately 3,800 suitcases, including 2,100 labeled by their owners; more than 12,000 pots and pans; almost 470 prostheses and braces; 350 camp uniforms ('stripes'); about 250 fringed prayer garments."[9] There are also six thousand works of art, two thousand of them made by prisoners in concentration camps, and, of course, more than two tons of hair.

Naturally I was thinking about all this when, leaving Block 4 on one of my subsequent visits, I paused near an empty flight of stairs. The stairs are in a space between what's "on show." (For how easy it is to view Auschwitz, with its glass cases of ordinary objects set up to be contemplated, not as a memorial but as a kind of gallery of "conceptual art.") Every step has two wide indentations where millions have worn down the gray, speckled concrete. At the turn of the stairs that day, a window stood awash with sunlight that caught the indentations and made them sparkle.

When I catch up with my group they're climbing the steps into Block 6, with its photographs of tattooed prisoners. "Tattoos were needed to identify corpses," explains the guide. "Babies were tattooed on their legs because their arms were too small." I record the number on a woman's arm: 95670. The lower the number, the earlier the prisoner arrived. Most blocks are closed, including Block 10, where hundreds of women, mainly Jewish, were treated as guinea pigs by SS doctors, including the gynecologist Carl Clauberg for his sterilization experiments. Then there is Block 11, the "Death Block," adjacent to a courtyard with a replica of the "Death Wall." You file past a room furnished with chairs and a table. Here the Gestapo sentenced people to execution. Further down are the women's and then the men's changing room, where victims were forced to undress before being taken into the courtyard. Near the Death Wall stand poles where prisoners were tortured.

In the cellar of Block 11 are more windowless cells. The Nazis used them to work out how to kill more efficiently. Here, in Cell 18, the "Starvation Cell," is a shrine to the Franciscan priest Maximilian Kolbe, prisoner 16770, who died on 14 August 1941. He had volunteered to replace one of ten men condemned to death after another prisoner escaped. Starved for two weeks, Kolbe was finally injected with carbolic acid by Dr. Hans Bock, the *Blockältester*, or block master, of the camp hospital. In Cell 20, the "Suffocation Cell," they trialed Zyklon B. Here too are tiny cells where four people at a time slept on their feet. One has been partly dismantled so that visitors can stand in it and try to imagine. But that's impossible. If you look down at the one left untouched, you see the small hatch where the prisoners crawled in. The walls would have reached the ceiling. These were stand-up coffins for four. "Je cherche la region cruciale de l'âme, où le Mal absolu s'oppose à la fraternité," quotes Styron from André Malraux's *Lazare* (1974) as one of his epigraphs: "I seek that essential region of the soul where absolute evil confronts brotherhood." With Maximilian Kolbe one might want to turn that around. His cell is a place, in the heart of Auschwitz I, where brotherhood confronted absolute evil. It stands witness to the triumph of human identity transcending a death meant to consign the heroism to obscurity.

Along the corridors, too, hang photographs of shaven-headed prisoners in striped uniforms who, for all the Nazis' attempts to render them alike, are unutterably individual. For each, the name, date of arrival, and invariably date of death are given. Regardless of the expression—terrified, calm, angry, defiant, shrewd—almost all these people died within three months. "The food ration was decisively insufficient even for the most frugal prisoner," writes Primo Levi. "Death by hunger, or by diseases induced by hunger, was the prisoner's normal destiny."[10] But some were shot, some beaten to death, some gassed. Some died from exhaustion, some from experiments, and so on. (The word *unzerweiter* comes to mind, as if I'm making notes, doing a job.) I choose two photographs, one of a man, one of a woman. Franciszek Swiebocki arrived ("przybyla") on 16 January 1943 and died ("zmarla") on 15 March. Two months, in bitter winter. His number is 88567. He wears a hat and looks away from the camera. I think at the time that this is defiance, but others are the same; he would have been told to adopt that posture. Josefa Bala I notice because she is looking down. Her number is 22512. She entered the camp on 13 October 1942 and died on 28 October. She survived fifteen days. On my second visit I record "Władysław Sadowski 12903," whose birth date and job are recorded as "28.06.1917 *rolnik* [farmer]." He died in 1941. A colleague and I now take students to Auschwitz every year. Since our most recent visit I've learned that a Polish prisoner, Wilhelm Brasse, was told to take these photographs. He recorded more than fifty thousand individuals but was most affected by the three shots he took of Czeslawa Kwoka, a fourteen-year-old Polish Catholic girl whom he recalled drying her tears and stemming blood from her lip before facing the camera. She died in the camp in 1943. On the next visit I will look for her.

On each trip so far we have walked out into balmy sunshine, crunching back over the gravel past the wrought-iron entrance, past the uniform brick blocks toward the barbed wire and watchtower at the end of the avenue. The about-to-leaf poplars cast skeletal shadows across the paths and mown grass. Their silvery branches weave like smoke in the blue sky. Just as the particles in the smoke had to come to rest somewhere, so too the Nazis would have had ash strewn in the vicinity. The crunch of the gravel paths is partly the sound of bone fragments. I lag behind the group but can just hear our guide explaining that "90 percent of the doctors and soldiers who worked at Auschwitz were never arrested." This included Josef Mengele. Eventually, after trudging past the site of murderously long parades, with its beam on two poles (not unlike goalposts) where prisoners were hanged in groups, you exit through a gap in the wire near the gallows where Rudolph Höss was hanged.

One of the many startling things about Auschwitz I is that the commandant's villa is a brief stroll from the crematorium. Stand at the gallows and the villa is a few hundred yards to your right. Look to your left and the grass mound maybe ten feet away is the back of the crematorium. The villa is private property. Peer over the fence and you see a pebble-dash building with a concrete wall shielding the garden. On the days I've been there, all the windows facing us have had blinds drawn, including the attic windows, beyond which, in Styron's imagination, Sophie pleaded with Höss. Walking past the gallows to the crematorium, you file into a concrete space the size of a long, narrow barn with a low, flat roof. The hint of daylight comes from the square gaps in the roof through which the gas was dropped. The air is dank and oppressive. Through a doorway to the left stand two pairs of ovens, reconstructed with original metal. Again, it all seems rather small scale and mundane—"functional." You feel as if you've been processed through the camp. But you don't say any of this. Again, on these particular days we emerge to warm sunshine. What we don't emerge to is chatter. I remove my headphones. The only sounds are birdsong and the trudge of shoes.

Auschwitz-Birkenau is a completely separate and different kind of site. Again, the shock is one of scale, but in terms of vastness. The entrance beneath the tower opens to a flat space the size of countless football fields, strewn with brick huts to the left and chimneys and the foundations of wooden huts to the right. Three hundred buildings once stood here, holding a hundred thousand prisoners. Seen from the tower, the area to the left is expansive but finite. The area to the right stretches beyond sight. Woodland smudges the horizon, but the ruins of Crematoriums I and II—blown up by the Germans to try to hide the evidence—are too far away to discern. In the middle, one of two rail tracks splits off to the right halfway to the crematoriums, leaving a space for selections. One restored hut shows sleeping quarters, while another retains rudimentary toilet facilities put in place to counter disease. Then you pass the single boxcar, turn left at the selection area, and walk to the ruins of the crematoriums.

If you take the six-hour tour, you will also walk on out through the grassland to what's left of Crematoriums III and IV, which is nothing but redbrick wall at ground level, marking out the dimensions. But some distance away though these crematoriums are, the entrance watchtower always remains in view, here miniscule between the silver birches coming into leaf. Circling back, you enter the building where arriving people were shorn of their possessions, clothes, identities. You walk through an opening above which the word *Untersuchungsraum* (Examination Room) is still visible in the plaster. Then, at the end of it all, you find a room with black boards covered in photographs. But these were not taken by the Nazis for their records. These are photos collected from the people themselves. They depict their prewar lives and identities. Many of them have a hint of the theatrical—self-aware poses in which the people look out at you as if to say, this is who I am. There are group photos from mealtimes, weddings, outings. A man is reading a book. A girl is talking into a telephone. A woman in white dress, white hat, and veil, her laughing husband beside her, holds out to you a full glass of red wine.

Auschwitz. There is the town of Oświęcim. There are the three sites. There are the testimonies, the historical documentation, and the preserved material. Then, as one attempt to articulate the meaning of the events, there is *Sophie's Choice*. Visiting Auschwitz changed my perception and raised new questions. Faced with Auschwitz I in particular, I ponder the question of accuracy, or, as I put it earlier, artistic license. We are told that out of one window Sophie can see a pastoral view where Höss's "splendid chalk-white Arabian stallion," Harlekin, gallops alone. Out of another window there's "a busy, overpopulated prospect of the railroad ramp where the selections took place and the grimy dun brick barracks beyond, a scene crowned by the arched metalwork sign" reading from there "in the obverse: ARBEIT MACHT FREI" (225). Either Styron uses license here or Sophie is recalling it inaccurately. The camp plan suggests that you couldn't see the platform, let alone the gateway. No higher than the blocks, the villa stands in the southeastern corner, while the tracks come in and finish on the northwestern side. Moreover, the sign wouldn't have "crowned" the scene, since even if it were not hidden by the blocks, it's much too low. Do such details matter? Even if *Sophie's Choice* were not fiction, Sophie is not one to adhere precisely to the facts, and exact recall would probably have been difficult anyway. My own experience of recalling a smell in the room of hair, where there was perhaps no smell at all, revealed that much.

More important is the question of how *Sophie's Choice* contributes to our understanding. The novel is fiction, yet the impulse driving both author and reader is the desire to see and know *fact*. Looking at the photographs of inmates, I recall how I was drawn to individuals: Franciszek Swiebocki and Josefa Bala, and the next time Sadowski Władysław. And the following year prisoners 31317, Pelagia Golgowska, "przybyla 25.1.1943," "zmarla 25.3.1943," and 22203, Maria Maria Roźenek, "przybyla 7.10.1942," "zmarla 20.12.1942," one a young woman who survived two months, the other an older woman who died just before Christmas and to whose photograph someone had attached an imitation red carnation. And next time Czeslawa Kwoka. To record individuals seems a way of honoring the human dimension amid the impersonality born of the sheer scale of the murders. This too is why at the United States Holocaust Memorial Museum you receive a booklet about a single person. The same impulse is at work when you focus on a plait of hair, a shoe, or that lady with a glass of wine, or when the designers (former inmates) set aside a broken doll. We need to contemplate individuality.

We have, therefore, the reality of Auschwitz and the fiction of *Sophie's Choice*. Should the two be kept separate? Should criticism concentrate solely on the work? Should the critic pretend to be outside time and without personality, or family, or emotional involvement? Perhaps that's easy enough at other times and with other works, but not, for me, with *Sophie's Choice*. As an older man, a parent, and one whose eventual journey to Auschwitz came about because many years ago I found the novel in a library in upstate New York, my provisional conclusion is that *Sophie's Choice* helps keep the place alive in our minds. In the manner that Christa Wolf meant when talking of Dostoevsky and St. Petersburg, memories of the novel profoundly affect my visits to Auschwitz. As well as the likes of Borowski and Lengyel, I can imagine, in those places, Sophie, Jan, Eva, Wanda, Bronek, or people like them that much more vividly, and the human reality hits home that much more strongly. So *Sophie's Choice* plays its small part in reinforcing the significance of the objects and photographs and places that the Auschwitz-Birkenau Foundation preserves, in terms not ultimately of fictional characters but of the real people and real lives these things represent. But my purpose in starting my rereading of *Sophie's Choice* with this contemplation of Auschwitz today is to contextualize the novel beyond its literary status—as a statement about the relationship between our own behavior and that of the bystanders as well as the perpetrators of this unparalleled atrocity.

Sophie's Choice is Styron's most important achievement. It contains a quality of craftsmanship that took decades to master, and in the service of a subject that warrants it. It's not without flaws, perceived or actual. There are episodes some find extraneous and elements some find offensive. Readers might wonder why Styron needed to put in a given detail. But it contains characters as memorable as any in literature in a multilayered narrative sewn of resonant scenes. It's not just about a young person's encounter with a Holocaust victim; it's about the relationship between atrocity and everyday behavior as well as about the extremes of experience, from horror to exhilaration, terror to tenderness. The following is not as full a reading as has been done elsewhere, but a homing in on scenes and substance to show how the novel works and why it resonates. The scenes I've chosen illustrate Styron's ways of dramatizing these larger concerns. The substance I focus on falls in a category I've called "reflections." It includes analysis of a specific motif, the window;

of the ways in which characters parallel or reflect one another; and of Styron's further deployment of a ghost motif. As the director, Alan J. Pakula, said of the film, so one can say of the novel: it's "about ghosts," and gradually we discover "what the ghosts are."[11] Styron is not seeking to represent the experience of Auschwitz—the province of survivors' accounts; he's merely opening a window onto it. But he's also contemplating the Holocaust in the context of ordinary life and reflecting on it in terms of the complexities of memory and of the ghosts that inhabit our lives.

My focus on the novel's scene-by-scene vividness is partly prompted by comments made by the novelist John Gardner. It seems significant that Gardner's most decisive praise comes not in his review in the *New York Times Book Review* but in a preface to its republication. The review is mixed. He calls it "a courageous, in some ways masterly book" by a writer with an "almost awesome" capacity for "justice and compassion," but feels that it contains too much "emotional and idealistic" southern gothicism. He is hence "moved" rather than "persuaded." But in his preface to the review's republication, he acknowledges his "disservice to Styron." "Scene after scene" has remained in his mind "with astonishing vividness—perhaps the most obvious mark of a masterpiece." His retrospective view regarding the subject matter is that Styron "stands alone—if one does not count personal diaries or memoirs—as a writer who could fully dramatize the horror, the complexity, and something at least approaching the full historical and emotional meaning of the thing." Nor, Gardner reflects, does the novel's power have to do merely with its core subject matter; it also derives from the "descriptions of Brooklyn life," the "analysis of the young writer's anxieties," the characterization of Sophie and Nathan, and the interplay of humor and horror. "Like Shakespeare (I think the comparison is not too grand)," he writes, "Styron knows how to cut away from the darkness of his material, so that when he turns to it again it strikes with increasing force." Gardner concludes by comparing the place of *Sophie's Choice* in American writing to that of *Crime and Punishment* in the literature of Russia.[12]

Gardner's sense of the novel's significance rests on those two things—scenes and substance—that shape the rest of this chapter. In addressing how Styron managed to create so vivid, engaging, and memorable a novel, therefore, I can now turn to the three examples noted earlier: the windows motif, the parallels between characters, and the ghost theme, all of which contribute to "the novel's staying power." One thing I would add, however, with regard to Gardner's initial distaste for its "emotional and idealistic" southern gothicism is that such elements are indeed there. The novel deals in extreme emotions, a fact recognized by Nicholas Maw, who wrote an opera that is remarkably faithful to it. But then it also deals with extreme experiences—both terrible and joyful—and all this goes into producing the power that Gardner refers to.

The window motif in *Sophie's Choice* tells us something about the circumstances, and the process of contemplation, that enabled Styron to write the novel. But also, in its mere physical invocation it has much to tell us about why this chiaroscurist novel, with light and dark in equipoise, is so vivid. Gardner's comment that "Styron knows how to cut away from the darkness" is a response not just to bleakness juxtaposed with levity but to a visual quality that reinforces the emotional chiaroscuro of "Sophie's Manichean reflection" (261). Windows are invariably a source of this light, but they also have a symbolic function. The effect is not just to increase the novel's vividness but to further the sense of inner and outer worlds and to strengthen connections between past and present scenes. Lastly, the motif connects with Styron's interest in film, in terms both of his allusions to the cinematic and of the impact of movies on his writing. In discussing this, I'll make passing use of the Slovakian psychoanalyst Slavoj Žižek's observations in his DVD collaboration with Sophie Fiennes, *The Pervert's Guide to Cinema 1, 2, 3* (2006), a serious study of the psychology of the medium, despite its disconcerting title. *Sophie's Choice* certainly invites psychoanalytical readings, but my interest here is primarily in Styron's use of and allusion to the cinematic as a mode of craft and perception.

Before looking at how Styron uses the motif, here are some thoughts about how it came into being. On the one hand, Styron stole it from *Madame Bovary,* in which Emma frequently witnesses events through her window or daydreams with her head against the pane. But just as Flaubert steals this window motif from Balzac, so Styron transforms it for his own purposes. To gaze through a window in *Sophie's Choice* may be to observe, reflect, reminisce, or daydream, but it invariably involves perception and imagination on the part of the character and the reader. Near the end of our final recorded conversation, in July 1998, with the sun setting over the waters around Martha's Vineyard, I asked Styron what he found most satisfying as a novelist. He said he treasured the knowledge that people regarded his work "as important in their lives." He knew that his "ulterior motive" for involving himself in a fictional world had been to make others feel that "emotional and intellectual effect."[13] One way he does this is through a quality discussed in an earlier chapter, *intimacy*, the sense that he has invited the reader to share his reminiscence. This led me to wonder how that effect occurs on the page and brought me to the window motif as a factor.

Styron's working circumstances during composition were something like the following. For years he and his family spent October to May in Roxbury, Connecticut, before decamping to Martha's Vineyard. In both places, he wrote through the late afternoon. In Roxbury, as described in an earlier chapter, he did so in the cottage adjacent to the main house. Each afternoon (as I envisage it) he turned right up the stairs to the single room in the eaves. Ahead as he entered would be his writing desk. Sitting at the large desk allowed a view through a low window of part of the garden, some trees, a child's swing, and a field. Spending the early summer of 1990 in this cottage, I'd sit there most days, but only recently have I connected the writing of the novel with gazing through a window. An e-mail from Al Styron to Jim West subsequently revealed that Styron's Vineyard desk too faced a window.[14] No wonder, then, that *Sophie's Choice*, a window onto the 1940s, became a narrative in which windows form a pivotal part.

We can imagine the novelist at his desk. He dreams of the past, he meditates once again on history, his own and that of his era. Perhaps he sees through the window—whether in Roxbury or Vineyard Haven—his youngest child, Al herself, who during these years was between eight and twelve years old. Perhaps he sees other children, or adults, or hears muffled voices or a passing car. Just as a window in the novel is also often a window onto memory or imagination, so, as he scratches away through the late afternoon, the present merges with memory and imagination; the sounds become those of history. He's Stingo smelling the fragrance of blossoms through the "open windows" of Sophie's room (67); Rudolph Höss "in his attic office" (264); Sophie viewing the "quietude" of the "evening woods," where "maps of color" hang "motionless, no leaf astir, in the light of the setting sun" (332). "*Scratch, scratch*" goes "the virginal Venus Velvet" (111). He's absorbed in thought, seeking *le mot juste,* or links between his themes and scenes, and gazing out, sometimes at sunshine, or the last shadows of the day, sometimes to the sound of wind in the trees or rain on the rafters. He is seeking, as he signals in his André Malraux epigraph, that "region of the soul where absolute evil confronts brotherhood." So, as he sets down his thoughts, page by page, with that intimate, conversational tone, the window becomes one of the novel's key motifs.

He tells us of that summer he "so vividly" remembers, taking us to its "sunny and mild, flower-fragrant" days and Stingo's youthful angst, just as Sophie will draw Stingo into her all-consuming past (3). Gazing through that window, he imagines true terror: the loss of your children, caused, in some obscure way, through your own fault. No horror, for a parent, can match that of losing a child. So he sits there as a father. But he also knows the tenderness people are capable of. He has himself this capacity for being terrorized, whether by demons, memories, or fears of catastrophe. But he also has the capacity to cause distress, to terrorize his family with his tempestuous rages and his gloomy preoccupation with madness and mortality. So he comes to write about Sophie and how she lost Eva (eight) and Jan (twelve) at Auschwitz, and the window becomes a portal back to 1947; back further to her experiences, to Styron's childhood loss of his mother; and further still to Sophie's childhood in Cracow.

The window is therefore, both as he writes and in what he writes, a portal to memory and to daydreaming. Styron creates a world that no longer exists but in important ways never did exist. Yet such is the mingling of memory with imagination that it would have seemed real to the author, seems real to the reader, and now, in a way, does exist. At the very least, in Picasso's phrase, it's an example of art as "a lie that makes us realize truth."[15] Yet further, the window becomes a symbol for considering characters' perspectives, and so for empathy ("brotherhood"). Hence the characters too view the world through windows and reveal themselves in doing so—whether the young author, the camp commandant, or the bereaved mother. (It seems significant that we never see Nathan's view through a window, and never indeed have access to his presumably unfathomable mind.) Many of the issues of *Sophie's Choice*, consequently, are linked by the window motif.

But windows in the novel also function as screens. Styron combines the motif with the cinematic chronotope.[16] It's here that ideas Slavoj Žižek puts forward come to mind. For what is Stingo if not the young voyager as voyeur, who senses that all glamor and excitement is beyond the window of his dreary abodes? Not unlike Hitchcock's Scottie Ferguson in *Vertigo* (1958), who first glimpses his imagined reincarnation of Carlotta through an alley door onto a fabulous florist's, Stingo yearns to find both what he has lost and what he has not yet found. Styron too uses the idea that the reader's relationship to the Holocaust, and to history, is not unlike that of a person watching a film. In both cases, perceived detachment mingles with the horror and fascination of connection. Physical spaces in the novel's time present—Sophie's room; the train to Washington; the room at the Hotel Congress—function as portals to remembered or imagined spaces of exhilarating fantasy and of darkest despair. While this architecture has something in common with the kinds of framing devices we find in, say, *Wuthering Heights* or Turgenev's *First Love*, and while the modernists obviously experimented with representations of time past in time present, *Sophie's Choice* works on a level that is complex, multilayered (one might say multiplex), but also reader, or rather viewer, friendly.

The following observations made by Žižek will help us to see what Styron is doing in the novel. Žižek begins with a scene from *Possessed* (1931) that provides a commentary on the "art of cinema within a movie." "An ordinary, working class girl from a drab, small, provincial town" approaches a train passing slowly by a crossing when she suddenly "finds herself in a situation where reality itself reproduces the magical cinematic experience." She "turns into a viewer imagining the magic of the screen." At the end of the final car, which has held a succession of scenarios from window to window, a man in a tuxedo, drink in hand, stands at the railing. "Looking in?" he says. "Wrong way. Get in and look out." The car window has become "the screen of her dreams." Žižek later makes the point that reality and fantasy are not opposites but intertwined. "If you take away from our reality the symbolic fictions that regulate it you take away reality itself." "Reality," he says, "is illusion itself," and if catastrophe occurs, "it shatters the co-ordination of our reality" and "we have to fictionalize it." As for "the art of cinema," it "consists in arousing desire, to play with desire but at the same time keeping it at a safe distance." The problem, we will see in *Sophie's Choice*, comes when individuals delude themselves that other's actual lives are merely cinematic.[17]

Sophie's Choice is about illusions and reality from the outset. Stingo is desperate to become someone in the world, but that someone will be an author, intent upon "transporting" people into an imagined reality. Sophie is a Holocaust victim whose "reality" was once motherhood, but her illusion of specialness and stability is shattered. She is forced to fictionalize both her past and her present, her very self, to survive. In turn she becomes the fantasy made flesh that Stingo yearns for, but the reality of this is, on one level, a fantasy become nightmare. Stingo begins by seeing Sophie and Nathan as little more than his projected fantasies. He doesn't want to become "the hapless supernumerary in some tortured melodrama." But soon after thinking this he enters Sophie's room, to be greeted by them, "dancing a little two-step" out from behind a Japanese screen, with "vaudevillian smiles" and dressed in thirties costumes. They thus almost literally leap "from behind the screen" into his world (62). No mere spectator, he finds himself involved and implicated in not just the events of that summer but the dynamics of human behavior in the wider world. It's as if the "actors" he's been watching have become part of his reality.

In *Sophie's Choice* it therefore makes perfect sense that the window motif is a major element of this cinematic chronotope. We witness characters not gazing through windows simply as windows (as with the eponymous heroines of *Eugénie Grandet* and *Madame Bovary*) but as they might at movie screens, and becoming imaginatively involved in the pictures they see, recall, and create. The novel produces a kind of cinematic experience, so that the reader feels as if separate orders of time are spliced together. Sophie renders her past so vividly, and Stingo imagines it so fully, that it seems to us to exist in the same summer as their friendship. As in a movie, we can witness two time frames in a single continuity. Seen through the window, the characters seem fixed. But we're experiencing a story in which the characters themselves often behave as if they were onlookers rather than participants. Stingo sees, hears, imagines Sophie's story, while Sophie, within that story, defines herself in relation to the events she witnesses. Very often this is drama-tized by what she witnesses through a window: a screen that is not in fact a screen at all, but a physical object separating her physically, but not necessarily personally, emotionally or morally, from the scene.

Window as memory and window as screen are particularly suited to the subject matter of this young American learning of Auschwitz through someone who was there. There is always a frame between us and the events portrayed. The narrator is often rendering the perception of his younger self. But he's also writing as someone now well informed about the Holocaust from a historical perspective. He's thus able to shift from Stingo's viewpoint to Sophie's first- and third-person viewpoint, as recalled across the years. The frame, however, is always implicitly there, allowing us only a partial, mediated perspective. It's through the third person that he describes Sophie as reflecting, alone with Nathan soon after they've met, not so much upon American ignorance, in 1947, of what occurred but on any outsider's ability to wholly empathize. She thinks that perhaps if she explains "the *rudimentary* part of" her experi-ence now, she might not need to go into more detail later.

Perhaps, too, it was absurd or offensive of her to be so enigmatic, so ostentatiously secretive about something which, after
all, should be common knowledge by now to almost everybody.
Even though that was the strange thing: people here in America,
despite all of the published facts, the photographs, the newsreels, still did not seem to know what had happened, except in
the most empty, superficial way. Buchenwald, Belsen, Dachau,
Auschwitz—all stupid catchwords. This inability to comprehend
on any real level of awareness was another reason why she so
rarely had spoken to anyone about it, totally aside from the lac-
erating pain it caused her to dwell on that part of her past. (143)

This gives psychological justification for Sophie's part refusal and part
inability to divulge the truth about her past, but it's also a reminder that
for those of us who didn't experience the concentration camps our only
access is through testimony, visits to the sites themselves, history books,
photographs, and newsreels and that *Sophie's Choice* honors that framework. Auschwitz exists for us screened, as well as literally behind glass
and on screen. We observe it horrified, moved, but always removed.
We're all, as Žižek would have it, moviegoers, viewing people and action fixed in motion. We who weren't there are visitors filing past items
behind glass.

The window motif begins almost immediately. Stingo scorns the "sad
outpourings" of unpublished writers from his "glassed-in cubbyhole
on the twentieth floor of the McGraw-Hill Building" (5). It continues
throughout, from the "festive little room whose open windows" admit
"a fragrance of spring blossoms" during an early day with Sophie and
Nathan (67), to the dream of the window through which he sees his
mother's "rain-damp ravaged face" gazing in agony from her open coffin
(462), to the implicit window through which he hears a church bell in
the "half-light" prior to his seduction by Sophie (496) and the one that
allows the "puddle of sunlight" he wakes in to discover that Sophie has
left him (498). It's there, too, "in the dim light" that reveals Sophie and
Nathan dead on the "apricot bedspread" (507). Everywhere in *Sophie's
Choice* there is not merely the visual sense that the mood of interiors is
sourced by window light but also an emphasis on thoughts, provoked by
sensations, memories, moods, or music, opening up vistas of visual sensation. Often we can imagine the author witnessing such a scene from

his window even as he writes. For instance, "the larghetto from the B-flat major piano concerto of Mozart" causes Sophie to think "of children playing in the dusk, calling out in far, piping voices while the shadows of nightfall" swoop "down across some green and tranquil lawn" (508).

To follow through on this motif is to trace the novel's all-important themes. The first of these has to do with Stingo's self-perception. Feeling uninvolved, he treats the view from his room at the University Residence Club as a cinema screen. Christening his neighbors "the Winston Hunnicutts," he fantasizes about their party guests (14). Then one night he experiences "a violent reversal of emotions" that causes him "never to gaze down into the garden again." Ogling "Mavis Hunnicutt's familiar posterior" from his "accustomed post at the window," he envisages that she's chatting with Carson McCullers and Aldous Huxley. Imaging their discussion topic to be Sartre, Joyce, or "vintage wines," he finally realizes that they're talking about their environment. "Mavis" whirls "in a half circle" and thrusts out "a furious little fist" that's "so prominent, so bloodlessly agitated" that she seems to brandish it "a scant inch" from Stingo's nose. To his "pounding chagrin," he's certain he can read her sentiments: "If only that goddamned *eyesore* weren't there, with all those *creeps* peering out at us!" (15).

The point of the scene is not just that suddenly the characters in his fantasy turn around and look at *him;* it's also that Stingo, encased in his self-centered vision, suddenly goes from judge of others (as with the McGraw-Hill manuscripts) to being the one judged. From being the "ape plucking vermin from his pelt" (5), he becomes one of "those creeps." This will be a novel as much about Stingo's behavior, strengths, and weaknesses as about Sophie's. Windows therefore function from early on as a symbol of perception. What characters see through a given window and how they respond reflects their situation, disposition, and outlook in both senses of the word. This episode is also the first example of the cinematic motif in *Sophie's Choice.* To watch action through a closed window seems, for Stingo here, little different from watching a film in that it gives him another chance to enrich his fantasies. (Similarly, he refers to a sexual fantasy as "an expertly constructed one-act play" the film of which on that occasion "jams in the projector" [45].) But his fantasy world spills into actual life. Just as he lacks empathy with Leslie Lapidus and Mary Alice Grimball, so he assumes here that those he watches can't see him. He's shocked that suddenly the gaze is returned; Mavis's fist is simultaneously a cinematic close-up and a kind of punch through the screen.

In a typically Styronian word echo, *creeps* will recur when Sophie refers to "creepy people" with their "unearned unhappiness" (130), and in a way Stingo, the moviegoer enthralled by fantasy, is guilty of "unearned unhappiness." But he's young and by no means a lost cause. His "relentless flame" (or "sacred fire," as Stendhal calls the qualities of Julien Sorel in *The Red and the Black*) may begin the summer as a "pilot light" (3), but his egotism and self-pity mingle with rebelliousness, ambition, and expectation.[18] His departure from McGraw-Hill occurs because these aspects of his nature clash with company etiquette. Again, his temperament and trajectory find expression in a window scene. "One of the few tolerable features of life at McGraw-Hill," the narrator tells us, was Stingo's "view from the twentieth floor—a majestic prospect of Manhattan, of monolith and minaret and spire" that reliably revived his "drugged senses with all those platitudinous yet genuine spasms of exhilaration and sweet promise that have traditionally overcome provincial American youths." Up until a fateful day, Stingo has contented himself with occasionally dropping "a sheet of paper from the window to watch its ecstatic tumbling flight as it sped across the rooftops, often disappearing far off into the canyons around Times Square, still tumbling and soaring." But finally, "inspired to buy a tube of plastic bubble material" and blow up "half a dozen of these fragile, lovely, iridescent globes, all the while anticipating their adventure upon the wind," he releases them "one by one into the smoggy abyss." The result satisfies every "infantile desire to float balloons to the uttermost boundaries of the earth."

> They glowed in the afternoon sunlight like the satellites of Jupiter, and were as big as basketballs. A quirky updraft sent them hurtling high over Eighth Avenue; there they remained suspended for what seemed interminable moments, and I sighed with delight. Then I heard squeals and girlish laughter and saw that a gaggle of McGraw-Hill secretaries, attracted by the show, were hanging out of the windows of adjoining offices. It must have been their commotion which called the Weasel's attention to my aerial display, for I heard his voice behind me just as the girls gave a final cheer and the balloons fled frantically eastward down the garish arroyo of Forty-second Street. (19)

High up, childlike, filled with the idea of adventure, gazing out over Manhattan, watched by admirers, turning the ordinary into the magical—this is the epitome of Stingo's fantasy-driven perspective. The act gets him fired, but only to release him on his own turbulent adventure through the summer and beyond.

These early window scenes anticipate more nuanced ones involving Sophie and her more complex concerns. She herself is a window onto the past for Stingo, even before actual windows figure within those memories. So intense are those memories and so compelling is her story that the narrative comes to resemble a series of dreams within dreams. We accept her past as a reality on a level with her time with Nathan and Stingo. Her story bursts into life in chapter 4, when she describes her Cracow childhood. Even when the narrator turns to her third-person narrative, he retains the feeling of dreams within dreams. Her "febrile doze—a half sleep in which the far past of Cracow" mingles with Dr. Blackstock's "sculpting hands"—leads to a waking dream of her father (100). So with Sophie the window motif informs both her conversations with Stingo and her memories within memories. The novel thus gains a miraculous multidimensionality. Not unlike in *The Confessions of Nat Turner*, dreams and memories compete with the novel's vibrant time present.

For Stingo the voyeur, as for the reader as voyeur, the window Sophie allows him to look through contains scenes that withhold and only gradually reveal. Her seduction of him involves a kind of undressing, but one that will not only fulfill his fantasy but also produce his nightmare. The body revealed is both sexual and mortal, and the last Stingo sees of Sophie is her corpse. Her secrets are far more horrific than wonderful. But more complex still, the window onto the past that Sophie offers can be traced through a succession of scenes in which she herself is looking through a window and so revealing her own situation, disposition, and outlook. Of several vivid instances, the following ones illustrate her changing circumstances and perspective. The novel is chronological with regard to the Brooklyn summer, but Sophie's story appears in a fragmented, nonlinear way to do with a psychological need at certain times to divulge certain things.

In chapter 10, for instance, we have a view through a window in Haus Höss that matches her own and Stingo's initial sense of Auschwitz as a distant place that doesn't involve them. Bronek, the "expert scrounger" whose "outward simple-mindedness" yet "extraordinary vigor" has caught Höss's attention enough to earn him a place in the villa, has brought Sophie some figs (258). Having secreted the package in her smock, she steals away to eat them in a "cubbyhole" (the same word used to describe the McGraw-Hill office where Stingo, too, felt special and apart). This is no ordinary treat but a moment of sensuous joy. "A film of tears" mists her eyes as the figs slide "richly down her throat." She devours them "wild with delight," hearing "herself panting with pleasure" (261). She then climbs the stairs toward Höss's office. From a landing window she can see events at the camp unfolding, but through glass and from a distance. She usually tries "to avert her eyes" from this familiar view of "nondescript subjects," but "not always successfully" (260). On the middle-distant platform, "too near to be ignored, too far away to be seen with clarity," "fragmentary and flickering apparitions" register "imperfectly, like the grainy shadow-shapes in an antique silent newsreel: a rifle butt raised skyward, dead bodies being yanked from boxcar doors, a papier-mâché human being bullied to the earth."

> The platform was too distant for sound; the music of the loony-bin prisoner band which greeted each arriving train, the shouts of the guards, the barking of the dogs—all these were mute, though upon occasion it was impossible not to hear the crack of a pistol shot. Thus the drama seemed to be enacted in a charitable vacuum, from which were excluded the wails of grief, cries of terror and other noises of that infernal initiation. It was for this reason perhaps, Sophie thought as she climbed the steps, that she succumbed from time to time to an occasional irresistible peek— doing so now, seeing only the strings of boxcars newly arrived, as yet unloaded. SS guards in swirls of steam surrounding the train. She knew from manifests which had been received by Höss the day before that this was the second of two trainloads containing 2,100 Jews from Greece.

"Curiosity satisfied," she turns away and opens the door to the salon that leads to "the upper stairway." There, in a room "flooded with sunlight," she finds Wilhelmine pawing "through a stack of silken female underwear" (261).

This scene is a good example, to repeat Picasso, of "a lie that makes us realize truth." As noted earlier, Sophie couldn't have seen all this from the villa. "A glimpse of the railroad platform" becomes a detailed description. The question is why. Sophie here may be at the camp itself—or at least in Höss's villa on the edge of Auschwitz I—and her worst experiences already behind her, but readers don't know the latter yet. Styron manipulates time and space to position Sophie in a way that mimics the general reader's perspective, which is to know of Auschwitz only through history, cinema, newsreels, and books. Watching like the reader from a place apart, she's aware of events but can choose whether to look. It's all there, but too far away to discern clearly or perhaps to need to. Only later will we learn of the memories that cause her "to blot out of her sight" these scenes, but for now her response is ours. We too can turn away from what we see, which is effectively the newsreels of the camp liberations, or perhaps a cinematic rendering of atrocity seen from afar. From behind the closed window the platform is "too distant for sound," so events seems to occur "in a charitable vacuum." Like a general reader, Sophie is appalled yet fascinated and takes the occasional peek, until, "curiosity satisfied," she turns away. Only when she encounters Wilhelmine does she again become a participant in the "drama." Sophie, in other words, is seeing Auschwitz not in a way that realistically renders what one might see from the villa but as an amalgam of newsreel, of survivors' accounts (this, for instance, is similar to Borowski's descriptions in *This Way for the Gas, Ladies and Gentlemen*), and of historical data and statistics ("2,100 Jews from Greece").

Further into chapter 10, after Wilhelmine has molested her, Sophie still views Auschwitz from behind glass, but with differences. Again on the landing she sees the "barren drill field sloping toward the melancholy stand of poplars" and "the countless boxcars in drab file" beyond, but now through "a partly opened window."

> Since her encounter with Wilhelmine the boxcar doors had been thrown open by the guards, and now hundreds more of the condemned voyagers from Greece milled about on the platform. Despite her haste, Sophie was compelled to halt and watch for an instant, drawn by morbidity and dread in equal measure. The poplar trees and the horde of SS guards obscured most of the scene. She could not clearly see the faces of the Greek Jews. Nor could she tell what they wore: mostly she saw a dull gray. (265)

While this scene is again "cinematic," it becomes something more. With the window open, "the sweet, pestilential stench of flesh consumed by fire" assails Sophie's nostrils. "The throng on the distant platform" blurs. "Involuntarily, with creeping horror and disgust," she puts "her fingertips to her lips" and, realizing where the figs have come from, pukes them up (266). The Auschwitz platform is no movie; she has eaten of its fruit. We recall the Rilke epigraph and the fruit of the tree of knowledge.

Sophie has already lost her children in the selection process at Birkenau. But it's really the reader, still ignorant of this, who must confront Auschwitz as "reality" rather than film, while Sophie does so symbolically rather than actually. This sleight of hand again illustrates art lying to reveal truth. Styron fabricates the dramatically necessary suggestion that Sophie, like Stingo and most readers, has not been subjected to the full reality of the camp in order to depict the truth that it's a delusion to think one can watch atrocity unfold from a safe, detached place.

Another example of the window motif within Sophie's memories, and of Styron's artistic arrangement of time, occurs when Sophie is with her children in Warsaw. In linear time this is obviously earlier, but the memory is told to Stingo later, in chapter 12, and Styron uses it to dramatize Stingo's changing perspective on the question of involvement. Sophie, in this memory, urged by Wanda to translate papers found in a Gestapo van in Pruszków, gazes "out the window at the wintry Warsaw desolation" and says that she cannot help. Wanda replies that it's "offensive" of Sophie to place herself "on a different level from others" (371). "Zosia," she says, "you have to make a choice!" Sophie sees her children "homeward bound in the dusk" after Eva's flute lesson. As she watches Jan explain something to Eva, her daughter's flute teacher, Stefan Zaorski, appears. Sophie leans "forward against the window." Zaorski, "ever the passionate pedagogue," has "hobbled after Eva in order to correct, or explain, or elaborate on something he had taught her in her most recent lesson," and Sophie is "both touched and amused."

> She pushed the window open slightly in order to call down to the group, now huddled in the entrance to the building next door. Eva wore her yellow hair in pigtails. She had lost her front teeth. How, Sophie wondered, could she play a flute? Zaorski had made Eva open her leather case and remove the flute; he flourished it aloft in front of the child, not blowing on it but merely demonstrating some soundless arpeggio with his fingers.

When Zaorski does blow some notes, they strike "antiphonal bells" deep within her soul, speaking "to her of all she longed to be—and all she wished for her children, in whatever future God willed." She grows "faint, unsteady," feels herself "in the grip of an aching, devouring love. And at the same time joy" that she finds "inexplicably both delicious and despairing," as it sweeps "across her skin in a cool blaze." The spell breaks as Zaorski pats the children good-bye and Jan pulls Eva's pigtail before they rush indoors. And there stands Wanda behind Sophie, again telling her to "come to a decision," to which Sophie replies, "I have already made my choice, as I told you. I will not get involved." "I mean this," she says, "*Schluss—aus!* That's final! (373–74).

The scene captures Sophie's adoration of her children, who define her very sense of self, but also her delusion that she can remain, as it were, safely indoors. The pull of parental love makes her not just lean against the window but push it "open slightly in order to call down to the group." Her last word, *final,* is deeply ironic in terms both of her children's fate and of the Nazis' use of the word. Her choice is not a solution. Yet this is also a scene about not just terror but tenderness on the part of Sophie in her parental love and amused view of Zaorski; on the part of Jan in his explanations to help his sister; and on the part of Zaorski in his concern to teach Eva to play the flute. Styron's description of Sophie's love for her children—"faint, unsteady," "aching, devouring," mingled with "joy" that is "delicious and despairing"—echoes her hunger in the earlier scene to devour the figs. It's as if the heaven of the figs and the hell of the puking are recaptured for the reader, and anticipated for Sophie, in the visceral feelings of parental love.[19]

There are many other examples of the window motif. For instance, in the previous chapter Sophie has told Stingo of Nathan's proposal of a suicide pact, made on a trip to Connecticut in their first fall together. She frames her reminiscence of his drug-fueled abuse of her with a view of the Connecticut foliage through their bedroom window. It begins with twilight, when she sees "past his hand and its poison" an "inferno of leaves" (332), and ends with her waking next to Nathan hours later, seeing "the bright and flaming woods," and realizing that she must tell him that she was once married and lost a son at Auschwitz. Standing by the window, she recalls trying, as a child, to see God's shape in the natural world. On this autumn day in Connecticut, she forgets herself and feels like that little girl again.

> There was a wonderful smell of smoke in the air and I saw smoke rising far off in the woods and I saw God's shape in that. But then—but then it came to my mind what I really knew, what was really the truth: that God have left me again, left me forever. I felt I could actually see Him go, turning His back on me like some great beast and go crashing away through the leaves. God! Stingo, I could see the huge *back* of Him going away in the trees. The

light faded then and I felt such an emptiness—the memory coming back and knowing what I would have to say. (344–45)

The window motif here becomes a memory portal, again freighted with
suggestion—the "inferno" of leaves, the smell of smoke—that accentu-
ates the distance between who Sophie believed herself to be and who
she feels she is now. The image of God's monstrous back "crashing away
through the leaves" may or may not be a deliberate reference to *Colos-
sus*, attributed to Goya, but it evokes it. Sophie's rejecter is not in the
clouds but a grotesque and smoky giant here on earth. The image recalls Stingo's introduction to Nathan, smothering Sophie in the "palsied
chiaroscuro" of a "forty-watt lightbulb" and "dominating the scene by his
height and force," while all Stingo sees of Sophie is "about a third of her
face" (47). Just as Nathan dominates Sophie's emotional life in America,
so no view, however beautiful, will ever for Sophie be the same again.
She'll always see the hulking shadow of God's back—the ever-present
memory of her doomed children and the crematorium smoke.

Later still, Sophie and Stingo take the train south. This is again a
journey of escape, albeit now physical too, from memories personified
by Nathan. Ensconced in the Hotel Congress, Stingo opens the window. An October breeze freshens the room. The far-off "clangor and
muffled hoots of the trains at Union Station," mingling with "the piping
self-esteem of a military band" (457), recall the trains of Auschwitz and
the camp's "loony-bin prisoner band" (261). Although on the one hand
the portal of memory and imagination has untold delights, it's also the
portal to nightmares. The world of Auschwitz impinges upon the world
of 1947 Washington regardless of Sophie's or Stingo's attempts to evade
it. From the very fact of a train ride (reflected again in the train with
boarded-up windows that takes Sophie and her children to Auschwitz)
to Stingo's suggestion of marriage, Sophie's past stands before her, as if
in the very space and time she and Stingo now occupy.

Beyond the window motif, many other strategies integrate *Sophie's
Choice*. These include parallels between characters, echoes of both
words and actions, and merging of time and place that suggests interplay
between inner and outer realism. Styron melds reality and fantasy in
his characters' minds to such a degree that we accept that their psychology extends to a depth far below anything they can articulate. To
chart these depths systematically would be an endless process, but a
few examples will suffice. Since the scenes with Sophie so far discussed

all have Stingo listening, or the older narrator shaping the narrative, I'll round off discussion of these two by looking at their eventual sexual coupling, a culminating episode in which Stingo finds his heart's desire, while Sophie seeks forgetfulness before choosing oblivion.

For some the episode is difficult to deal with for reasons beyond the fact that it's graphic. Concerns have been raised over the years as to whether it should coexist with scenes about Auschwitz, and whether there's sufficient distance between Stingo's experience and the narrator's reimagining of it. Whatever else, the former concern testifies to the novel's cinematic vividness. The juxtaposition of scenes gives the impression that events occur in close proximity, whereas in fact they belong to two distinct time frames. But the documented history of Auschwitz shows that death camps and all manner of sexual behavior were hardly incompatible, whether between staff, between staff and prisoners, or between prisoners. Such activity was present everywhere, from the camp brothel to the Nazis' abuse of inmates, including the activities of Irma Griese, whose beauty evidently so matched her depravity that it "entranced" internees even though her visits meant "roll call and inspections for the gas chambers." "Were a novelist to compose such a scene," writes Olga Lengyel, "his readers would accuse him of the wildest imagination."[20]

Indeed, as Susan Sontag points out in "Fascinating Fascism," sexuality was part of the dynamics of Nazism, which "converted" it "into the magnetism of leaders and the joy of followers." Moreover, while Styron considered a relationship between Höss and Sophie, he opted to show Höss acting out what Sontag describes as "the fascist ideal": seeing the woman "as a temptation" but choosing "heroic repression of the sexual impulse." Hence Höss accuses Sophie of "flirting shamelessly" (279) and tells her he "would risk a great deal to have relations" with her, but instead sends her away (282). Sophie's labeling as "temptress" remains with her in America: that she is "a perfect replica" of Griese is one of Nathan's accusations in Connecticut (335). But her sexuality, both with Nathan and with Stingo, and her human physicality rather than idealization seems a deliberate contrast to the Nazi aesthetic.[21]

As for the narrator's perspective compared with Stingo's, he is aware of the latter's limited understanding of Sophie's mental state, but he still celebrates passionate, animalistic sexuality, in contrast to Sontag's observation of the Nazi emphasis (in art) of "a utopian aesthetics" of "physical perfection" or a "spiritual" force. He also celebrates the human capacity for passion prior to the aging process (implicit in his middle-aged self's envy of the youth he once was). When Sophie tries to delay Stingo's sexual response, Stingo reflects that he would happily remain aroused until his hair grows "thin and gray." The two orders of time—Stingo's and the narrator's—collapse in the moment's intensity, even though the narrator believes that while Stingo is clasping in his arms "the goddess" of his "unending fantasies," Sophie is more likely to be engaged in "a plunge into carnal oblivion and a flight from memory and grief" (496). The scene is not only in keeping with Sophie's sensual nature and sensitivity to Stingo's yearnings but also an apt conclusion to their hours of talk. "Sex is a profoundly semantic act," writes George Steiner. "To speak and to make love is to enact a distinctive twofold universality: both forms of communication are universals of human physiology as well as of social evolution."[22]

As for the graphic descriptions, these are not least of interest in terms of a reader's response in juxtaposition to the main subject matter. Styron leaves little to the imagination, but if we wish that he had, we might ask ourselves why. Whether it has to do with distaste, prudery, embarrassment, or a concern with who might read it—and what, be corrupted by it?—the scenes make us ask ourselves how we can square any such feelings with our voyeuristic response to details, here or elsewhere, of atrocity. Why might the juxtaposition of lovemaking with atrocity seem distasteful? Why are we horrified and incredulous that Sophie must choose between her children, but not offended? In other words, the novel challenges us with regard to any moral position we might take as to what is or is not included. For rather than being gratuitous or pornographic, these scenes merely, and rightly, describe humans as sexual beings.

Sophie is both Stingo's seductress and his "instructress"—initiating him into all manner of knowledge about the world, but also far more of a flesh-and-blood woman than perhaps any other tragic heroine in literature (496). What she is not, crucially, is any kind of exemplar of the Nazi ideal that Höss would envisage. In a tacit admission that the twenty-two-year-old male virgin behaves much as one would expect, some critics opt to blame the author for the graphic description. But the scenes are moral in two senses of the word. They are about Eros conquering Thanatos, and ring true in relation to Sophie's intensely sensual rather than spiritual nature. But they are also judgmental of Stingo's perverse attraction to Sophie not just as a woman, and a mother-figure, but as doomed. When the narrator suggests that on the most basic level Sophie's motives have to do with "animal passion" (496), he is inviting recall of her description of how the Nazis "turned people into sick animals" and her recognition of how "easy it was for you to act like an animal too" (286). Styron again draws parallels when Stingo sees "her eyes closed and her expression so beautifully tender and drowned and abandoned in her passion" that he has to "avert" his "gaze" (497). He uses virtually the same phrase when Sophie tries to "avert her eyes" from the Auschwitz platform (260). Styron thus amplifies the moral connection between fascination with atrocity and the misfortune of others and Stingo's infatuation with Sophie. To critics of the episode one might thus say, with Stendhal: "Son miroir montre la fange, et vous accusez le miroir!"[23]

But the sex scene also calls to mind other themes, and not least the interaction between fantasy and reality. It's a culmination of the tension Stingo experiences when he fantasizes about Mavis Hunnicutt only to have her shake her fist at him. His feelings for Sophie grow from the powerful fact that she is simultaneously fantasy, reality, and memory. She starts as a romantic stranger, face half hidden by Nathan's shoulder. She becomes a flesh-and-blood woman. But she's also—from the beginning of the novel to the end—only ever now a memory to the narrator. On the one hand (unlike any nineteenth-century heroine), she urinates, climaxes, and wears dentures. On the other hand, she's the goddess of Stingo's "unending fantasies" and a trigger for memories of Maria Hunt and Stingo's mother. Her very physicality is part of the unease she invokes in Stingo. As Žižek might put it, she's the disastrous nightmare of fantasy fulfilled; the very flesh and blood that is erotic and sensual is also subject to, and a reminder of, destruction and decay. "When a fantasy object—something imagined, an object from inner space—enters our ordinary reality," suggests Žižek, "the texture of reality is distorted." Hence "desire is a wound of reality." Sophie has returned from death-in-life, has been, as it were, miraculously resurrected. She is both flesh-and-blood and phantomlike, a fantasy fulfilled that will wound Stingo forever because she reveals far more than he bargained for: a deep, dark knowledge of human weakness, of our capacity for cowardice, cruelty, and contempt.[24]

Beyond this, Sophie lets Stingo taste, to use Žižek's words, "the deepest levels of our desires which we do not even admit to ourselves." She follows on from Mavis Hunnicutt in becoming the "object" who "returns the gaze," but far more consequentially.[25] For just as their fathers resemble each other, if only in their nostalgia, so Sophie, the childless mother, is a reminder to the narrator that he is a motherless son. Even a biographical detail is the same, in that Sophie once hoped to study piano in Vienna, just as Styron's own mother actually did between the wars.[26] But it's not just that she is patently a mother figure, resurrected by Stingo to meet unconscious desires; it's also that her destroyed sense of self is emblematic of the fragile delusions of anyone's self-identity, the very thing that in Styron's work is held up as achievable through self-realization. For even as Stingo begins his journey of self-discovery, he meets someone who had achieved an identity only to have it ripped away. "I am not '*other women*,'" she has told Wanda. "I'm *myself*. I have to act according to my conscience. You don't have children" (370). Mature identity, for Sophie, is inextricable from parenthood. But, Žižek points out, fiction and reality are intertwined, and "if you take away from our reality the symbolic fictions that regulate it you take away reality itself." Likewise, illusion contains reality, so that if "the co-ordination of our reality" is shattered, "we have to fictionalize it." Hence the very beauty of body and soul that Sophie presents to Stingo is indeed the fiction she has constructed to mask the destroyed fictions that once made up her sense of self.[27]

Evidently stemming from Styron's waking dream of seeing the name Sophie on the bedroom closet door, *Sophie's Choice* is unquestionably born of intense psychological complexity.[28] Its myriad parallels, echoes, mergings, and suggestions are beyond cataloguing. In the memory and imagination of the author, sitting there at his window-facing desk, Sophie comes into Stingo's life like a dream and will disappear like the ghost that on one level she is. Miraculously reunited with her after she has left with Nathan "forever" (290), he feels that "just as her presence had begun to spill over" him "like a blessing," she seems "once more to be on the verge of vanishing" (304). The word *blessing* reminds us that, for all his talk of the "blessed," "Almighty novel," the true subject of Stingo's devotion that summer is Sophie herself (112). A little later he sees her across the Maple Court, and "whether by accident or celestial design, a shaft of dusty sunlight" catches "her head and hair for an instant" like a "quattrocento halo" (305). Sophie is no saint, and, as Stingo discovers when he sees her haggard face without the false teeth, no beauty either. But this motherless son and womanless man needs the ghost he creates of her, even as Sophie, with her all-too-real story, draws him into the world not just of evil but also of good: her selfless compassion balances his selfish passion. Thus are Stingo and Sophie united in terror and tenderness.

If Sophie is a kind of ghost, she has her own ghosts to contend with, of course, including the ghost of religion and the ghost of her past.

They come together, as we have seen, in her vision of God as a dark giant turning His back on her. In this sense, God and Nathan, both of whom she feels she has lost, are equated, and both distinctly resemble apparitions. God is Sophie's ultimate ghost, the "dis-embodied gaseous vertebrate," as Styron puts it in *Set This House on Fire*, the all-powerful concept, unlikely in actuality yet much yearned for, that represents a morality external to the individual (294–95). Nathan is Sophie's dark past, an embodiment of her sense of guilt and despair even as he is her life force. Sophie contrives to find a way to present herself to the world despite these ghosts.

In other words, it's entirely in keeping with what we might broadly term the novel's religious impulse that Stingo should worship Sophie just as he worships art. For Sophie is a work of art both in the sense that Stingo projects his fantasies onto her and in that she re-creates herself after Auschwitz. As one of my students, Rebecca Parry, pointed out, Stingo's naivety is palpable when he describes Sophie's face without her teeth as resembling "a mask." "Stingo is wrong," she wrote. "It is not her toothless face that is the mask. It is her cheerful nature that masks the suffering."[29] Sophie's "old hag" face, "crumpled in upon itself" with "a mouth like a wrinkled gash and an expression of doddering senescence," is the reality (131). The *mask* is the face Sophie presents publically, with its gentle beauty and "peals of laughter" at moments of forgetful joy (514). Sophie, by the end, believes only in her own self-re-creation, aided by Nathan. She ends her letter to Stingo, "FUCK God and all his Hände Werk" and goes off to die with Nathan in costume, wilfully playing to the end her final role (500). That it is indeed Sophie's decision, not something Nathan has bullied her into, is apparent not just from her journey back to New York but from the music "on the top of the stack," which was probably the last they heard: "Jesu, Joy of Man's Desiring" (508). Way back in chapter 5, when Stingo was still getting to know her, he hears this same piece from Bach's Cantata 147. "That's Sophie who put the music on," Nathan explains. "I try to get her to sleep late in the morning when she doesn't have to go to work. But she says she can't" (117). Bach, therefore, is Sophie's final choice.

As for Nathan as ghost, the more I reread the novel, the more he resembles an apparition who embodies Sophie's overwhelming sense of guilt, the shadowy Jew sitting in judgment of her survival. She cannot escape this wild-eyed man of the mind, this fabulator who feeds Stingo's daydreams and transports Sophie, Stingo, and the reader into ever wilder realms of fantasy and nightmare. Never seen without Sophie, he's her shadow from start to finish. Described by Morris Fink as a "golem" (60, 501), he seems able to disappear without trace (though the narrator surmises that he may have "sought refuge with his brother in Forest Hills" [416]) and reappear with a phantom's ease as "a shadow, dark gray," detaching "itself from the blacker shadows surrounding the front porch" (414), to reestablish "himself with Sophie on the floor above" (415). It all "seemed so natural," recalls the narrator, "that to this day I cannot remember when or how he transported back all the furniture and clothing and paraphernalia he had decamped with that night, replacing them so that it appeared that he had never stormed off with them at all" (417). Nathan distills the novel's Dostoevskian interplay between the real and the imagined, functioning both as a facilitator of all that's tender and welcoming for Sophie and Stingo in postwar Brooklyn—the music, food, flowers, generosity, and love—and as the shadowy symbol of terror—the reminder of Sophie's guilt; the debunker of Stingo's literary fantasies; the violent perpetrator of the punishment Sophie feels she deserves.[30]

If the novel causes one to reflect on Auschwitz itself and can be better understood by way of the window motif and the ghost theme, a final reflective element has to do with character parallels and contrasts. These Dostoevskian pairings include the fathers of Sophie and Stingo; Leslie and Mary Alice; Nathan's brother, Larry, and Wanda; and Morris Fink and Bronek. As I mentioned earlier, the two fathers have attributes in common even though they're so different. Both are figures from a bygone age, even if one is a would-be Nazi collaborator and the other a liberal.[31] Similarly, Wanda and Larry Landau parallel each other in their decent, sane dependability. Leslie and Mary Alice and Morris and Bronek offer rather simpler echoes. But the most interesting parallel is between Stingo and Rudolph Höss. Indeed, while Nathan is the third of the three friends sharing the Brooklyn summer, Höss is as important to the novel's scheme. Rather than paralleling one another, Nathan and Höss provide oppositions. Where Nathan abuses Sophie, Höss is almost a model of rectitude. Where Nathan is an insane fantasist who seems closer to the realms of the supernatural than to the natural, Höss is depicted as an unimaginative functionary. Instead, the narrator draws parallels between Höss and Stingo, which in a way is to say with himself.

This is not a facile comparison nor simply a case of parallel dispositions, as if Stingo, under other circumstances, might have grown up to be a Höss. In paralleling these two figures, Styron shows how forms of individual behavior, belief systems, and impulses toward egotism, self-preservation, and self-mythologizing are common to all kinds of people. But the parallels should also be seen as the narrator's projection of himself into his imagining of Höss. They are an act of confession, or a demonstration of intelligent awareness that the seeds of such behavior, and of such a destructive life, exist within the narrator himself. This, to cite the Malraux epigraph, is precisely "that essential region of the soul where absolute evil confronts brotherhood." In seeking to empathize with others, however noble or monstrous their actions, the narrator projects himself onto the Höss of the historical record. Nevertheless, psychological links exist between Stingo and Höss just as between Sophie and Stingo and between Professor Biegański and Stingo's father. The details by which Styron suggests links between Stingo and Höss are often as minute as a speck of light in a Vermeer.

Just as Sophie is interesting because she is "both victim and accomplice," so Stingo, and even Höss, can also be seen in dual terms (219). To view Stingo as simply sexist is like complaining that Höss is too family orientated. That Styron created Stingo's outlook as more than a little flawed is evident in the contrasting sensitivity with which Styron himself, as a young author, dealt with Peyton's sexual encounters in *Lie Down in Darkness*. Stingo is first seen, full of self-pity, at his job as "junior editor" (4), where, "denied the opportunity to read manuscripts of even passing merit," he must plough "daily through fiction and non-fiction of the humblest possible quality." In turn, insistent "that the written word exemplify only the highest seriousness and truth," he treats this work of "a thousand strangers' lonely and fragile desire" with the "abstract loathing of an ape plucking vermin from his pelt" (5). Later we're told that Höss feels that "there is real cause for this absolute loathing" of Poles (279). The parallels thus begin early on. Like Höss, Stingo is involved in a selection process, dealing with strangers, working from the top of a building, set apart from the masses. His self-pity echoes that of the historical Höss, who writes in his autobiography that lest his "natural emotions get the upper hand," he "had to watch coldly, while the mothers with laughing or crying children went into the gas chambers" (152). Both display attitudes that Hannah Arendt explains as a psychological trick that allows perpetrators to justify their actions and avoid compassion. Styron quotes her as saying that perpetrators do this by "turning those instincts around, as it were, in directing them toward the self"—thinking not "What horrible things I did to people!" but "What horrible things I had to watch in pursuance of my duties, how heavily the task weighed upon my shoulders!" (153). Stingo's equivalent attitude is evident, on a lesser scale, in his determination not to be sucked into Sophie and Nathan's troubles. Similarly, his behavior toward Leslie and Mary Alice may not be lethal, but he resembles Höss in his failure to empathize.

The parallels continue. Both men, as Crane observes, tend toward "the solitary."[32] Stingo begins by describing "a morbid and solitary period" of his life when he "lacked both the opportunity and the initiative to make friends" (11). Meanwhile, Höss tells Sophie that he "was never one of the fellows" and has "always been aloof. Solitary" (281). Both have a quasi-religious temperament. Stingo immures himself "like a half-mad anchorite" (11) intent on producing his "sacred Novel" (112). Meanwhile, in the "sanctuary" of his attic office, Höss, the "bureaucrat with priestly sensibilities," executes "his most personal, confidential and momentous work." Such phrases not only strengthen the parallels between Stingo and Höss but also again reveal Styron's awareness that the Höss he creates, albeit based on historical data, is a projection of his authorial self. As with Nat Turner, Styron becomes Höss, or the Höss he creates becomes self-evidently a man with whom he can begin to identify, or at least identify with Stingo: someone whose self-image is of a lonely, misunderstood, conscientious, and ultimately sympathetic figure. Höss's room is adorned with a portrait of Hitler that "might have been the portrait of Christ" (223). Just as Stingo's devotion to writing echoes Höss's devotion to the cause, so too Stingo's fantasies about being near to famous writers echo Höss's boast to an SS visitor, overheard by Sophie, that his mounted, antlered stag was killed in 1938 "on the slopes above the Königssee so deep within the very shadow of Berchtesgaden that the Führer, had he been in residence (and who knows, perhaps he had been!) might have heard the fatal crack!" (394). Devoted to writing, Stingo agonizes over correct word usage even when reporting on manuscripts: "Should I say 'undoubtedly Kleenex' or 'indubitably'? 'Host' of human needs or 'horde'? 'Mass'? 'Mess'? During its composition I would pace my cell distractedly, uttering soft meaningless vocables to the air as I struggled with the prose rhythms" (13). Höss is as scrupulous with his reports. "'There can be no question'—no, that's too strong. I should say something less positive?" he asks Sophie, accepting her view that the phrase "in all probability" will allow "the Reichsführer more leeway to form his own judgment" (224).

All sorts of other incidental details connect Stingo and Höss. Stingo chain-smokes, and Sophie worries about his cough. Höss, also "a chain-smoker" (222), in Sophie's memory "coughed a phlegmy smoker's cough" as he gazed out the window, his "face wreathed in blue tobacco fumes" (223). Even their early sexual histories are similar. Höss confesses that although he "never consorted with prostitutes," he did once, when young, go to a brothel (281). Stingo too has had, prior to Sophie, a "single pathetic crumpling" with a prostitute (122). Both men are, if only for a while in Stingo's case, company men. Stingo doesn't feel like one of McGraw-Hill's "regimented minions" (17) any more than Höss feels himself to be a piston in the Nazi machine. But their egotism deludes them. More subtly, they parallel each other in their romanticism. Each responds to the bucolic while turning away from the unpleasant. In further examples of the window motif, the narrator contrasts Stingo's "serene, almost pastoral" view of Prospect Park with "urban, cacophonous" Flatbush Avenue "short blocks away" (37). Not only is this strikingly like the split scene Höss sees with Sophie from his window when the smoke of Birkenau is briefly blown away to reveal "in the clear sunlight the great glorious white stallion" (275), but the stallion in itself calls to mind Stingo, who, thanks to Leslie's verbal encouragement, achieves a "stallionoid condition" (165).

Nowhere are the links more exquisite than in two gestures separated far apart in the novel. In the first, Nathan, Sophie, and Stingo are returning from Coney Island.

> "Oh, we're *all* going to become great friends!" Sophie echoed him suddenly. A lovely phosphorescence enveloped her face as the train plunged toward sunlight, out of the claustrophobic tunnel and into the marshy maritime reaches of south Brooklyn. Her cheek was very close to my own, flushed with contentment, and when once again she linked her arms in mine and Nathan's, I felt on cozy enough terms to remove, between my delicate thumb and forefinger, a tiny thread of sauerkraut clinging to the corner of her lip. "Oh, we're going to be the *best* of friends!" she trilled over the train's rackety noise, and she gave my arm a tight squeeze that was certainly not flirtatious but contained something in it more than—well, casual. (76)

This first scene is of the fragile tenderness of a three-way friendship. Sophie soothes Stingo's loneliness while Nathan, we imagine, watches unconcerned. Stingo desires Sophie, but innocence here prevails. Yet we're also aware of her vulnerability, wedged between two men capable of being predators and rivals. Her repeated assertion of friendship, itself an echo of Nathan's words, underlines the forced and temporal nature of this conviction. Two of these people will not survive the summer. The narrator knows this, and the moment's melancholy beauty becomes more poignant on a rereading. This is not least the case in that a quite different scene parallels it. In this one, Sophie has tended Höss during a migraine attack and explained to him how she came to be in his house.

> "And here," he interrupted, "here you are." He gave a sigh. "You have had good luck." And what he did then caused her electric amazement. He reached up with his free hand, and using the utmost delicacy, plucked a little something from the edge of her upper lip; it was, she realized, a crumb of the chocolate she had eaten, now held between his thumb and forefinger, and she watched with grave wonder as he moved his tar-stained fingers slowly toward his lips and deposited the tiny chestnut-brown flake into his mouth. She shut her eyes, so disturbed by the peculiar and grotesque communion of the gesture that her heart commenced pounding again and her brain was rocked with vertigo. (273–74)

To follow the contours of Styron's prose is to be constantly surprised by minuscule nuance. On the surface there is the parallel of Höss, like Stingo, taking something from Sophie's lip. But that is only the start. The act might be construed as tender. Höss's desire for Sophie, his human interest in her, which is not purely sexual, is evident in his sigh, and in his completion of her sentence. But then he puts the chocolate into his own mouth, and in a way suggestive of his own appetite, his own predatory nature. His tar-stained fingers add to our revulsion, and Sophie's response, far from the tender, comforted, and comforting response to Stingo's gesture, is one of unnameable terror. But there are yet other layers to contemplate. While Stingo's gesture is the first we come across, both he and we are oblivious, at the moment it happens, to the fact that for Sophie it would probably have sparked a memory of Höss. The fragility of her happiness, of their friendship, the transience of it all, is made the more powerfully three-dimensional on a rereading. Sophie, like the reader in a small way, once aware of the full story and so recalling the events, can never escape its tyranny. The tenderness of the first moment, ambiguous in itself, is on any rereading forever balanced with the terror that shadows it.[33]

All this said, the differences between Stingo and Höss are just as important, as is the fact that the Höss we see in the novel, we must again remind ourselves, is in large part the narrator's creation not only through Sophie's descriptions and the self-image presented in the autobiography but also by way of the narrator's confession of his own failings. The differences between them are not just of circumstance but of age and intelligence. Stingo's reaction to Farrell's "brief, desolating story" of his son's death shows he's capable of empathy, and to depart from McGraw-Hill is to absent himself from his "smug and airless self-deprivation" and enter "the chaotic Manhattan streets" of life itself (24–25). In turn, if Stingo were not simpatico, Sophie would not tell him her story. From his comments about Höss's autobiography, we know that Styron sees him as a man of limited intelligence and self-justifying behavior. But just as Styron says of Nat Turner that he gave "him dimensions of humanity that were almost totally absent in the documentary evidence," so he gives Höss "dimensions of humanity" beyond the evidence of the autobiography. To do so is to prove oneself better than the Nazis, while to do otherwise would be to fall into their own delusion of seeing others as less human than themselves. "Maybe the truest thing to be said about racism," Henry Louis Gates Jr. writes, "is that it represents a profound failure of the imagination." If we see this to be so, then it follows that it's important to give Höss humanity as a counter to the impulses that allowed Nazism to happen.[34]

Styron does this in interesting ways. For instance, what do we make of this passage, in which Sophie describes Höss's reflections on the horse?

["]That beautiful Arabian horse was still in the field down below and Höss was leaning against the window, gazing down at it. The smoke from Birkenau had lifted up. I heard him whisper something about his transfer to Berlin again. He spoke very bitterly. I remember he used words like 'failure' and 'ingratitude,' and once he said very clearly, 'I know how well I have performed my duty.' He didn't say anything for a long while then, only kept looking at that horse, and finally I heard him say this, I am almost sure they were his exact words, 'To escape the body of a man yet still dwell in Nature. To be that horse, to live within that beast. That would be freedom.'" She paused for an instant. "I have always remembered those words. They were just so . . ." And Sophie stopped speaking, her eyes glazed with memory, staring toward

the phantasmagoric past as if in wonderment.
("They were just so . . .") *What?* (282–83)

Such a moment calls to mind Gardner's comment about Styron's "justice
and compassion." Here we have the commandant of Auschwitz, a man
who wrote a self-justifying autobiography. More even than in the case of
Nat Turner, we have his very words to show what kind of a man he was:
not an evil brute, but an ordinary bureaucrat, the kind one encounters
frequently enough in normal life, an apparatchik of limited intelligence,
limited imagination, limited empathy, and a desire to follow the rule
book and "get on in the company." But Styron portrays this character
type with great subtlety. He has Sophie witness this man at vulnerable
moments. Once again, Höss's gaze through the window represents his
perception of himself and of the world. It reveals his self-pity, conformity, romanticism, and self-justification. At this point, too, he sees
himself as a victim. In charge of the most horrific set-up humanity has
yet known, even he feels trapped in the role he has acquired, whether
through a certain mundane managerial ability, petty vanity, misplaced
ambition, or mere cowardice. He wears the uniform and he cannot remove it. But his desire to escape is something that, on a human level,
as the atrocities that he presides over just for a second blur into the
background, Styron makes us at least see.

The point is to imagine how this man views himself. It's pretty convincing, not to say discomfiting. To what extent do we explain away
any of our own roles or actions? We may not run a death camp, but
most of us turn away from things done in our name. Then, subtlest of
all, when Höss wishes he could "be that horse," Sophie's reaction is all
the more powerful for not being articulated. Perhaps there *is* no way to
describe Höss's wish to find "freedom." Are his words dumb, pitiable,
crass? Or are they somehow weirdly moving? Could the commandant of
Auschwitz say something . . . beautiful? Styron's masterstroke is to leave
Sophie's response unarticulated. Perhaps she doesn't know herself what
she feels. Take the words out of context; give them to, say, a Bosnian
peasant, or an Indonesian sweat factory worker, and they become un-
contentious. But when they come from Höss we don't know, any more
than Sophie, how to put our feelings into words. More powerful still is
Sophie's physical response on relating this moment. She hides her face
in her hands, but the tears seep through, and Stingo lets "her cry in
silence" (283). Perhaps silence is best. Even Stingo is lost for words. Perhaps the only response to Höss's romantic escapism is to judge him as he

surely, as a historical figure, deserves. Perhaps such a clichéd sentiment is the best this dull little middle manager of atrocity is capable of dredging up. But Styron's genius ensures that such a scene, in what in another writer might be a straightforward scenario, lingers long in the mind.

The complexity of emotions doesn't end there. While Sophie bends her head toward the table at the Maple Court, Stingo is quietly overjoyed to have her back after her latest breakup with Nathan and to "be simply breathing her face and body once more" (283). So the time present of this "rainy August afternoon" of 1947 Brooklyn, remembered by the narrator years later, takes on a visceral immediacy. Sophie is drinking whiskey, both as an anesthetic for anguish and, paradoxically, to help her express her memories. She tells Stingo for the first time that her "child was there at Auschwitz" and that "that afternoon when Höss was looking down from the window," she pleaded for help in saving Jan (284). We find ourselves both in the Maple Court and in Höss's office at Auschwitz. Stingo watches her gazing "into that past which seemed now so totally, so irresistibly to have captured her" (285). She talks more of Poland, of the refugee center in Sweden. She pauses again, locking "her eyelids shut as if in savage meditation," then gazes "once more out onto the baffling distances" before describing the scene with Höss to the end of the chapter (286).

The effect is of an immense fluidity between past and present. Sophie is drowning in the depths of her past, surfacing to the present long enough to take hold of Stingo's "hand in a numbing grip" "as if seeking whatever semblance of present reality" Stingo can offer. This, we might note, echoes her "tight squeeze" of Stingo's arm after he plucks the sauerkraut from her lips, perhaps evoking memory of Höss. The pull of the past is so powerful, so present, that her fragile edifice of identity is being pulled apart by memory's undertow. Her grip on Stingo's hand also imitates her description of clutching at Höss's shirt and the way he grabs her wrist and pulls it away. Sophie tells of falling to her knees and pressing her face "against his boots." Finally, she relaxes her grip, to look him full in the face and tell him how she surrounded Höss's boots with her arms, pressing her "cheek up against those cold leather boots as if they were made of fur or something warm and comforting" and maybe "even licked them" (286).

The psychological complexity of this scene is mesmerizing. It's as if Sophie clings to Stingo to haul her above water. But at the same time, in layer on layer, the grief and despair that she's *remembering* so overwhelms her that she's willing to cling to, even to kiss, this Nazi bureaucrat who is directly responsible for implementing the orders to execute men, women, and children, including, as we later learn, her own daughter, Eva. The intensity of this rendering of layers of despair almost certainly owes something to the author's own inescapable grief: that sense, if we think of his unresolved childhood mother-loss, to "be simply breathing her face and body once more." It's a measure of the novel's scope, and its author's capacity for compassion, that read in youth it evokes in us some immediate empathy with Stingo in his mother-loss and emotional fragility but that an older reader, especially a parent, would have to be emotionally stunted not to be moved by Sophie's anguish. On both an emotional and a technical level the scene captures, with multidimensional lucidity, our ability to experience the past in the present.

Sophie's Choice is therefore several kinds of novels in one. Originally subtitled a memoir, it's a ghost story, or at least a story about ghosts; a novel about how we imagine ourselves into others' situations, how others' memories activate our own imagination; a novel about empathy as well as the failures and limitations of our capacity for empathy; and a novel about windows into the past, the future, and the lives of others. The source of its vividness is this melding of truly substantial subject matter and integrated structure built in melodic prose scene by cinematic scene. More generally it combines the modernist innovations of Joyce, Woolf, and Faulkner with the strength of classic realism. *Sophie's Choice* has a first-person narrator who is also effectively omniscient. Styron is thus able to show how powerfully, through memory, research, and a capacity for compassion and empathy, we can envisage others' lives.

This, moreover, is not a step back to an older tradition but a realignment of that tradition. I wrote earlier about Styron's use of cinematic innovations to reshape the novel form. This is evident as early as *Lie Down in Darkness* but just as important in *Sophie's Choice*. Fay Weldon has noted a couple of things that seem relevant to this. One is that, for her, "guilt is to the soul as pain is to the body: it indicates what we ought and ought not to be doing and should be listened to." *Sophie's Choice* exudes compassion precisely because Sophie's and Stingo's capacity for guilt stems from their empathic natures. In Sophie this is partly parental instinct. Any normal parent would suffer unbearable guilt at feeling they are the cause of their child's suffering. But her friendship with Stingo is also built on tenderness; she understands that from his youthful perspective he too suffers on a hefty scale. Stingo has his own motives for listening to Sophie, but he's not without the capacity for empathy and compassion, as his mature self illustrates in the act of composing the narrative. The other observation Weldon makes, however, is that "on an individual level, the world's a kinder place these days. Fiction and film have allowed us to experience what it's like in someone else's shoes."[35] Perhaps it's no coincidence that this compassionate novel makes such use of the cinematic technique of allowing us to see events as if through Sophie's eyes, even Höss's eyes, as well as Stingo's and the narrator's. Only Nathan, whose chaotic, irrational, unpredictable mentality prevents this, must remain beyond empathy, a force of nature—a personification of Sophie's sense of guilt.

To conclude, let's imagine once again the author at his desk facing a window, dreaming up this remarkable narrative and coming, after four years, to its end. In discussing *Set This House on Fire* I evoked Dostoevsky to suggest that *novel as a drama of self. Sophie's Choice*, while about much else besides, is also open to such an interpretation. One man tells this story, so everything, however vividly evoked, comes through his mind. Sophie especially is such a presence that this is hard to believe. The narrator allows her to tell her story in all its immediacy. Styron uses cinematic technique and our cinematic habits to achieve this in a way that prior to cinema a novelist probably would not have attempted. This is part of his importance as an innovator of the novel form. But even though Sophie is so present, so "real," she is also—as both sympathetic and hostile critics have seen—a manifestation in the narrator's mind of his own dead mother. So as with Höss, we see Sophie filtered through the narrator's mind. The window motif remains valid. These characters are, again, carved of air and light. They are memories built in the portal of reflection. The novelist sat at his window-facing desk, reminiscing and dreaming, and out of that long process came Sophie, the reminiscing woman who can hardly bear to articulate to Stingo, or to herself, the truth about her life.

In its uncensored obsession with human behavior, *Sophie's Choice* is something of an uncomfortable read. But great art, Kafka reminded us, is not about making us comfortable and may need to "be the axe for the frozen sea inside us."[36] *Sophie's Choice*, though, is as much about tenderness as about terror. Styron at the end has Stingo himself cry. It works because Stingo is not at the last self-pitying. He is letting go his "rage and sorrow" for "the beaten and butchered and betrayed and martyred children of the earth." We cannot, try as we might, emotionally ingest the deaths of "the six million Jews or the two million Poles or the one million Serbs or the five million Russians," but we know what it means to have loved ones (515). We understand the nature of loyalty and betrayal. We can empathize by concentrating on individuals, with those who loved, lost, felt joy and terror. Styron created Sophie and Nathan and Wanda and Jan and Eva to help in that process, with that same instinct that makes visitors to the United States Holocaust Memorial Museum pick up an identity card. Mine is #1118, Ezra Zelig Szbasson and his family, "never heard from after 1941." This is the same instinct that made me record the names of a handful of inmates whose photographs hang in the corridors of Auschwitz I—Franciszek Swiebocki and Josefa Bala the first time; Sadowski Władysław, Pelagia Golgowska, and Maria Rożenek on later visits—without of course forgetting that more than 90 percent of those who died were Jews whom we remember not from individual prison photographs complete with names and dates but from prewar snapshots, from their possessions, and from their hair. That *Sophie's Choice*, which I first read as a young man not so unlike Stingo, should have led me to these attempted acts of empathy, however minor and inadequate, and to writing this seems to me to be a measure of the novel's lesson in compassion, its merging of terror and tenderness. What more is there to say? On the wall of the Memorial Museum, in the city where we last see Sophie alive, is the Hebrew word for "Remember."

רובזל

CHAPTER 8

Train to the Tidewater

A Journey of Rediscovery

Awaiting the train from New York to Newport News one mid-September morning, I pondered how to end this critical memoir. If all books are journeys, Styron himself was adept at structures that expressed both the linear trajectory of a life and the cyclical nature of memory. *Lie Down in Darkness* follows Peyton's parents through the day of her funeral but also traces her life by way of characters' reminiscences. *Set This House on Fire* joins Peter's and Cass's ruminations on the events in Sambuco. *The Confessions of Nat Turner* involves the time present of Nat's reflections and the author's implicit meditation on history. *Sophie's Choice,* the most complex of all, builds reflections upon reflections; the narrator remembers his young self in Brooklyn and his Virginia childhood as well as Sophie's revelations that summer as he recalls them across the years. Boarding that train to the Tidewater, I thus decided to reflect upon the literal journey of rediscovery I undertook to research the book. The primary purpose of the trip that September and early October was scholarly. I'd be examining Styron's correspondence with Random House and with his first agent, Elizabeth McKee, at Columbia University; reading the notes and manuscripts of *Set This House on Fire* and *The Confessions of Nat Turner* in the Library of Congress, and those of *Sophie's Choice* at Duke University; and trawling through whatever other unpublished material I might find. But I also wanted to remind myself of the man behind the work, both through his correspondence and incidental writings and through the environment of his youth.

Like others, I was drawn to the man through the writing rather than vice versa, and while it's equally true that this physical journey possessed a personal dimension, the archives showed my own responses in context. They confirmed that while Styron's evocation of apparent intimacy has no home in conventional critical analysis, it nonetheless exists for many a reader. In letter after letter correspondents tell Styron that they are not in the habit of contacting authors but that they must tell him how his writing has affected them. There are letters from high-school and university students, including a 1960s one from Alabama undergraduates apologizing for phoning Styron drunk. A sixty-year-old member of an "American Negro Group" thanks him in 1968 for putting African Americans "smack in the middle of American history." A man from Lagos asks to live with Styron to learn the craft of writing. A Holocaust survivor praises him for his description of the social structure of the camps and for revealing the way individuals veil bad qualities beneath a guise of benevolence. Barry Hannah writes that Styron and Cormac McCarthy are among the few writers who could capture the American landscape. Dr. Seuss (Ted Geisel) is so moved by the screenplay "Dead!" that he sends "the only fan letter I've ever written."[1] Yet more letters simply thank Styron for *Darkness Visible* as a book that helped to save correspondents' lives, or at least to restore them to health. And then there are the numerous, more generalized letters from young people, one of whom was me.

In turn, Styron's sense of responsibility toward individual readers is palpable. He routinely instructed his agent to decline requests from organizations. He was not above sending acerbic replies to the more absurd of such letters, such as the one, referred to in an earlier chapter, from the executive director of a library association.[2] But as Al Styron attests, her father "responded to almost everyone who wrote him," and when these were readers moved simply to put pen to paper as a gesture of gratitude or solidarity, regardless of their eloquence or eccentricity, he did so with invariable grace and good humor.[3] For what mattered to him as an author was precisely the passionate engagement of the individual reader.

That ability to draw people into his writing also drew a number of readers into his actual life. His writing's blend of insight, intimacy, and compassion forged in some a loyalty to the man, even as his forthrightness and refusal to compromise his vision brought enemies enough, whether among decent people put off by his blind spots or among ideologues, bigots, *agélastes*, spurned critics, or the occasional librarian. He was combative in the face of stances he thought wrong and refused to appease special-interest pleaders. As one of those drawn to the man himself, I have thus felt it natural not only to describe rereading the work but also to revisit environments of his youth, and so to "reread" the settings of some of his fiction. Reflecting on those settings aids understanding of his work. For saturated art—art that is integrated and textured on many levels—rewards focus on any specific element. The individual attributes complement and enhance the whole. Knowing from close reading that Styron's best writing exemplifies this saturation, I thus roamed Manhattan and Brooklyn, then caught that Newport News train to Washington before turning inland for Durham, North Carolina, and during my time there drove up into Virginia to visit Courtland and Newport News. This final chapter records some observations I made in doing so and expresses, through this as well as thoughts on "Shadrach," "A Tidewater Morning," and an unpublished essay, "State of Writers in America," my sense of Styron's links to contemporaries and his literary legacy.

I referred at the start of this book to Christa Wolf's meditation on the levels of reality involved in reading or rereading an author and the complex relationship between fiction and fact. If it's true that "to begin writing you must first be someone to whom reality is no longer self-evident," it may be equally true that close study of complex novels implies the same of the reader. The world readers experience is shaped by the writings that have mythologized it, and in this sense there is, as Wolf states, "a truth outside the important world of facts." "The reality of Crime and Punishment goes beyond the topography of a city," to reprise Wolf, in being "certainly St. Petersburg," but one that "would never have existed" but for Dostoevsky. Similarly, my awareness of Styron's novels affected my experience of the places I visited. That's to say, with Wolf, that the "reality" of these places, like all our realities, involves projection. Not to acknowledge this would be to deny a truth all too easily denied: that critics are personally involved in the stories they unfold.[4]

Peter's description early in Set This House on Fire of revisiting Port Warwick clearly matches Styron's sense of revisiting Newport News. His "home town," says Peter, "had grown vaster and more streamlined and clownish-looking" than he thought "a decent southern town could ever become." Acknowledging that "it had always been a shipbuilding city and a seaport" rather than "one of the ornaments of the commonwealth," he still recalls how he "had known its gentle seaside charm" and shaken loose for himself its "own peculiar romance." In place of the sights and sounds he remembers, he finds that the magnolias have "been hacked down to make room for a highway along the shore," and "a Yankee-built vehicular tunnel" now pokes its "snout two miles beneath the mud at Hampton Roads." In this town of "the rootless and uprooted," he hunts "in vague panic for a familiar scene" (10). Driving with his father through the city, he stops at a garage and realizes that right there, "several fathoms beneath the foundations of this Esso Servicenter," he had once hunted, aged twelve, for crawfish and "had almost drowned" (17).

> Yet here on the identical spot, years later, I thought that nothing could be the victim of such obliteration. My great-grandchildren's cleverest archaeology will strive in vain to unlock that sun-swept marsh, that stream, those crawfish, that singing trolley car. Everything was gone. Not just altered or changed or modified, not just a place whose outlines may have shifted and blurred (new growth here, no growth there, a new-fledged willow, a deepened cove) but were still recognizable, dependable, fixed—my marsh had vanished, a puff into thin air, and nothing of it remained. (18)

Peter is left feeling estranged. The place where his identity formed now only exists in imagination. Moreover, this place where only a black fisherman's intervention had prevented him from drowning is where he'd felt a "sudden tumultuous love" for his "fleeting life" (17). It's where life had left him "shorn of illusions and innocence." But all that is now "shadow." Only in his mind do gulls flash overhead while the trolley car sways, "chiming, as if through the light of centuries, like a phantom" (19).

As often in *Set This House on Fire*, an excellent scene, ironically itself buried beneath the novel's unsightly architecture, deserves better surroundings. Peter's memory merely leads him to contact Cass in his quest to "find the answer to at least several things" (19). But what lingers is this observation of transience, of careless destruction and construction, and of a landscape altered forever, and I had the scene in mind during much of my search for places of his youth. On the one hand, to travel the region where Styron spent his early years confirms the truth of this passage composed in the 1950s, only far more so. But while at times you wonder if anything much remains of the world he knew, at other times, in unexpected ways, tantalizing glimpses of that past and links with that literature still emerge. They do so, moreover, in ways beyond mere awareness of a world that, except through the magic of art, is "irretrievably lost" (18).

For instance, trains feature in Styron's first and last novels, and while to travel down the Atlantic coastal route in the twenty-first century is obviously very different from how it would have been in the 1940s, similarities surely remain. You may buy your coffee at Tom Horton's Fast Food Joint nowadays, but heading south from New York you still await the train, as Stingo and Sophie did, in "the bowels of Penn Station," not least because the Beaux-Arts structure Styron would have envisaged Stingo and Sophie hurrying into was demolished in the early sixties and only the bowels remain (447). Then, as you pull out—in my case on the 95 Carolinian at 10.35 a.m.—there's still the ride itself, first out from under New York for the short haul to Newark and then through the New Jersey landscape. Just as, through history and literature, voices and images from the past and from imagination populate our present, so on such a journey there are passengers beyond those physically in the carriage with you. Like the reflection in the train window of his "little boy self" that Stingo thinks he sees beyond his own in the "sunless cavern" of the Philadelphia station (452), so other presences seemed intermittently to visit in tunnels or against the whizzing autumn colors.

The morning train Stingo and Sophie take to Washington on the way to Virginia stalls on the trestle opposite the Wheatena factory in Rahway. During this brief stop Stingo takes "hopeful stock of the future" (447). He watches Sophie sleeping against his shoulder, encircles her with his arm, and puts his lips to "her tousled blond hair." Wrapped up in his egotistical fantasies, he hugs her softly while thinking of his book. His thoughts jar horribly with the reality of Sophie's story. He has, for instance, "a moment of gloom" over whether he has "the insight to portray this young suicide." Can he "make it all seem *real*?" (449). He's forgotten that within the novel's reality he holds in his arms another suicidal woman, desperate to *escape* the "*real*."

The train lurches forward. Sophie wakes and asks Stingo to fetch some water. He returns to find her drinking whiskey. "The clickety-clack momentum" hurtles them "across New Jersey's satanic industrial barrens" (451). The conversation turns from Stingo's boyhood to Sophie's desire to write about Auschwitz to his declaration of love, interrupted by her announcement that she needs the bathroom. As the train leaves Baltimore he finds her slumped, grief stricken, at the back of the car. Both characters' minds are on the past. Stingo is returning to the supposed idyl of his home region in his unconscious desire to rebuild a family life ripped from him in childhood and from Sophie in parenthood. Sophie, caught up in her memories, mimics her desire to return in the other direction, if not to the past then to Nathan and New York, by stumbling back toward the rear of the train.

The trackside detritus that accompanies this journey south from New

York still seems much as Styron describes it—"squalid slums, sheet-metal sheds," "warehouses," "parking lots" (451). But equally, there's foliage and the prospect of warmer weather, along with fellow passengers and the luxury of contemplation, occasionally interrupted by a reminder that dangers may still lurk.

"Ladies and gentlemen, this is the 95 for Newport News. Your safety is important. If you see something, say something."

"Ladies and gentlemen," came the intercom voice a little later as we passed an abandoned factory with "Morley Mackay Co." faded white on the brick wall and broken windows reflecting blue sky or gaping black. "This is downtown Newark, New Jersey. Look and see you have all your belongings. Downtown Newark, New Jersey, this stop."

We pulled out of Newark past more derelict factories, more smashed windows, more rust. Orange-clad railroad workers clambered across the rails in front of pastel-colored clapboard houses. Twenty minutes out of the city sunlight splashed the car as we passed greenery, a playground, sports fields, houses with pools, hoops in the driveways. By 11:25 we were crossing the Delaware at Trenton.

"Nineteen forty-seven I came out of the army," an old black guy across the aisle from me tells his companion. "That was a great time."

"We had no hard times," she replies. "They was all good."

With their voices in the background, I think of Stingo, drunk, disheveled, and distraught after finding Sophie gone, reading his Bible aloud with "a fudge-colored lady of majestic heft and girth" on the train north all the way from the outskirts of the District of Columbia until his "dark priestess" alights at Newark promising him that "ev'ything gone be all right" (505–6).

On our train, heading in the opposite direction six decades later, the couple gathered their bags at Baltimore. I asked the old man where he'd been stationed in the war. "Guam," he explained. "Thank you for taking an interest." So, like Styron, he had been in the Pacific. With the couple gone, the rest of the way to Washington I had nothing to listen to except more distant murmurs from fellow passengers, and nothing to do but gaze at the whizzing foliage, and later more pine forests, punctuated by rivers and lakes, so I thought back over my time wandering Styron's New York.

My first stop after the subway down from, coincidentally, my West Eighty-eighth Street accommodation on the very stretch between Riverside Drive and West End Avenue where Styron finished *Lie Down in Darkness,* had been the McGraw-Hill Building. I had never before thought of finding this building, though I'd seen a painting of it in the New York Public Library. It turned out that I'd unwittingly passed it many times. "An architecturally impressive but spiritually enervating green tower on West Forty-second Street" (5), it looms shadowlike behind the Port Authority, where I'd dozed on many a night in youth so that I could roam the city by day. Now, amid the passersby, I thought of *Sophie's Choice* and imagined Stingo on the twentieth floor about to get fired for that balloon escapade. I pictured the "majestic prospect of Manhattan" that reliably revived Stingo's "drugged senses with all those platitudinous yet genuine spasms of exhilaration and sweet promise that have traditionally overcome provincial American youths." Looking from window to window, I wondered from which one Stingo had watched a sheet of paper's "ecstatic tumbling flight as it sped across the rooftops, often disappearing far off into the canyons around Times Square" (19).

The blue sky held no "fragile, lovely, iridescent globes" adventuring "upon the wind" in fulfillment of "every buried, infantile desire to float balloons to the uttermost boundaries of the earth" (19). But even in the brilliant sunlight, the McGraw-Hill Building's box-on-box modernist solemnity looked as grim as Styron had described it. Its blue and green tiles seemed to suck in the sunlight. No one else was paying it attention, let alone likely to be reflecting on that scene from *Sophie's Choice.* But for a moment I thought I glimpsed an old, heavily bearded Norwegian, windswept from the Minnesota steppes, enter 330 Forty-second Street hoping to receive the time of day from an otherwise supercilious young manuscript reader. Could that, I wondered, be Gundar Firkin, the only unpublished writer to whom Stingo shows compassion? As if! Decades had passed, and Styron had probably invented him anyway. I walked east toward the Chrysler Building and caught the 1 Train downtown.

Nowadays when we look up in Manhattan at a sky of unblemished blue we think not of balloons but of airliners. Sheets of paper swirling through the canyons have other connotations too. I was there because of *Sophie's Choice,* but I also found myself thinking of Don DeLillo's *Falling Man.* Perhaps this was not least because it happened to be the ninth anniversary of 9/11, so—since atrocity and history were always Styron's subject matter—I rose from the subway at Canal Street and joined a crowd across Broadway near City Hall to watch two banner-waving groups confront each other about the proposed Islamic center to be built near Ground Zero. An imam megaphoned the crowd that Muslims had become the bogeymen and that we could live together in peace. As I turned west down Park Place to Ground Zero, his voice lost out to a Christian speaker denouncing terrorism and proclaiming one nation under an Almighty, or a "gaseous vertebrate" so far as *Lie Down in Darkness* (384), *Set This House on Fire* (294–95), and *Sophie's Choice* (505) were concerned.

I continued down Trinity Place toward Broadway and eventually reached Greenwich Village to stroll along leafy West Eleventh Street, where Stingo first lives at the University Residence Club before moving to Brooklyn. Not far past the New School for Social Research I came across a heavy, tanned man in his fifties reading Jonathan Safran Foer's *Extremely Loud and Incredibly Close* on the shady steps of a brownstone. With his graying hair swept back in the manner of the photo on the dust jacket of *Sophie's Choice*, he resembled the Styron of the seventies.

"Is there a University Residence Club around here?" I asked.

"I don't know it," he said, "and I've lived here thirty-six years."

"William Styron describes it in *Sophie's Choice*. It may not exist now if it ever did. His biographer mentions only a 'residence club.'"[5]

"Geez," said the gray-haired man, rubbing his tanned face pensively. "William *Styron. Sty*-ron!" He intoned the name as if it were that of an acquaintance with whom he'd long ago "mysteriously parted company" (4). "*Sophie's Choice!*" he sighed. "Wow—yes. I remember. Styron!"

I thought about engaging him in further conversation but went on my sun-dappled way, imagining him sitting there on the shady steps no longer reading his Foer novel but thinking back to when he first moved to West Eleventh Street thirty-six years earlier. I thought about how he'd have been Stingo's age when *Sophie's Choice* appeared and how he'd perhaps had literary pretentions himself. Maybe it had meant a great deal to him. I imagined that I'd set him off daydreaming, and, of course, on my way to Brooklyn I continued my own daydream, so that by the time I reached the bridge the man had become Styron himself, not catching up on recent literature but about to write *Sophie's Choice*. Pondering "the relativity of time" and our "elastic definitions," I worked back thirty-six years and, realizing that it was "simultaneously, a long time ago and only yesterday," considered the dizzying notion that there on the steps of that brownstone on the very street where Styron first lived on in Manhattan I'd been talking to the ghost of William Styron circa 1974 and had reminded him of his own youth back in the city in the 1940s.

I was beginning to see what it meant to roam Styron's New York, and what a strange activity it is to delve into the past in this way, in search of a world part lost and part imagined. My youthful projection of Styron as the great writer, I realized, involved encountering the right novelist at the right moment. But he too spent much of his time reconstructing his own semi-imaginary past and its relation to history. The intertwining of his life with mine, his imagination with my imagination, was not merely my fantasy but actually the way humans are constructed, and if I was to write honestly I would have to make it part of the book. This, after all, is the essence of rereading. To live is to reread.

As I crossed Brooklyn Bridge in the strong sunshine, the stanchions and their shadows created a strobe effect against the distant borough. Alexandra Styron had agreed to meet at a restaurant called 5 Front Street, just beneath the looming bridge, to talk about her father. 5 Front Street turned out to be closed for refurbishment; indeed the whole Dumbo area seemed under reconstruction, the dug-up streets muddily reminiscent of how they might have been in the nineteenth century. But we found a sandwich bar and talked at a corner table about her view that her father's inability to write another novel was what "killed him." I'd met Al in the nineties, but it was curious to chat with one of Styron's children now that he was gone. She was coming at him from one perspective, and I from another. She was an insider, while I was an outsider. Apart from the fact that we're of the same generation, our experiences of the same man, the same novelist, could not have been more different. But somewhere there was a meeting place. She pointed out that we don't necessarily know our own parents better than others do, just differently. She talked, as did Jim West and others, of how taciturn her father was, of how he "wouldn't talk about stuff." She also said how averse he was to modern technology. "I tried to show him my computer," she said. "He wouldn't even look at it."

At the time we met, *Reading My Father* had yet to appear. I had only seen the *New Yorker* article with the same title. But among the things her book confirmed was that she too felt that the Roxbury cottage where her moody and unpredictable father worked her childhood away had a sense of "foreboding" and a "haunted vibe." What her book dispels, if it needs dispelling after a certain age, is any "romantic idea about the private lives of famous writers in general, and Bill Styron in particular." But the main common ground between us, I felt, was awareness of the incredible struggle that must have been involved in putting one's heart and soul, and years, into huge, handwritten manuscripts so painstakingly constructed in terms of both the "architecture" and the sentences. I knew that he "labored over every word," because the more I read the two final novels, the more their pieces fell into place, like puzzles that have an intellectual completeness. She knew it because of the hours her father devoted to his writing and because she had tried to reconstruct *The Way of the Warrior* after his death.[6]

No passage in *Reading My Father* is more powerful than that about her discovery of the jumbled manuscript and her realization that it had become an ever more complex puzzle without much hope of resolution. Leafing through the manuscript, organized as best he could by Jim West, she "found that the first page was page 5 and began in the middle of a sentence. The second page was page 11, after which the manuscript moved on sequentially till page 33. The page after that was 39, and then the numbers began to run backward, then forward again." "On and on it went like this. Hundreds of pages jumbled, others omitted entirely. In the order they were in, the manuscript made no sense at all." She moved on to open the second folder, holding 100,000 words. Only the third was sequential, from page 1 to page 159, with a handwritten note from her father dated 2 February 1985. Her conclusion on surveying this huge volume of writing, with its "crafted sentences," "avenues of thought," and "great loops of memory and emotion," was that she had found the source of her father's depression. With a degree of compassion that I had not myself felt (being too wrapped up, no doubt, in the romance of a famous writer's life) when as a young man I'd sat in awe of the manuscripts, she writes of how "the whole pile vibrated with the strength of his effort. And with a certain madness."[7]

Whether Styron "was depressed, and then he couldn't write" or whether he was "unable to write" and this was what "drove him completely mad" is probably not answerable. When she put it to Bob Loomis that the inability to write was what made him ill, Loomis said that it was the other way around: Styron's illness destroyed his ability to write. In any event, Al's conversation and eventually her book helped me ponder the human dimension far more deeply. Anyone who tries to put together a book with any level of complexity knows the feeling of not being able to see the wood for the trees, of chapters that refuse to take shape. Styron, who rarely found writing easy, had experienced this to the point of no return in later years. My rereading of his work was reminding me in fresh ways that his kind of novel was a construction of immense complexity but achievable completion. "It's like a jigsaw puzzle," he said in 1988, a matter of piecing it together "and finding that it actually *does* fit."[8] His work was designed to reward the most careful reading, so the pain of failure would have been akin to discovering that a puzzle you had spent decades on had pieces that would never be found or, worse still, like an anti-parable by Kafka, or Borges, or Calvino, was made up of unconnected fragments of a picture that could never exist.

After lunch the subway sped me over Brooklyn to Flatbush. I didn't expect much from the area Styron had immortalized in *Sophie's Choice* as symbolizing, among other things, a young writer's "hungriest aspirations" (3). Still, I stepped out at Church Avenue to take in "the pickle-fragrant air" while walking blocks of browning sycamores to 1506 Caton Avenue (33). In the "Reading My Father" essay, Al had warned that the Pink Palace was "long gone." I'd now find a "concrete box, where a Dr. Duddempudi no doubt conducts serious business despite her Seussian name," "the Kingdom of the Jews renationalized by more recent colonizers," and the air full of "truck exhaust."[9] But I had one pleasant surprise. While it's true that 1506 Caton Avenue as Styron would have known it doesn't exist, right by it, at 1522, stands what Styron would surely have described as "a large, rambling wood and stucco house of the nondescript variety erected, I should imagine, sometime before or just after the First World War." Like the Pink Palace, this too might once "have faded into the homely homogeneity of other large nondescript dwellings that bordered on Prospect Park," but it alone seems to have survived since the days Styron wrote about. Dark-windowed, camouflaged by enormous sycamores, barricaded by high fences as surely as Haus Höss, and with a NO TRESPASSING sign by the front door, on that sun-drenched day it really did suggest a place "isolated, remote, almost bucolic," and certainly it gave off, in seventies parlance, "bad vibrations" (45). It would have made as appropriate a setting for "A Rose for Emily" as a double for the Pink Palace. It was neither the house Styron had lived in nor painted pink, so perhaps I simply latched onto something meaningful in this otherwise thoroughly twenty-first-century neighborhood. But there again, since the house combined pale yellow wooden panels with a lilac framework, viewed through the dappled sunlight between the sycamores it indeed seemed a pale pink. Moreover, times and places, as we know—on earth and beyond, in our redshift perception of stars— tend to acquire a pinker tinge as they recede. The Pink Palace exists only in a work of fiction, and Styron could as easily have been inspired by a neighborhood house—by this house—as by 1506 Caton Avenue. Is the Pink Palace really "long gone"? Perhaps not, but maybe it was never pink, just remembered that way.

Vaguely satisfied, I walked around Prospect Park and the lake where Sophie fed the swan she called Tadeusz among shades of "gold-flecked green" beneath majestic trees "that loomed over meadow and rolling grass" as if "prepared to shelter a *fête champêtre* in a scene by Watteau or Fragonard," and imagined Sophie depositing herself beneath one with "a marvellous luncheon picnic" and choosing from her "sourly fragrant, opulent, heroic squander of food" (90–91). But I knew not only that there was no way into long gone, 1940s Brooklyn but that the Brooklyn moments of *Sophie's Choice* had never existed except in the mind's engagement through the power of words, rhythm, voice.

In truth, my Flatbush interlude was all but over. I did take the train out to Coney Island, and my memory of doing so is now infused with rereading the ending of the novel in manuscript at Duke. The final, published paragraphs seem so unified that I was surprised to find that between Stingo drinking himself "into a netherworld of hallucinations" and standing "beneath the blazing stars," Styron originally wrote of him "being mugged in an alleyway." This "rather civilized affair" costs Stingo "a clout on the side of the head" and four dollars. Inconsequential, it needed cutting, but it reminded me, as did all the insertions and deletions, of the fantastic effort of the long creative process that produced a novel that is now a part of our literary landscape. Still, like Stingo, if not "in the night's starry hours," I can at least say that "I stood on the beach alone" (514). Like Stingo, too, I found nothing at Coney Island itself to speak of but the sand and sea air—in this case balmy with an autumnal tinge—and it dawned on me what an image of lonesomeness I must have presented: a middle-aged man searching a foreign city for imagined events in time-altered settings involving people invented by a long-dead friend. I felt ready for that train ride south.[10]

"Ladies and gentlemen, we'll be in Washington, DC, in three to four minutes. Look around to see you have your belongings. Union Station, Washington, DC, next stop."

The guard's voice aroused me from my reminiscences, and I alighted at Union Station. Like Sophie and Stingo, though with no reason to pretend to be the Reverend Entwistle, I booked into a hotel near the "nation's Capitol" and within hearing of the distant "clangor and muffled hoots of the trains" (456–57). It's in the Hotel Congress that Sophie completes her horrific story and then, so soon after initiating Stingo into "the bitter bottom of things," fulfills his sexual longing (412). But I'd given little thought before this journey to the fact that between the revelations of the Choice and the sexual denouement Stingo and Sophie actually spend two hours sampling Washington. While he talks of peanuts they pass the floodlit White House. When she reminds him that she has with her the wedding clothes Nathan bought her, and Stingo finally sees the "intolerable distance" between them, they're on Constitution Avenue. Struggling for words, he sees over her shoulder the Washington Monument, "a blazing stiletto in the night sky" (492). They follow Fourteenth Street, "L'Enfant's stylish oblong spaces luminescent all around," but can't appreciate the city's "symmetry" or "air of wholesome and benevolent peace." Washington seems "paradigmatically American, sterile, geometrical, unreal." They end the evening at a table in Herzog's seafood restaurant at Eleventh Street and Maine Avenue, "overlooking the sparkling, moon-flecked Potomac" (493). Sophie sees for the first and last time "the dark shores" of Stingo's intended destination, Virginia, a place "removed by staggering dimensions of time and space from her own benighted, cursed," and nearly "incomprehensible history" (495).

What Styron does, in a way I failed to appreciate before attending to the details of setting, is reveal the chasm between the Enlightenment-born American ideal and the reality of hellish corners of history. Perhaps it's too big a leap to link that with 9/11 and the twenty-first century, or maybe such juxtaposition is inherently Styronian. For the essence of *Sophie's Choice* is this "ability," to borrow F. Scott Fitzgerald's phrase, "to hold two opposed ideas in the mind at the same time and still retain the ability to function,"[11] and to create art out of operatic contrast. Who would we be to judge whether Sophie is still in denial when, looking out over the moonlit Potomac, she tells Stingo that "nothing would have changed anything" (495)? From that point on, *Sophie's Choice* speeds toward its close and ends not with judgment day but "morning—excellent and fair" (515).

Styron's readers are unlikely to settle for reading over "getting out in the world and *living*," or windowless research rooms over sampling a city like Washington.[12] I spent most of each day in thought and shadow but eventually always ventured out into the world of movement and sunshine beneath the same deep blue, cloudless sky that accompanied my whole trip. It was a journey both inward and outward, and the two elements sustained each other. I contemplated both dusty manuscripts and the dazzling Capitol—the latter mildly reminiscent of the white building Nat Turner dreams of: a symbolic America, the heart of the ideals, the aspirations, the mystery, the contradictions—and spent the late afternoons walking, walking. A Rembrandt self-portrait in the National Gallery of Art became my metaphor to explain what I gained from visiting the settings of Styron's novels. Look at a photograph of that 1659 portrait and you see just one more of Rembrandt's versions of his extraordinarily humane, world-weary face. But the painting itself has a quality that no reproduction could capture. The paint of the face is so thick that if you look at it aslant, you see congealed flecks and lumps, but if you view it straight on, it's so miraculously modulated, so saturated, as to seem to be the face of Rembrandt himself gazing across the centuries. It was a jolting juxtaposition, and faintly embarrassing, to then enter a room where a guide was extolling a modernist painting of Mt. Katahdin, Maine, by Marsden Hartley, to two attentive but baffled students. But my point is merely that visiting the settings of Styron's novels reveals the flecks and lumps of his world in a way that a reading based purely on imagination of setting cannot replicate. To see the thing itself—person, setting, painting—is to experience a reality otherwise unavailable.

Soon enough I was on the train south from Washington. If the routes are the same, another curious parallel between American train travel in the early twenty-first century and in the era depicted in *Sophie's Choice* is the fact of delays. In *Sophie's Choice* Styron uses the power failure that causes the train to stall in Rahway to dramatize Stingo's fear that Sophie has left the train. On my journey, the delay had to do with a cost-cutting experiment whereby Amtrak joined two trains together, one bound for Durham and beyond and the other for Newport News. This involved the guards, in their white shirts, red ties, and peaked caps, struggling for two oil-smeared, grunt-and-curse hours to uncouple the carriages at Rocky Mount. So in fact we were still far from Durham when, at the scheduled arrival time of five, the car floor filled with sunlit yellow squares worthy of Edward Hopper's *Chair Car* (1965). Later still, I looked up from reading *Lie Down in Darkness* to find a sunset beyond the window like that in *Compartment C, Car 193* (1938), and finally lighting a fire across the horizon like that in *Railroad Sunset* (1929). The North Carolina night was almost upon us. The years of the Hopper paintings that reflected the dying light beyond the carriage seemed to draw me back from Styron's early middle age to youth to childhood. It was after seven, and downtown Durham a silhouette against the purple sky, before the Carolinian chugged to an unhurried halt.

After that day-long journey to Durham, ensconced in a time warp of a hotel beside a spindle of pines not far from Duke campus, I spent a week walking back and forth along the sandy curbs to the flint-stoned chapel and through the quad to the Perkins Library. I'd viewed the Duke collection just before meeting Styron, more than twenty years earlier. The archives, while much expanded, had a familiar feel, but whereas once I'd viewed the material in anticipation of meeting the author, now I was middle-aged, the author dead, and the sclerotic deposits of our acquaintance part of the record in the form of the letters I myself had written.

But what had most drawn me then still drew me now: the handwritten holographic manuscript of *Sophie's Choice*. Styron's readers know the litany: "Number 2 Venus Velvet pencils," "yellow legal pads" (35). But the holograph is an amazing monument to "doggedness," "self-discipline" (Jim West's words) and dedication to a vision. Reading the novel in manuscript is like reading a 985-page letter. The fascination it creates is partly in the fact that, excised pages aside, you are reading a virtually clean copy of the novel as published. But while it's true that "the drafts are nearly flawless," since "Styron perfected each sentence and paragraph in his mind before setting it to paper," the few insertions and deletions were precisely what I looked for. This was not least because of my awareness that Styron sought to saturate his work with multileveled allusions and meanings. So where Sophie watches her children through a window in wartime Warsaw while Wanda begs her to help the Resistance, Styron adds emphasis to her visceral emotion. His insertion that Sophie is "in the grip of an aching, devouring love" and beset by a "delicious and despairing" joy that sweeps "across her skin in a cool blaze" renders her love for her children a physical phenomenon. Another example of Styron intensifying the language to match Sophie's emotional response occurs in the Choice itself, where the description of her screams—"tormented angels never screeched so loudly above hell's pandemonium" (438)—is also an insertion. But elsewhere he deletes rather than inserts. An example of this occurs where Sophie originally says that she wishes she knew Jan was dead. Styron changed this so that the line becomes: "'It would almost be better that—' and her voice trailed off into silence."[13]

Of the several other interesting insertions and deletions, there are those that have to do with the need to provide or withhold information. For instance, Sophie's reticence about the fact that she had two children is dramatically important. The withholding of this information is evident early in the manuscript when Styron deletes the phrase "and Jan and Eva" from Sophie's comment that "the Germans came . . . and I had to go." Indeed, throughout there's the sense of Styron as his own reader. As he said in that 1954 *Paris Review* interview, each day he would pick up whatever he'd "been working on and read it through." Evidently this would often be the time for important insertions and deletions. One of the novel's most memorable phrases, for instance—that Nathan was "utterly, fatally glamorous"—is just such an insertion.[14]

While in Durham I hired a car and drove up through Courtland to Newport News. The weather was exceptionally hot that week, so setting out in the damp coolness of first light was pleasant enough, despite the prospect of a four-hundred-mile round trip. I didn't know what, if anything, I'd find, but the journey felt necessary. In Brooklyn I'd had Al Styron's comments to supplement the descriptions in Sophie's Choice. With Courtland I had Styron's 1965 essay "This Quiet Dust." If Al's essay warned that her father's Brooklyn had all but disappeared, Styron's essay equally suggested that the most I might hope for was to come away with some feeling that momentous events had occurred in the place. I was in for a couple of surprises.

I reached this strangely secluded and half-deserted town after a drive north along I-85 into Virginia. I'd left with the pink light of dawn splitting the pines, and it had taken the dew-soaked windshield two or three miles along the freeway to clear. Reaching Virginia within an hour, I soon turned east on Highway 58, between cotton fields in such full bloom that loose roadside clumps danced to the passing traffic. Nearing Courtland after a second hour, my apprehension grew. In 1985 Ray Lane, of the Washington Post, had written Styron that traveling through with his wife, he'd "felt something funny about the place." His wife had mentioned The Confessions of Nat Turner, which he had read on his return to Washington.[15] Courtland does indeed feel set apart. I crossed a rusting bridge with a derelict factory to the left and turned right onto a near-deserted Main Street. At first nothing seemed significant, but then, on the right, gleaming in the morning sun, loomed the Southampton Court House, where Nat Turner had been sentenced to hang. With its blinding white pillars and bright red brick, the building seemed too grand for its surroundings. Further down on the left I spotted the Southampton County Historical Society and pulled onto the gravel to take a closer look. It was shut. I headed back up Main Street to the Walter Cecil Rawls Library and asked about Nat Turner. The librarian, Betty Anne Beard, showed me the collection of books, and there, among them, was my own. I told Betty I'd written it. Would I sign it? Would I have my picture taken? Would I like to meet Rick Francis, the great-great-grandson of the actual Nathaniel Francis whom Styron had portrayed as a character in the novel? Sure, I said, not thinking about Styron's version of the man.

"He knows everything about Nat Turner," said Betty.

"Everything," said a man named James Glascock at the counter.

Rick, clerk to the County Court, agreed to meet me in half an hour. Meanwhile I could look at the Vaughan house, which had been brought out of the backwoods to be renovated behind the Historical Society.

I felt at first that it would be intrusive to climb into this medium-sized, two-storey house, mistaken by Styron in 1961 for the Whitehursts'. It had once been not just a home but the scene of horror: the place where the last murders occurred. But it was nothing now but wood hammered together. Besides, a ladder leaned invitingly where the front door would have been, and I wasn't likely to awaken any Vaughan ghosts from a morning lie-in. They would have to be mighty resilient to have withstood the relocation and restoration. So in I climbed, stepping over a pile of new planks to stand in the dust-flecked gloom. The house comprised two downstairs rooms, a staircase between them, immediately to the right inside the doorway, and one large space in the eaves above. But there were only wooden supports for inner walls, so how the house would actually have looked in 1831 was hard to envisage. Much of the wood had been replaced with chipboard, and light new wood interspersed the beams. Through an open window lay a sunlit meadow. Rays streamed through gaps in the panels. Somewhere a dog barked. A broken window lay against a wall. I climbed the stairs and ducked between the rafters half expecting bloodstains or axe wounds to the wood. A fragment of newspaper hung from the end wall. "The Pip[--] Chapter 9," I read. "[--]adad's eyes widened at John Severance's unusual method of seeking an introduction."[16] Not a little spooked, I clambered down and out of the house, leaving it to the dust motes.

While I waited to meet Rick Francis by the Court House in the sunny breeze of the deserted Main Street, I leafed through *The Confessions of Nat Turner* to remind myself just how Styron had described this man's ancestors. While slave owners came in numerous varieties, Nat tells us, from "the saintly" to the "barely tolerable," with just "a few who were unconditionally monstrous," none were more "bloodthirsty" than Nathaniel Francis, a "hairless man with a swinish squint." His wife, Lavinia, is "a slab-faced brute of a person with a huge goiter and, through the baggy men's work clothes she customarily wore, the barely discernible outlines of a woman." "A winning couple," we are told (299). Worse still, "perhaps in reaction to his wife or (it seems more persuasive to believe) goaded by her after or before or during whatever unimaginable scenes took place upon their sagging bedstead, Francis achieved pleasure by getting drunk at more or less regular intervals and beating his Negroes ruthlessly with a flexible wooden cane wrapped in alligator hide" (299–300). Francis was away during the insurrection, but Nat, in telling this, judges him "almost the only white man in the county who owned a truly illustrious reputation for cruelty" (416).

Out came Rick Francis. Tall with graying brown hair, he put out his large hand, greeted me, and fetched me a soda and a beaker of peanuts.

"Have a seat," he said, tapping a pile of papers on his desk. "All this is Nat Turner." He pointed to filing cabinets. "And all that." Lastly he indicated bookshelves. "All Nat Turner. So what's your interest in him?"

I offered my explanation while Rick quaffed his own beaker of peanuts. Before I finished my response he'd put the beaker down. I had the feeling that a cloud had crossed the sky-blue day.

"And what's your view on it all?"

I told him. "And yours?"

"On Styron?" He grunted. "He's a sonofabitch is what he is."

"Well, he's dead."

"He's still a sonofabitch. He slandered Nat Turner and he slandered my ancestors. If it hadn't been for Henry Tragle and his book on Turner, my impression of them would be a lot different. I don't have any problem with Tragle, or Stephen B. Oates, or any of them folk, but Styron?" He took a gulp of soda. "I wasn't here, of course, but I'm told he came down and looked at the papers for about a half-hour and then he went off and wrote that stuff."

"He wrote a novel, not history," I said.

"I grant you that," said Rick, swigging his soda again, "but he should have stuck to the historical record. It was sloppy research."

"Do you think Turner had a wife?"

"Well, there's no evidence until after the fact, but Nat Turner would have protected his wife in the confessions. Reese mentions a wife name of Cherry. In the Richmond papers there's an anonymous piece about her being put under the lash, but anyway, there's no evidence whatsoever for all that stuff about Margaret Whitehead."

Nor would there be, I thought, given that if it existed it would hardly have been something he'd have divulged to Thomas Gray as the recorder of his confessions. Had he somehow ended up doing so, the white lawyer in turn would never have included any overt reference to such interracial attraction. Besides, Styron's reasons for not giving Nat a wife seemed aesthetic rather than political or pernicious. A note on an endpaper of the Drewry book (reproduced in West's biography) reads, "perhaps Nat had seen his wife seduced by Travis," one of his owners.

Styron thus considered it but chose to portray Nat, as noted elsewhere, along the lines of Erikson's psychological study *Young Man Luther*.[17] Still, intense responses are always interesting, and Rick Francis was certainly not indifferent to Styron and his novel.

"What would you say to Styron," I asked him, "if he were here now?"

Rick smiled. "Well. Ha ha," he laughed grimly, swigging his beaker of peanuts as if it were a drink. "What would I say?" He shook his head and crunched. Just as Styron had filled gaps in the original *Confessions,* so I'd have to use my imagination. We sat for a moment in silence. "See, what you have to understand is that we Virginians are up on our heritage. We feel loyalty and anger about someone attacking a person's name. We're still fighting Appomattox."

"As Faulkner said, there is no such thing as *was,*" I ventured.

Rick took another swig of peanuts. "Yup," he chomped.

I returned to Nat Turner. "Where was the tree they hanged him from?"

"A couple of miles away; there's barely a dent in the ground."

Rick gave Nat Turner tours, so I asked about that. "If I had time to take the tour, what would I see? How long would it take?"

"About four hours. They covered twenty-seven miles that first full day of the twenty-second August. Drewry has his add-ons, but he's pretty accurate about chronology. It's a roundabout route because Nat Turner went to houses he was familiar with, perhaps to recruit slaves he knew."

"And is there much to see?"

"Not a lot. We're not even sure of all the locations. We have a committee to confirm some of them, or try to."

"And the Vaughan house," I said. "Have you been instrumental in bringing that into Courtland?"

"I have," he said. "People had been taking wood from it and the farmer was going to pull it down, so we brought it into town."

"And this was the house Styron wrote about in 'This Quiet Dust?'"

"Yeah, and was wrong about. Sherriff Ryland Brooks showed him around. He's still hereabouts. He's a nice guy, but he didn't know much."

"So nothing could persuade you that Styron's approach had any validity or that you might have had a dialogue about the subject?"

"Like I say, I grant you that he wrote a novel, but I want nothing to do with anything connected with Styron."

"Yet his novel brought me here," I said. "We're sitting here talking about Nat Turner because of it. That's not a bad thing, is it?"

"I would rather have Nat Turner sitting where you are now than

William Styron. I would shake Nat Turner's hand before I would shake Styron's. I have no time for him, none whatsoever."

I needed to get back on the road to Newport News. We stood up and shook hands, and I drove on, not displeased with my discoveries and encounters. My overall impression of Rick Francis was that he was a man loyal to his family and his family name. Adamant as he seemed in his view of Styron and the novel, such indignation is understandable. As with Sophie's sighting of the platform of Auschwitz and the inverse AR-BEIT MACHT FREI sign from Haus Höss, Styron used artistic license. Indeed, I later checked on what was known of Nathaniel and Lavinia and found that while he survived because, alerted to something amiss, he'd gone to his sister's house, Lavinia had been eight months pregnant with the first of nine children. A slave had hidden her between the roof's gables. The Francis family Bible verifies that she gave birth a month later.[18]

On my way to Newport News I pondered the ambiguities of fact and fiction. On the one hand it may be true that Styron came to Courtland and spent little time with the public records. On the other hand it's mere hearsay. There are reports that Nat Turner had a wife, but there's no record of her from the time. Styron discarded evidence, but he was writing a novel. It's true that had Nat had a wife, any mention would have endangered her, for reprisals were precisely what the slave owners would have sought. But it's equally true that if Nat had feelings for Margaret, he would hardly have divulged them. Such arguments and counterarguments take on the dimensions of religious debate about the unknowable: there is no evidence that God exists but no proof that he doesn't, just as, to use Bertrand Russell's analogy, there's no evidence either way as to whether a teapot is "revolving around the sun in an elliptical orbit."[19] Cherry, as I'll call her, may have existed, because there's no proof that she didn't and reason to suppose why that evidence is missing. Likewise, Nat and Margaret's mutual attraction—c'est la même chose. Styron's version of Nathaniel Francis would seem to have virtually no connection to the historical figure, but merely to draw on the testimony of former slaves like Frederick Douglass, to depict one kind of owner. Perhaps Styron should indeed be faulted for disparaging the name of an actual person, but I left Courtland feeling that I had at least some inkling of how a nineteenth-century white Virginian might have seen the world.

Newport News is not somewhere you're drawn to by reputation. You're either born there or have family in the city or get posted or employed there. Styron's reasons, as a fourteen-year-old, for wanting "*to get the hell away*" were multiple, if his comments in *This Quiet Dust* are anything to go by (57). It was the place of his mother's excruciating death. It was also where his stepmother, Elizabeth, caused him another kind of grief. But it was also his birthplace, his beloved father's home, and the source of his identity. In his fiction, Newport News/Port Warwick is either the setting of family, and of grief, or the place one leaves, or the place Stingo is alternatively homesick for or nostalgic about. But it was not a place to pursue youthful ambition, and even if Styron or any of his characters were to one day return, first and foremost he, and they, had to get out.

Myself, I had a little trouble getting in. That's to say that my arrival in the leafy neighborhood of Hilton Village, adjacent to the James, took some time. Where Styron introduces us to his urban landscape by way of the train ride into *Lie Down in Darkness,* I drove in over the James River Bridge and, imagining the city to be a rather small town that would now have Styron Square at its center, headed for downtown. Once again, I'd done inadequate homework. Hilton Village is north of the bridge, so I quickly learned something of the city's long, narrow geography by driving it. Situated on a peninsular between the James and the Atlantic, it's only a few miles across but twenty-six miles from the north of the city south to the shipyards where Styron's father worked. Perhaps it was always a curious place, but there's a startling contrast between downtown and uptown. Downtown is Main Street America, but set against the "jagged silhouettes of cranes," which Styron in "My Father's House" describes as reminiscent of "the shapes of prehistoric birds" he'd seen in *The Book of Knowledge* (132). On the way uptown, before the tree-lined highway takes you out of the city, is the riverside interlude of Hilton Village and the new town of Port Warwick, named after the city as it's known in *Lie Down in Darkness.*

Thanks to kind folk at a downtown gas station who wrestled with my map as the sea breeze whipped around the forecourt in the high-noon sunshine, I finally reached Hilton Village. Memory being a merging of fact and imagination, I took notes and photographs. Quigley's store, as Styron calls it in "A Tidewater Morning," is now a restaurant. The red brick elementary school still looks out on the James, and you can locate the James River Country Club, where some *Lie Down in Darkness* scenes are set; the movie theater where he worked; and the old C&O train station, where, in his imagination, the mourners meet Peyton's coffin. Hilton Village itself is bucolic, small-town America, its streets lined with trees. The modest house at 56 Hopkins Street reminded me of Flaubert's

comment on the smallness of Emma's house and the immensity of her
dreams. It must have been dreadful to live there as an only child with
a dying mother and a distraught father. The boy would have been, like
Robert Frost, a swinger of birches, or whatever he could find, seeking
escape in the imagination, literature, cinema, but also in the short walk
past the school to the small beach and the sun-bleached jetty that takes
you out onto the expanse of the James.

I wandered out along the jetty past locals fishing, the estuary
breeze blew in across the sparkling river. The water at the end was only
a few feet deep, perfect to swim in. To the left the bluish cranes leaned
against the horizon. The James River Bridge arced across like a stroke
of gray watercolor. But beyond the vista, as Styron writes in *This Quiet
Dust*, shimmers "the river's prodigious history." Here Styron would have
been faced with "the absolute and dominating physical presence" of his
youth, and the history of this part of America would have sparked his
mind (315). Caressed by the mild air, I sensed both how it dawned on
him that he had "*to get the hell away*" and yet how this environment
imprinted his "hyperintense sense of place" (57).

I ended my visit to the city with a dreamlike stroll around Port
Warwick. It was as if I had experienced the timeline of Styron's life,
from his birthplace to the community through which his hometown has
memorialized him. He knew that a writer's posterity is not a given, and
no doubt many who live there never wonder about the man for whom
Styron Square was named. Equally, many may not know the significance
of Herman Melville Avenue, Emily Dickinson Square, James Baldwin
Street, Philip Roth Street, and Nat Turner Boulevard, to note some of
the places Styron personally named. But it seemed a good place to leave
him, surrounded by his own literary heroes, one or two literary friends,
and with his name entwined on the street signs with Nat Turner's. It was
time to drive the three or more hours home through the sunset and into,
as Styron puts it in the final words of *Lie Down in Darkness*, the oncoming night.

Driving back over the James, past Courtland and down into North
Carolina, I thought of Styron and his world. This book would be not just
a critical study but an act of remembrance, an attempt to express the
significance of his work in terms of actual life rather than as something
set apart for literary study. The library stacks at Columbia, Duke, or any
library are a somber reminder that, for all the fervor of composition,
books line up like gravestones, many unvisited for years. Indeed, this

was one reason why I was pleased to see *The Novels of William Styron* in the Courtland library. Styron's writing is alive in the act of reading and rereading, and in that precious activity of discussion and reflection beyond as well as within universities.

The image that resonated as I drove away was of the water lapping the jetty. It reminded me of Styron's beloved Martha's Vineyard, just as that place reminded him of Hilton Village in what, in "My Father's House," he calls "the cramped little bungalow of my childhood" (114). The September days I spent before and after this visit in Cass's home state of North Carolina were as blazing as the weather in which he and Peter discuss events two years after Sambuco. There was nothing much to look for there. I suppose I might have found my way to the Ashley River or the Oregon Inlet. But I had more papers to examine at Duke, after which I'd return to New York, not to find the nonexistent Nathan and Sophie in their death's embrace in the nonexistent Yetta Zimmerman's nonexistent Pink Palace, but merely to fly home.

As for visiting settings, a fuller appreciation of any novel wedded distinctly to place is likely if one has that opportunity. Reading *Wuthering Heights* is never the same after a (preferably wintry, rainswept) trip to Haworth Parsonage, the graveyard, the moors. The same is true with St. Petersburg for *Crime and Punishment*, Paris for *L'Assommoir*, Eastwood for *Sons and Lovers,* or Boston's North Shore for the novels of John Updike. Witnessing Styron's settings adds immeasurably to one's sense of place in his work. Art can be appreciated without such insight. After all, we can't return to earlier eras, and we can't go everywhere even if we wanted or needed to. But especially when there's a historical dimension, so that the real and the fictional intertwine, it adds immeasurably to the reading experience.

On the train back from Durham up to Washington I reread *A Tidewater Morning*. I have already commented on its first story, "Love Day," but the other two felt pertinent since both have to do with homecoming. "You can't go home again," asserts the title of Styron's early influence, Thomas Wolfe's posthumously published novel (1940). But we make enormous efforts to do so, whether in writing, reflecting, remembering, or reading, or through physical journeys. Like migrating birds, we seem hardwired to return. Written during the composition of *Sophie's Choice*, the second tale, "Shadrach," is about a former slave who returns home at age ninety-nine to die. As recalled from childhood by Paul Whitehurst, Shadrach manages to tell his story to Paul and his friends, the

Dabney family, whose forebears owned him in youth. The Dabneys have long since lost all wealth and gentility but still possess a modest piece of land. Shadrach, they gather, has made it "home to Ole Virginny," the best part of a century after being sold in the 1850s, so as to "be buried on 'Dabney ground.'" Moreover, just as he probably "journeyed those six hundred miles to Alabama on foot and in the company of God knows how many other black slaves, linked together by chains," so he seems to have mostly walked his way back (56).

At Shadrach's request the Dabneys take him to a millpond. Pondering this ancient man gazing at the Dabney children swimming, Paul thinks maybe Shadrach, after years of "poverty and hunger and humiliation, of the crosses burning in the night, the random butchery and, above all, the unending dread," might have made his "solitary journey from the Deep South" in search of this pond and a "glimpse of childhood." He senses that Shadrach now "recaptured perhaps the one, pure, un-troubled moment in his life" (73–74). For the tale, even as it expresses this yearning to glimpse the precious past, is about the brutality of life. When Shadrach dies, his request to be buried on Dabney land proves illegal. The impoverished Dabneys must pay to have him buried at "one of the colored churches" by a "colored undertaker" (69). "Death ain't nothin' to be afraid about," says Mr. Dabney. "It's life that's fearsome. *Life!*" (76).

"Shadrach" is also another meditation on time. For Paul, Shadrach is a link with Virginia's slave-owning past. He doesn't discount the pos-sibility that these were Shadrach's "happy years." But the admission that "this incredible pilgrimage" might have more to do with an instinct to revisit a moment of childhood happiness perhaps wards off accusations that the story of a former slave returning home to "Ole Virginny" risks sentimentalizing Virginia slavery as relatively benign (56). Moreover, like *The Confessions of Nat Turner,* the story does document the economic history of the Tidewater, "that primordial American demesne where the land was sucked dry by tobacco" (45). It also documents the racism of the 1930s South, whereby, even in death—when, as Mr. Dabney notes, as much of race as of where you're buried, "nobody knows the differ-ence"—segregation was the law (78).

Mr. Dabney's sentiment that life is "fearsome" hovers behind much of Styron's writing, but the source of his awareness is laid bare in "A Tidewater Morning" like a long-hidden wound exposed to salty, seashore wind. The story deals directly with memories at the heart of Styron's pre-occupation with the art of self-realization. I began this study by looking at his essays, which are the closest we get to his direct voice, unrefracted by the needs of fiction. But I also suggested that the voice of his later fiction and that of his essays intersect. "A Tidewater Morning" is a case in point. Its importance lies not just as Styron's equivalent, if you will, of Tolstoy's "The Death of Ivan Illych" or Kafka's "Metamorphosis"—a distillation of a worldview—but as his most direct expression of the tragedy of his mother's death, which haunts his fiction from first to last. It's his final statement on his own psychology as a child of the Depression, who grows up in a household dominated by terminal illness and then grief, and then war, including the probability of his own involvement and likely demise. In this the story brings his career full circle, merging the author in his twilight years with the child whose early experience of "the bitter bottom of things" produced the impetus for his literary achievement.

Rereading "A Tidewater Morning," I reflected upon how much one forgets. From earlier readings I recalled the newspaper route, the setting, the mother's pain, the father's anguish, the onset of war. But there is much more. The setting is beautifully evoked. The fan's "puny puff of air," so ineffective yet dutiful a gesture against the smothering climate, comes to represent the human struggle to barricade against the elements (88). The southern gothic is in evidence: the mother's nurse has twelve digits; a horror-film scream captures the awfulness of a loved one's slide toward death; Paul feels as if his room is "a dungeon" (92). The start of war, evoked and ironized by the dying mother's longing for Europe, is there again at the end, when Paul recalls the day to have been the eleventh of September, 1938, a time when, in the newspaper headlines, "Prague Awaits Hitler's Ultimatum" (142). Finally there is, in the juxtaposition of Montaigne, Nietzsche, and Schopenhauer set against religious dogma, the evocation of a world faced without hope even as the religious impulse helps to sustain the spirit, as in the dogged determination of the father coercing his son into chanting Psalm 46: "*Yet alone shall I prevail*" (142).

Like "Shadrach" (and much of Styron's short fiction), "A Tidewater Morning" is the story of a young person realizing the inescapability of death. But this story in particular touches the pulse of all Styron's work not just in its depiction of his harrowing childhood experience but in Paul's discovery of what is and is not worthwhile. We witness the tiny family dissolving amid the juxtaposition of mean-spiritedness, bickering, and the profundity of love. We see Quigley's sordid kingdom, which seems to represent the kind of petty, pointless meanness one can find anywhere. We feel the sticky heat of the Tidewater summer and the agony of grief. But we also see what sustains human dignity in the face of a mindless universe and a finite time on earth. For "A Tidewater Morning" is also about the power of art, and human relations, to prevail against horror. The main sources of survival here are words, music, and the father's desperate determination to shield and nurture his son. Like Pauline Styron, Paul's mother is a singer, and the father's response to her death is a diatribe against religion, accompanied by his defiant playing of Brahms. He turns the music up so high that its "hymnal sonorities" envelop everything: "the busts of Schubert and Brahms and Beethoven, the portraits of the great virtuosi," even an image of Paul's mother, "captured in a flicker of bygone merriment." The sound shakes Paul "with such ferocity" that he thinks he sees her "seated at the piano by the window, her voice raised exultantly as it had been long before" (140). Synthetic as the music is (it ends, and the father removes the needle), and feeble beyond its effect on the human spirit, it's at least human sound—and the father's gesture a human stand—against the silence of eternity.

The final words of the story are the final words of fiction that Styron published in book form in his lifetime. "We each devise our means of escape from the intolerable," he writes at the start of the last paragraph. In the paragraph itself, Paul and Styron become one in a kind of into- and out-of-body experience. "I let myself be elevated slowly up and up through the room's hot, dense shadows," says Paul. "And there, floating abreast of the immortal musicians, I was able to gaze down impassively on the grieving father and the boy pinioned in his arms" (142). This is the transcending power of art. The artist's function, Styron told me, is to stand apart. That's the soul of art: the proof that there is a life, of sorts, beyond the physical life. The mind, at least, can travel back through time and relive and reshape events, and so reread the past. Memory is rereading, reliving, reinterpreting the palimpsest of time. And this final image really is at the core of Styron's work. For in a way the older man holding the younger man is both father and son, and the older man holding his young self in memory. It's an image of youth and age, of the beginnings and endings of life, and of reconciliation between the two.

So the end of "A Tidewater Morning" returns us to the beginning. Father and son are together, as are the older Styron and his boyhood self at the very moment that propelled him into his novelistic universe. The older man peers into his own origins as an artist. "Mothers and fathers—they're at the core of one's own life somehow," we recall Sophie saying (462). Ghosts and memories: I see myself before the house on Hopkins Street, just as I see myself before what was once my own parents' home, where strangers now live. "I Years had been from Home," wrote Dickinson on behalf of us all.[20] But I also think of the "In Vineyard Haven" vignette that ends *Havanas in Camelot* and that "soft collision" of "harbor and shore" (161). Even as my train trundles into Washington, in my imagination I am beside the James as well as up there in Massachusetts, on Martha's Vineyard. I see Styron on his Vineyard Haven lawn, grunting at my suggestion that he's a distinguished man of letters. But his contribution is real. As with Stendhal, Flaubert, Dostoevsky, his few books have qualities that make quantity irrelevant.

In Washington I completed my research at the Library of Congress and found, in the final box, an unpublished essay—perhaps written as a lecture or address—in which Styron placed his work in a literary context. The essay felt tentative and incomplete but was interesting enough for me to copy pages to reread on the train from Washington up to New York. Its date is uncertain, but its location and sixties references suggest that Styron wrote it soon after *Set This House on Fire*. I contemplated his meandering views across the years as if he were my companion on the Carolinian. Given his conversational style, and that I was reading his handwriting, it felt like another letter, albeit one that reached my doorstep half a century after it was mailed. I listened with middle-aged patience as this thirty-something man sought to contextualize his vision before a word of *Sophie's Choice*, and in all likelihood *The Confessions of Nat Turner*, had been written.

Entitled "State of Writers in America," it melds a concern with the nature of good and evil with an interest in existentialism and responsibility. It begins with a comment on Paul Goodman's *Growing Up Absurd* (1960) as a way into discussing the Beat movement in terms of both its less impressive qualities ("its indifference to learning, its general tackiness and aimlessness, its spurious religiosity and ignorance of tradition, its bad art and so forth") and its more impressive ones ("self-reliance," "the quality of action as opposed to reflection," and its "relatively healthy and easy-going sexuality"). For Styron, at least in this unpublished essay, the Beats were "the embodiment of our national love principle, our national need for love." He then segues into an argument that while America doesn't want or need to be a nation with a creed based on hatred, its culture perhaps too often becomes unbalanced toward the need for love, as if hatred were not a facet of human nature. To love, argues

Styron, one needs to know about hatred. By way of existentialism, he later compares Dostoevsky and Camus. Concluding that the final section of *Crime and Punishment* is a cheat, he contrasts Raskolnikov's redemption through Christian love with the end of *L'Etranger,* where there's really *no* hope of reconciliation between humans and an evidently indifferent universe. He forgives Dostoevsky because we have, after all, Raskolnikov's personal drama. But he argues that serious modern writing cannot ignore Camus's basic bare truth about the human condition. Happiness, he seems to decide, must be earned through confronting the fact that individual acts make a difference.[21]

The argument is a little torturous, but this "mind in the act of finding" (to use a Wallace Stevens phrase) was precisely what drew me.[22] There was Styron, in the early sixties, situating himself in the great river of literature with regard not merely to his American forebears and contemporaries but also to the wider realm of European writing. But what, now that his writing is done, is there to say about his influence on his peers and about his literary legacy? Like his hero in this regard, Orwell, Styron is so individualistic a writer that it might at first seem incongruous to think in such a way. His idiosyncratic stance has not always served him well when it comes to critical response, for in the short term critics try to make canons and for a number of reasons already touched on Styron's work is often seen as tangential. As Henry Louis Gates Jr. writes, he perhaps "deserves a greater critical presence than he has." But as Gates also writes, in *Loose Canons,* "it is a commonplace of contemporary criticism to say that scholars make canons," when "just as often, writers make canons, too, both by critical revaluation and by reclamation through revision." I will thus end with observations on how, with Styron, that process has already begun. He has a clear legacy as a role model to the likes of Dunne, McGinniss, Mewshaw, and Harington, but there's also the question of his impact on his contemporaries. Some of these, like John Updike and Philip Roth, were his friends; others, like Saul Bellow, Joyce Carol Oates, and Don DeLillo, were acquaintances; while Norman Mailer, we know, saw himself as a rival.[23]   There is little specific to be said about any connections between Styron's work and that of Bellow or Updike, so different are they as writers from him. The writing of Mailer, Oates, Roth, and DeLillo, on the other hand, shares with his a willingness to portray historical figures in a fearless and direct fashion. Hence Mailer's *Armies of the Night* uses fictional techniques to present a factual event, while *The Executioner's Song* depicts the 1977 execution of Gary Gilmore in Utah. There are also such books as *Marilyn:*

A *Biography* and *Portrait of Picasso as a Young Man.* Oates's first foray into the hybrid realm between fact and fiction begins with her author's note for her 1969 novel, *them,* although her declaration that the characters she portrays as living in Detroit at the time of the 1967 riots turned out to be fabrication. In later years, however, she's been bolder, with her portrayal of "The Senator" and an intern named Kelly Kelleher in *Black Water,* a novella self-evidently about Ted Kennedy, Mary Jo Kopechne, and Chappaquiddick; with *Blonde,* about Monroe ("Norma Jeane"), John F. Kennedy ("The President"), and Arthur Miller ("The Playwright"); and other fact-based novels such as *Zombie* and *My Sister, My Love: The Intimate Story of Skyler Rampike.* Oates in particular, shares with Styron that audacity of stealing directly from documented events and portraying actual people. With Roth's, Styron's work shares a fascination with history, too, although Roth is less given to the kind of direct interventions we see with Styron and Oates. But however differently they deal with them, Roth's *The Ghost Writer* is a miniature version of some of the tensions existent in *Sophie's Choice,* just as *The Plot Against America,* which imagines Charles Lindberg becoming a Fascist American president during World War II, reveals a similar sense that significant fiction often grows from contemplation of historical possibilities. Finally, in this regard one might think of DeLillo, in that *Libra,* about Lee Harvey Oswald, and *Underworld,* his Cold War novel, are examples of an American contemporary writer wading in the river of history.

While such family resemblances are not in themselves necessarily examples of influence, the work of two writers, Cormac McCarthy and Toni Morrison, illustrates that Styron's influence on other major writers is already palpable. In McCarthy you can hear rhythms and voices common to southern writing, to be sure, but also shades of Styron. As Harold Bloom notes, the link between Styron and McCarthy is Faulkner. In Bloom's view, McCarthy only broke out from under Faulkner with his 1985 novel, *Blood Meridian.* In truth, McCarthy's style is at times Styronian. This is not obvious on a casual read, since *Blood Meridian* is so different and irredeemably darker than anything Styron ever wrote. But even McCarthy, in *The Road*—which also has Styronian echoes in being a meditation on history and in its treatment of the father-son theme—has since let glimmers of light into the darkest of worldviews.

Indeed, home in on specific passages of *The Road* and McCarthy echoes Styron in subject and style. In depicting a world that's deserted, past, ghostlike, McCarthy's details and rhythms suggest *The Confessions of Nat Turner* as a source. For example, Styron writes of a room "dismantled of everything that could be moved—of crystal chandeliers and grandfather's clock, carpets and piano and sideboards and chairs," and of how "only a lofty mirror, webbed with minute cracklings and bluish with age, embedded immovably between upright columns against the wall, remained as sure proof of past habitation: its blurred and liquid depths reflected the far side of the hall, and there four immaculate rectangles marked the vanished portraits of Turner forebears" (230–31). One can compare this with a passage typical of *The Road*, this one involving father and son in a deserted house.

> They stood listening. Then they stepped back in a broad foyer floored in a domino of black and white marble tiles. A broad staircase ascending. Fine Morris paper on the walls, waterstained and sagging. The plaster ceiling was bellied in great swags and the yellowed dentil molding was bowed and sprung from the upper walls. To the left through the doorway stood a large walnut buffet in what must have been the diningroom. The doors and the drawers were gone but the rest of it was too large to burn.[24]

It's not so surprising that *The Road* should reprise the contemplative scenes of *The Confessions of Nat Turner*. Both novels are about that slow process of appreciating the world. Both pursue a need for contemplation. Styron's pervasive emphasis on silence signals the novel as meditation. It's a kind of floating back and forth in historical time from before humanity to beyond humanity. When Nat is alone at a deserted Turner's Mill, the emphasis on silence recurs. There's "no wind," and "the trees in the surrounding woods" are so quiet that "this very stillness" seems "a solid mass stretching out on all sides" of him "in perfect circumference to the last boundaries of the world." He feels as if "nothing but this still and ruined plantation" exists and the mill is "the very heart of the universe," and Nat himself "the master not alone of its being at the present instant but of all its past and hence all its memories" (232).

McCarthy follows Styron in theme. Like Nat Turner, his father and son are "between two existences" (299). Hence, when Samuel Turner says that "all this we see here will be gone too, and the mill wheel will crumble away and the wind will whistle at night through these deserted halls" (220), it could almost be a sentence from *The Road*. But McCarthy also follows Styron in sound and tone. The latter's description of a dying culture, dramatized by the collapse of Turner's Mill, contains rhythms evident in McCarthy. Styron writes:

Slowly these sounds diminished, faded, became still altogether, and the fields and rutted roadways lay as starkly deserted as a place ravaged by the plague: weeds and brambles invaded the cornfields and the meadows; sills, frames, and doors fell apart in the empty outbuildings. At night, where once glowing hearths lit each cabin down the slope, now all lay in suffocating dark like the departure of the campfires of some army on the plains of Israel. (225)

In Styron's wake, McCarthy describes a journey through a similarly benighted land:

By then all stores of food had given out and murder was everywhere upon the land. The world soon to be largely populated by men who would eat your children in front of your eyes and the cities themselves held by cores of blackened looters who tunneled among the ruins and crawled from the rubble white of tooth and eye carrying charred and anonymous tins of food in nylon nets like shoppers in the commissaries of hell.[25]

Not only is there an evocation of a ruined land (as there often is in McCarthy) but a similar "voice" is evident. There is, too, that same dwelling on specific detail that's then linked, by both writers, to a vaster canvas through a biblical illusion. While Nat looks forward to the future, we look back to the past and say: indeed, it was so, it happened, just as our own world will dissolve into a history imagined by future generations. In turn, McCarthy anticipates a future that will one day be past and in that present moment evokes the past that has gone. This is literature in the river of history, meditating both on its own moment and on the past and future: "adrift," to reprise *The Confessions of Nat Turner*, between that which is past and "those things yet to come" (228).

As noted, one might argue that the connection between Styron and McCarthy is largely about both being southern writers with that common link of Faulkner, a penchant for rhetoric and a feeling for place. The influence of Styron on Toni Morrison, though, is rather different. It's not an influence of rhythm or even of structure beyond a certain point, but of subject matter. Morrison's only written reference to Styron is in *Playing in the Dark*, where she describes Nat's dream of "the sealed white structure" as Styron's "allegorical figuration of the defeat of the enterprise he is engaged in: penetration of the black-white barrier." But her comments in person reveal her regard for him as a writer. In 1988 she said that she was "very pleased" with his attempt to dramatize Nat Turner's life. "He went into territory that *is* his territory," and "that was admirable." She said she might have done some things differently but that that didn't matter. The question, therefore, is not just how Morrison did in fact do things differently but also what elements their books have in common.[26]

Perhaps it's the case that their novels of slavery can stand like bookends. Indeed, in a way, my rereading of *The Confessions of Nat Turner* has been as much in light of *Beloved* as my comments on *Beloved* evolve from rereading Styron. Despite having Faulkner as their common forefather, their styles could hardly contrast more. They may share his circling around and into subject matter, but Styron models his narrative on the kind of voice Douglass, Washington, and Du Bois use to address a mainly white audience. Anachronistic as this may feel for some, Styron was surely wise to do this. It's always implicit, through Gray, that the novel is in dialogue with a white consciousness. He could hardly have done as Morrison does and write in the vernacular. But the respect in which the novels complement one another is as meditations on past and present. Returning to Styron's novel with close knowledge of *Beloved*, perhaps one is bound to take more notice of the ghost theme. Nat and Beloved herself provoke equally mixed responses. Both are victims who turn violent. Both haunt the present. Both materialize by way of water, with Nat drifting into the novel on a small boat and Beloved rising from a river. Both novels too use a grave marker to memorialize the victims of slavery; Nat's grandmother's foreshortened name, "Tig," is succeeded by Sethe's inability to pay the stonecutter for the full phrase, "Dearly Beloved" (208).

But in terms of the treatment of history the influence on *Beloved* comes less from *The Confessions of Nat Turner* than from *Sophie's Choice.* For if voice is Styron's legacy with McCarthy, with *Beloved* it is story and theme, and on that score Morrison's novel would surely not exist in the form it does if not for *Sophie's Choice*. The parallels may be disguised initially simply because the authors' ways of telling a story are so utterly different, but they are demonstrably there. Indeed, early in *Sophie's Choice* there is even a passage that just might, consciously or otherwise, have inspired Morrison, who in reading Styron's attempts to link this European atrocity with American slavery must surely have thought all the more about producing her own novel of slavery. In the passage, the narrator is describing his slave-owning grandmother in order to explain how he came to receive part of the proceeds of Artiste's sale, buried before the Yankee invasion. "Born in 1848," he writes, "my *own* grandmother at the age of thirteen possessed two small Negro handmaidens only a little younger than herself, regarding them as beloved chattel all through the years of the Civil War, despite Abraham Lincoln and the articles of emancipation. I say 'beloved' with no irony because I'm certain that she did very much love them" (28). Just as Beloved's foreshortened gravestone name echoes Nat's grandmother's, so Morrison, coincidentally or otherwise echoing this passage, would seem to have picked up and run with the phrase *beloved.*

But this is an incidental, if intriguing, suggestion of a profounder link. The parallels between the actual stories show that Styron's influence is incontestable. Like Styron's, Morrison's approach is the personal within the historical. As in *Sophie's Choice,* a mother's choice dramatizes the true ghastliness of a historical atrocity. That choice can again be construed as deliberate sacrifice for which the mother suffers debilitating guilt. Again we have men (Stingo, Nathan, Paul D) ambiguously involved in her struggle for recovery and a younger person (Stingo and Denver, respectively) coming to understand something of the horrors of history. Both novels involve not just people haunted by past actions but ghost stories of the resurrected dead (whether that's Sophie as Stingo's mother, Stingo as Sophie's son, or the "golem," Nathan, or with Morrison, Beloved as the ghost of the child or of black Americans' consuming past). Not unlike Sophie, Beloved is a flesh-and-blood phantom. Both novels mix sensual pleasure with physical horror; where the wounded Sophie seeks solace with Nathan and then has sex with Stingo, so the wounded Sethe and Paul D seek sexual gratification, while Beloved then seduces Paul D. Albeit for very different reasons, Sophie and Beloved are even connected (one of the more unusual links in literature) in that they lose their teeth. Even Morrison's dedication to "sixty million and more" feels comparable. So while *Sophie's Choice* and *Beloved* no more read like similar novels than do others where the latter is in fact influenced by the former (*Madame Bovary* and *Anna Karenina; The Trial* and *L'Etranger; Ulysses* and *The Sound and the Fury*), analysis of the bones of each novel makes the genetic link abundantly clear.

Such, at least, was how I thought about Styron's legacy as the train trundled north out of Newark past turning leaves alight in the October sun. A critic's pronouncements need not be his or her only view of a given author or book. In truth, one can argue differently, even conversely, depending upon what aspect of an author or book one chooses to scrutinize. But American writing has a tradition, too, of celebrating contradiction and process over dogged consistency: Emerson, Whitman, Dickinson, William James, Fitzgerald, and Oates, for example, all make statements to this effect. Fluidity, process, journey—these are American watchwords, distilled by the writings of pragmatism, classical American philosophy, and much American literature.

In "State of Writers in America" Styron makes an extended statement that fits that pattern. "The difference between truth in a novel" and truth in a lecture or essay, he writes, "must be painfully apparent to anyone who has first written novels and then tries his hand at this other form of expression." Truth in a novel "is second-hand, if not downright facetious. The author utters a portentous statement, or has one of his characters make what appears to be a wise observation—and as readers we take them or leave them; we are aware that we are, after all, only in the world of fiction, a facsimile of life, where most of our truths end up being half-truths anyway." In an essay, in contrast, dissimulation is less easy.

> Any statement you make begins to register a kind of magisterial authority in spite of itself; half-truths tend to proclaim themselves most nakedly; but most troublesome of all is the knowledge that anything you say does, in fact, have somewhere a lawful antithesis, an almost equally valid opposite. I say "almost," and that, of course, is the word that saves us; we cannot be too reticent about our beliefs. So we plunge ahead, somehow confident that if we are honest enough, searching enough, we shall hit upon insights truthful enough to provide a lawful antithesis for someone else. And in this cumbersome way we arrive at final truths and revelations.[27]

This Jamesian emphasis on process is everywhere apparent in Styron's vision, from his view that "tragedy is so provisional" to the provisional endings of his novels.[28] So it seems that the most apt way to end this book is not to conclude but to state a kind of anticonclusion, a call to continue rather than a final sealing of my own or anyone else's response to Styron's life and work. "There is continuity in literature," he wrote to an admirer, Jeffrey Gibbs, in one of the last of the *Selected Letters*. "How gratifying it is to me to think that my work may have inspired you in some way to create your own." Books, he added, "are lifelines to the future" (638).

These thoughts I had about Styron's legacy as the train approached
New York offer an example of how we might articulate and value his
innovations, ambition, and breadth of vision, but there have been and
will be others. He knew as well as anyone that fame is fickle. Even now
his profile is less pronounced than in his prime. And while such factors
as his refusal to compromise, his ability to offend, and the complexity
of his writing might account for this, the sliding of his reputation also
perhaps had an effect on him in later years. From knowing the man to
some extent, and from reading West's biography and Al Styron's memoir,
it seems clear that his confidence became fragile. But while Styron may
have doubted his own legacy at times later in life, my analysis of his
work and this sample of his legacy might have reminded others what a
remarkable body of work he left us.

So yes, I thought to myself as the train entered the tunnel beneath
the Hudson into Manhattan, William Styron is a writer to reread in both
senses of the word. When I think back over his writing certain images
recur: the Sunday morning sunshine on the suburban lawn where Milton's drinking is at least controlled and Peyton still a child; Peter's fraz-
zled drive from Rome to Sambuco; Nat as master of a deserted Turner's
Mill, with empty walls where family portraits once hung; Sophie's "festive little room" where Stingo, glass foaming with Budweiser topped up
by Nathan, entranced by the "sunny June day, the ecstatic pomp of Mr.
Handel's riverborne jam session" and the "fragrance of spring blossoms,"
experiences "the gestalt" (67). There are gloomier recollections, too:
Helen's and Milton's inconsolable grief; Mason's destructive puerility;
Nat's treatment by the likes of Moore and Eppes; Sophie's experiences in
Poland and with Nathan in Connecticut; Paul and his father as "A Tidewater Morning" ends, clinging to the wreckage of their homelife. Light
and dark are always in equipoise in Styron, even if, as Gardner puts it,
Styron knew "how to cut away from the darkness of his material so that
when he turns to it again it strikes with increased force." But the images
I retain also include the train rides that begin and all but end his career,
from the trains that lead us into and out of *Lie Down in Darkness* to the
train Sophie and Stingo take to Washington and Stingo takes alone back
to New York. "I treasure that ability," as Styron said on his Vineyard
Haven lawn in his seventies, with his great work behind him, "to have
been able to transport people," to have produced something that they
"regard as important in their lives," and to have made "other people feel
that ultimate emotional and intellectual effect."[29]

Well, Bill, my own train rolled into Penn Station that autumn day, and my physical journey through your world ended. But as Bellow wrote, "Travel is mental travel."[30] One might add that all narratives are travel narratives. The real journey has been my own intellectual voyage, embarking upon and completing, for now, my self-imposed task of rereading William Styron. And that too is done. No conclusion, no final judgment—only a flight home and a book, not necessarily excellent but perhaps enlightening to others and, I would hope, honest and fair.

PERMISSIONS

NOTES

CHAPTER ONE

1. Jorge Luis Borges, *Labyrinths: Selected Stories and Other Writings*, ed. Donald Yates and James Irby (1964; repr., Harmondsworth, UK: Penguin, 1987), 66.

2. Henry James, *The House of Fiction: Essays on the Novel*, ed. Leon Edel (London: Rupert Hart-Davis, 1957; repr., London: Mercury, 1962), 76. James writes that a novelist must achieve "saturation with his idea. When saturation fails no other presence readily avails." For an example of Styron's own version of this, see his 16 December 1955 letter in *Selected Letters of William Styron*, ed. Rose Styron with R. Blakeslee Gilpin (New York: Random House, 2012), expressing his disappointment that Peter Matthiessen has failed to "transform" a scene into "a dramatic powerhouse" with all its "crannies and corners" filled out (216). The value of Styron's nonfiction is surely enhanced now by the publication of *Selected Letters*. My scant in-text references to this remarkable volume merely reflect the fact that its publication has come too late for detailed inclusion in this book.

3. William Styron, *Letters to My Father*, ed. James L. W. West III (Baton Rouge: Louisiana State University Press, 2009), 69, 67. Subsequent in-text references are to this edition.

4. James L. W. West III, "William Styron: Public Author," *Critique* 51, no. 2 (2010): 150.

5. Gavin Cologne-Brookes, "Appendix: Extracts from Conversations with William Styron," in *The Novels of William Styron: From Harmony to History* (Baton Rouge: Louisiana State University Press, 1995), 232, 244. Styron may have acquired the term from Henry James, who writes of Turgenev's "want of 'architecture'" in *Partial Portraits* (New York: Macmillan, 1888), 315.

6. Wallace Stevens, "Reality is an Activity of the Most August Imagination," in *The Palm at the End of the Mind: Selected Poems and a Play*, ed. Holly Stevens (New York: Alfred A. Knopf, 1971; repr., New York: Vintage, 1972), 396; David Bromwich, "The Novelists of Every Day Life," in *The Revival of Pragmatism: New Essays on Social Thought, Law, and Culture*, ed. Morris Dickstein (Durham, NC: Duke University Press, 1998), 370–76. For a more detailed explanation of this intellectual position, see Gavin Cologne-Brookes, *Dark Eyes on America: The Novels of Joyce Carol Oates* (Baton Rouge: Louisiana State University Press, 2005), 3–5.

7. Christa Wolf, *The Reader and the Writer: Essays, Sketches, Memories* (Berlin: Seven

Seas, 1977), 41–42.

8. Ibid., 43–44.

9. Ibid., 44.

10. Cologne-Brookes, "Appendix," in *Novels of William Styron,* 237, 226.

11. William Styron, *Sophie's Choice* (New York: Random House, 1979), 512. Subsequent in-text references are to this edition.

12. Pearl K. Bell, "Evil and William Styron," in *"Sophie's Choice": A Contemporary Casebook,* ed. Rhoda Sirlin and James L. W. West III (Newcastle, UK: Cambridge Scholars, 2007), 7.

13. William Styron, *This Quiet Dust and Other Writings* (New York: Random House, 1982; rev. and expanded ed., New York: Vintage, 1993), 96, 97. Subsequent in-text references are to this edition.

14. Bell, "Evil and William Styron," in Sirlin and West, eds., *"Sophie's Choice,"* 4; Leo Tolstoy, "Why Do Men Stupefy Themselves?," in *Recollections and Essays,* trans. Aylmer Maude (Oxford: Oxford University Press, 1937), 81. Tolstoy is citing the artist Bryullov's making a small change to a pupil's drawing and telling him that "Art begins where the tiny bit begins."

15. Notable exceptions are Robert Coltrane, "The Unity of *This Quiet Dust,*" *Papers on Language and Literature* 23, no. 4 (1987): 480–88; and Melvin J. Friedman, "William Styron's Criticism: More French than American," *Delta* (Montpellier) 23 (January 1986): 61–67.

CHAPTER TWO

1. William Styron, *Grateful Words about F. Scott Fitzgerald,* limited-edition pamphlet of an address to the F. Scott Fitzgerald Society (Hempstead, NY, 1997), 5.

2. Borges, *Labyrinths,* 70; James L. W. West III, *William Styron, A Life* (New York: Random House, 1998), xii; Arthur Miller in Joel Foreman, "William Styron: A Portrait," 1982, Box AV 7, William Styron Papers, David M. Rubenstein Rare Book & Manuscript Library, Duke University, Durham, NC (hereafter Styron Papers, Duke). See also Mikhail Bakhtin, *The Dialogic Imagination: Four Essays,* trans. Caryl Emerson and Michael Holquist, ed. Michael Holquist (Austin: University of Texas Press, 1981), 256: "It is just as impossible to forge an identity between myself, my own 'I,' and that 'I' that is the subject of my stories as it is to lift myself up by my own hair."

3. Alexandra Styron, *Reading My Father* (New York: Charles Scribner's Sons, 2011), 209; Borges, *Labyrinths,* 282–83.

4. William Styron to Don Harington, 4 April 1964, in "The William Styron–Donald Harington Letters," ed. Edwin T. Arnold, *Southern Quarterly* 40, no. 2 (Winter 2002): 115.

5. Primo Levi, *The Drowned and the Saved,* trans. Raymond Rosenthal (London: Abacus, 1988), 22.

6. Joe McGinniss, *Heroes* (New York: Viking, 1976; repr., New York: Touchstone / Simon & Schuster, 1990), 64–66.

7. Ibid., 175.

8. Michael Mewshaw, *Do I Owe You Something? A Memoir of the Literary Life* (Baton Rouge: Louisiana State University Press, 2003), 18, 35, 237; Alexandra Styron, *Reading My Father,* 237. The letter Mewshaw refers to also appears in *Selected Letters,* 424–26. See also Arnold, ed., "William Styron–Donald Harington Letters."

9. Joyce Carol Oates, "Transformations of Self: An Interview with Joyce Carol Oates,"

by *Ohio Review,* in *Conversations with Joyce Carol Oates,* ed. Lee Milazzo (Jackson: University Press of Mississippi, 1989), 47; Albert Camus, *Discours de Suède* (Paris: Gallimard, 1958), 13, quoted in *Literature and Responsibility: The French Novelist in the Twentieth Century,* by Rima Drell Reck (Baton Rouge: Louisiana State University Press, 1969), 56; Gavin Cologne-Brookes, "Looking Back: A Conversation with William Styron," *Mississippi Quarterly* 62, no. 4 (2009): 509.

10. A. N. Wilson, *Tolstoy* (London: Hamish Hamilton, 1988; repr., Harmondsworth, UK: Penguin, 1988), 267–68.

11. Mewshaw, *Do I Owe You Something?,* 33; Arnold, ed., "William Styron–Donald Harington Letters," 118.

12. William Styron, "Why I Wrote *Sophie's Choice,*" interview by Michel Brandeau, in *Conversations with William Styron,* ed. James L. W. West III (Jackson: University Press of Mississippi, 1985), 254; Dmitri Merejkowski, *Tolstoy as Man and Artist* (Westminster, UK: Archibald Constable, 1902), 178.

13. Kurt Vonnegut, *Slaughterhouse-Five* (New York: Delacorte, 1969; repr. London: Triad, 1983), 136–37; Styron, letter to the author, 20 October 1987. This letter has subsequently been published in *Selected Letters,* 586–87.

14. William Styron, *The Confessions of Nat Turner* (New York: Random House, 1967), 3. Subsequent in-text references are to this edition.

15. Michel de Montaigne, "Of Glory," in *The Essays of Michel de Montaigne,* trans. Charles Cotton (London: G. Bell & Sons, 1913), 347.

16. Alexandra Styron, *Reading My Father,* 4.

17. William Styron, letter to the author, 3 March 1988.

18. Alexandra Styron, *Reading My Father,* 154; William Styron, letter to the author, 3 March 1988; Cologne-Brookes, "Appendix," in *Novels of William Styron,* 228.

19. Blaise Pascal, *Pensées,* trans. A. J. Krailsheimer (Harmondsworth, UK: Penguin, 1966; rev. ed., 1995), 8; F. Scott Fitzgerald, "Early Success," in *The Crack-Up, and Other Pieces and Stories* (Harmondsworth, UK: Penguin, 1965), 53.

20. Ronald Bryden, *Spectator,* 17 February 1961, 232–33; F. Scott Fitzgerald, *The Great Gatsby* (1925; repr., New York: Charles Scribner's Sons, 1953), 5.

21. Styron, letter to the author, 20 October 1987.

22. Styron, letter to the author, 3 March 1988.

23. Philip Roth, *The Ghost Writer* (New York: Farrar, Straus & Giroux, 1979), 5.

24. Tolstoy, *Anna Karenina,* 302. William Styron, *Set This House on Fire* (New York: Random House, 1960), 250; subsequent in-text references are to this edition. Alexandra Styron, *Reading My Father,* 81.

25. Alexandra Styron, *Reading My Father,* 196.

26. This appears in longer form in Cologne-Brookes, "Appendix," in *Novels of William Styron,* 237–38.

27. See West, *William Styron,* 208 and 242, for a description of this 1952 first meeting and of Rose later checking out the wrong *Lie Down in Darkness.* West's chronology differs from mine, as does Alexandra Styron's (*Reading My Father,* 120), and is no doubt correct.

28. Alexandra Styron, *Reading My Father,* 26–27.

29. James Baldwin, "My Dungeon Shook," in *The Fire Next Time* (New York: Dial, 1963; repr., Harmondsworth, UK: Penguin, 1964), 3.

30. James, *House of Fiction,* 33.

31. For the full transcript of the conversation, see Cologne-Brookes, "Looking Back."

32. Emily Dickinson, Poem 1455, in *The Complete Poems of Emily Dickinson,* ed. Thomas H. Johnson (1890; repr. London: Faber & Faber, 1960), 617.

33. In ibid., 459.

34. Styron, letter to the author, 23 January 2003.

CHAPTER THREE

1. In an attempted fictional treatment of depression, written prior to *Darkness Visible,* Styron writes of Hemingway, "I loved a great deal of his work but I don't think I would have liked him much as a person, for he was inescapably a braggart and a poseur, and no other illustrious writer has left behind him a spoor of accounts testifying to so much atrocious meanness. But that night I was not pondering his character or his talent; I was thinking again of his terrible ending, which made me reach out to him in tenderness and brotherhood." Early holograph fragment, 20–21, Box WS 12, Styron Papers, Duke.

2. See Styron's exchange with Mailer documented in West, *William Styron,* 278–96. While Styron never publically responded to Mailer's attacks on him and other writers, he did offer his private opinion. In a postcard of 18 June 1963 to John Dodds, he wrote: "Like you, I'm sure that *Esquire* would be delighted to have me write a rebuttal to Mailer's piece. It was a marvellous Machiavellian goulash of steaming envy, mean spirits and pure malevolence—all mixed up (as you no doubt noticed) with my friendship with Jones, which is what bugs him the most of all human events, and which I'm sure was the impulse for the article." Box B, Don Congdon Papers, Rare Books & Manuscript Library, Columbia University, New York. Among several observations now available in *Selected Letters* is Styron's admission to the fiction editor Rust Hills that his "revulsion" at Mailer's attacks on fellow writers was "tempered by a kind of grudging admiration that *Esquire* should allow a convicted wife-stabber and, to my mind, moral imbecile so captiously and naggingly to lucubrate on the conduct of others" (349).

3. Cologne-Brookes, "Appendix," in *Novels of William Styron,* 223.

4. Vladimir Nabokov, *Lectures on Literature* (London: Weidenfeld & Nicolson, 1980; repr., London: Picador, 1983), 146; Styron to Harington, 3 May 1964, in Arnold, ed., "William Styron–Donald Harington Letters," 118.

5. Cologne-Brookes, "Appendix," in *Novels of William Styron,* 237. See also James Campbell, "Styron's Voice," *Times Literary Supplement,* 15 January 2010, 3–4. Campbell asserts that Styron's writing has a "voice" rather than a "style" (4). True or not, the later works, *Sophie's Choice, A Tidewater Morning,* and *The Suicide Run,* employ the same recognizably Styronian speech patterns.

6. John Barth, "The Literature of Replenishment: Postmodernist Fiction," *Atlantic Monthly,* January 1980, 70.

7. West, *William Styron,* 377; Cologne-Brookes, "Appendix," in *Novels of William Styron,* 223. See also Styron, *Letters to My Father,* 115: "I don't mind getting all this additional reward," he wrote to his father in June 1951 of the public success of *Lie Down in Darkness,* "especially after knowing that first and foremost I was honest, that the book represented hours of real sweat and pain, and that I did my level best, in every word of it."

8. Joan Didion, *A Year of Magical Thinking* (New York: Alfred A. Knopf, 2005; repr. London: Harper Perennial, 2006), 24.

9. William Styron, *The Suicide Run: Five Tales of the Marine Corps* (New York: Random House, 2009), 200. Subsequent in-text references are to this edition.

10. Cologne-Brookes, "Appendix," in *Novels of William Styron,* 223.

11. Ibid., 217, 214, 222.

12. William Styron, *Havanas in Camelot: Personal Essays* (New York: Random House, 2008), 121–22, 122–23. Subsequent in-text references are to this edition.

13. See West, *William Styron*, 36–38, for more detail on Elder Michaux and Bishop Grace.

14. Michael West, "An Interview with William Styron," in West, ed., *Conversations*, 230.

15. Jeffrey Berman, "Darkness Visible and Invisible: The Landscape of Depression in *Lie Down in Darkness*," in *The Critical Response to William Styron*, ed. Daniel W. Ross (Westport, CT: Greenwood, 1995), 64, 78; Alexandra Styron, *Reading My Father*, 232.

16. William Styron, *Darkness Visible: A Memoir of Madness* (New York: Random House, 1990), 34, 9, 78. Subsequent in-text references are to this edition.

17. For a discussion of depression and *Sophie's Choice*, see Bertram Wyatt-Brown, "William Styron's *Sophie's Choice*: Poland, the South, and the Tragedy of Suicide," in Sirlin and West, eds., *"Sophie's Choice,"* 117–27.

18. For a more detailed discussion of this, see Cologne-Brookes, *Novels of William Styron*, 158–63.

19. Wyatt-Brown, "William Styron's *Sophie's Choice*," in Sirlin and West, eds., *"Sophie's Choice,"* 117.

20. Tolstoy, *Anna Karenina*, 250–53; Gavin Cologne-Brookes, "Written Interviews and a Conversation with Joyce Carol Oates," *Studies in the Novel* 38, no. 4 (2006): 563; William Stafford, *Writing the Australian Crawl: Views on the Writer's Vocation* (Ann Arbor: University of Michigan Press, 1978), 17.

21. West, *William Styron*, 160; Cologne-Brookes, "Looking Back," 505. See also Styron's 1981 interview with Michel Brandeau, "Why I Wrote *Sophie's Choice*," in West, ed., *Conversations*, 254: "In a letter to his publisher, Joseph Conrad explained that every time he'd open the door to his study, see his work on the table, and white sheets of paper, he was close to bursting into tears."

22. Friedman, "William Styron's Criticism," 61–67.

23. Fitzgerald, *Great Gatsby*, 48.

24. West, "William Styron: Public Author," 150, and "An Accidental Boswell: Writing the Life of William Styron," *Sewanee Review* 119, no. 3 (2011): 449. For chemists' response to *Madame Bovary*, see Francis Steegmuller, *Flaubert and Madame Bovary: A Double Portrait* (London: Robert Hale, 1939), 385: "All the pharmacists of the Seine-Inférieure recognized themselves in Homais, and some of them discussed the advisability of calling on Flaubert and slapping his face." The letter I refer to is from David R. Bender, executive director of the Special Libraries Association, New York, 16 February 1983, in Box C 9, Styron Papers, Duke. It not only expresses regret at Styron's portrayal of librarians in *Sophie's Choice* but asks him to consider presenting a more up-to-date characterization in any future work and offers the association's help in providing appropriate information. Styron's handwritten note reads: "<u>ANS</u> said he was ridiculous." In *Selected Letters*, Styron writes to Frederick Exley in 1972 about the opening of Styron's play *In the Clap Shack* that he is steeling himself "for the inevitable attack, a mean little book of essays entitled, 'William Styron's *In the Clap Shack*, 10 White Urologists Respond'" (487).

25. Wilson, *Tolstoy*, 267–68; Tolstoy, *Anna Karenina*, 148; Cologne-Brookes, "Appendix," in *Novels of William Styron*, 230. On Styron's relationship with his stepmother, see West, *William Styron*, 72–73. As for *Selected Letters*, I'll give just one example of Styron's

libertine rejection of what he would presumably have viewed as priggery. In a letter to James Jones critiquing the manuscript of *Go to the Widow-Maker* (1967), he complains of a character being so "insanely jealous" of the possibility of a partner's adultery and puts it down to "a particular moral hang-up which seems to posit absolute purity and decency on the one hand and absolute treachery and evil on the other, either one depending upon whether one has inserted a throbbing piece of flesh into a more or less throbbing orifice, or whether one hasn't" (401).

26. West, *William Styron*, 277.

27. See ibid., 191–92 and 308–10. With both *Lie Down in Darkness* and, in Britain, *Set This House on Fire*, Styron's writing was subject to censorship in terms of language deemed offensive. With his first novel this included excision of references to "sex organs," "menstruation," "underwear," "dog shit," a "cowboy belt," and a "tube of jelly." The British publisher of *Set This House on Fire*, Hamish Hamilton, wary of falling foul of the 1959 Obscene Publications Act, replaced coarse language and softened the stronger profanities. The publishing house was particularly prim about the word *shit*. Hence, "grinning like a shit-eating dog" became "grinning like a big hairy dog," while "I shit on Him because I do not believe" became "He is a monster! He is the devil!" Even with such changes, the British edition eventually had to be printed in the Netherlands.

28. Reck, *Literature and Responsibility*, 56; Stendhal [Marie-Henri Beyle], *The Red and the Black*, trans. Catherine Slater (Oxford: Oxford World's Classics, 1998), 520.

CHAPTER FOUR

1. James, *House of Fiction*, 188; Cologne-Brookes, "Looking Back," 505.

2. James, *House of Fiction*, 187.

3. See Styron's long explanation of an idea for the novel, a brief reading from a potential opening, and a subsequent discussion of it in Cologne-Brookes, "Appendix," in *Novels of William Styron*, 231–45. He later said this idea was no more than a pipedream.

4. McGinniss, *Heroes*, 64.

5. Cologne-Brookes, "Looking Back," 502.

6. Jack Griffin, Jerry Homsy, and Gene Stelzig, "A Conversation with William Styron," in West, ed., *Conversations*, 54; Louis D. Rubin, *The Faraway Country: Writers of the Modern South* (Seattle: University of Washington Press, 1963), 186; Tamsen Douglass Love, "Defining Postmodernism: Styron's 'Complicitous Critique' of Faulkner," *Southern Literary Journal* 28, no. 1 (1995): 20–21.

7. Peter Matthiessen and George Plimpton, "The Art of Fiction V: William Styron," in West, ed., *Conversations*, 13; Douglas Barzelay and Robert Sussman, "William Styron on *The Confessions of Nat Turner*: A *Yale Lit* Interview," in ibid., 107; Matthiessen and Plimpton, "Art of Fiction V," in ibid., 19; Cologne-Brookes, "Appendix," in *Novels of William Styron*, 214, 222–23.

8. Virginia Woolf, "Modern Fiction," in *Collected Essays*, ed. Leonard Woolf, vol. 2 (New York: Harcourt, Brace & World, 1967), 106; Barth, "Literature of Replenishment," 70; Michael West, "Interview with William Styron," in West, ed., *Conversations*, 231; Cologne-Brookes, "Appendix," in *Novels of William Styron*, 215.

9. Cologne-Brookes, "Appendix," in *Novels of William Styron*, 266; Joyce Carol Oates, *New Heaven, New Earth: The Visionary Experience in Literature* (New York: Vanguard, 1974), 24; Griffin, Homsy, and Stelzig, "Conversation with William Styron," in West, ed., *Conversations*, 54; Cologne-Brookes, "Appendix," in *Novels of William Styron*, 214, 227;

Dawn Trouard, "Styron's Historical Pre-Text: Nat Turner, Sophie, and the Beginnings of a Postmodern Career," *Papers on Language and Literature* 23, no. 4 (1987): 496.

10. Love, "Defining Postmodernism," 23–29.

11. For more detail on this early version of the novel, see James L. W. West III, ed., *Inheritance of Night: Early Drafts of "Lie Down in Darkness"* (Durham, NC: Duke University Press, 1993).

12. Matthiessen and Plimpton, "Art of Fiction V," in West ed., *Conversations,* 19; John Gardner, "A Novel of Evil," in *Critical Essays on William Styron,* ed. Arthur D. Casciato and James L. W. West III (Boston: G. K. Hall, 1982), 248; Berman, "Darkness Visible and Invisible," in Ross, ed., *Critical Response to William Styron,* 78, 64.

13. Norman Mailer, *Advertisements for Myself* (New York: Putnam, 1959; repr., London: Panther, 1968), 379–80.

14. Isaiah Berlin, *Russian Thinkers* (London: Hogarth, 1948; repr., Harmondsworth, UK: Penguin, 1994), 30.

15. William Styron, *Lie Down in Darkness* (Indianapolis: Bobbs-Merrill, 1951), 342. Subsequent in-text references are to this edition.

16. Edward Murray, *The Cinematic Imagination: Writers and the Motion Pictures* (New York: Ungar, 1972). For Murray, the phrase is pejorative; he thought the influence of cinema detrimental. Styron's "cinematic imagination" would later lead him to experiment with film script itself. *Selected Letters,* for instance, shows him writing to his father in 1961 that his interest in Nat Turner might "shape up much more as a movie than a book" (308). See also his screenplay coauthored with John Phillips, "Dead!" *Esquire,* December 1973, 161ff.

17. Woolf, "Modern Fiction," in *Collected Essays,* 2:106.

18. Bakhtin, *Dialogic Imagination,* 247, 248.

19. For a more detailed discussion of influence, see Cologne-Brookes, *Novels of William Styron,* 34–43.

20. For a useful delineation of the narrative structure of each of Styron's novels, see John Kenny Crane, *The Root of All Evil: The Thematic Unity of William Styron's Fiction* (Columbia: University of South Carolina Press, 1984), 128–64.

21. Love, "Defining Postmodernism," 23, 29.

22. Further evidence of the young author's attempted hatchet job on Helen comes from the fact that we now know she was a version of his stepmother, Elizabeth. Juxtapose this passage with Styron's comments in "A Case of the Great Pox," in *Havanas in Camelot,* 54–55, that she was "an ungainly, humorless, pleasure-shunning, middle-aged spinster" and that "I thought her a prig; she considered me a libertine," and the word *prig* jumps out. Included in *Selected Letters* is a 1983 diatribe against Elizabeth to her relative by marriage Mary Buxton based partly on a "hateful and poisonous" letter Styron's "vindictive step-mother" sent him when he was twenty-two and recovering from hepatitis in New York. Elizabeth blamed the young man for bringing the illness on himself by way of a debauched lifestyle. "I still hate Elizabeth for that loathsome, disgusting letter with its terrible freight of puritanical malice," wrote Styron. "The only reason—as always—that I didn't write back and tell her to go fuck herself was because of my father, and my desire not to make that good man unhappy. How he lived with her for so long in apparent bliss is a cosmic mystery" (563).

23. William Styron, "Moviegoer," in *Havanas in Camelot,* 103–7. Judging from such books as Magny Claude-Emonde, *The Age of the American Novel: The Film Aesthetic of Fic-*

tion *Between the Two Wars,* trans. Eleanor Hochman (1948; repr., New York: Ungar, 1972) and Murray's *Cinematic Imagination,* the mid-twentieth century would seem rather a late date. See Carolyn Geduld, "Film and Literature," *Contemporary Literature* 15, no. 1 (1974): 123–30. Geduld argues that Claude-Emonde "believed that novelists were unconsciously or consciously imitating cinema technique" and "traced the beginnings of this tendency directly to the 'objective' novels that appeared in America after World War I: the works of Dos Passos, Hemingway, Steinbeck, Hammett, Caldwell, James M. Cain." Murray, also reviewed by Geduld, thought that "virtually all the twentieth-century writers who were less than five years of age in 1903 when Edwin S. Porter made *The Great Train Robbery* have been consciously or unconsciously overwhelmed by film technique and that film technique has thus changed and even defined all of modern literature since." Writers Murray discusses include the modernists, as well as Nathanael West, Graham Greene, Steinbeck, and Robbe-Grillet.

24. F. Scott Fitzgerald, *The Last Tycoon,* in *"The Great Gatsby" and "The Last Tycoon"* (London: Bodley Head, 1977), 199.

25. Wilder's film, inspired by Charles Jackson's 1944 novel, doesn't contain this particular image, but much is made of the way the protagonist peers into his drinking glass as if into a goblet of magic potion that will enable him to see the world differently.

26. Again, see West, ed., *Inheritance of Night.*

27. Carlos Fuentes, "Unslavish Fidelity," *Times Literary Supplement,* 16 May 1968, 505.

28. Love, "Defining Postmodernism," 24.

29. See West, ed., *Inheritance of Night,* 137. Styron's own scrawled comment in the margin reads: "Would like to write a war novel: these people give me the creeps!"

30. Berman, "Darkness Visible and Invisible," in Ross, ed., *Critical Response to William Styron,* 61–80.

31. Mewshaw, *Do I Owe You Something?,* 19.

32. Berman, "Darkness Visible and Invisible," in Ross, ed., *Critical Response to William Styron,* 64–68, 77.

33. Joyce Carol Oates, *A Widow's Story: A Memoir* (New York: Ecco, 2011; London: Fourth Estate, 2011), 287.

34. Alexandra Styron, *Reading My Father,* 4.

35. See Samuel Coale, "Styron's Choice: Hawthorne's Guilt in Poe's Palaces," *Papers on Language and Literature* 23, no. 4 (Fall 1987): 514–22, for a provocative discussion of the ways in which, in Coale's view, "Styron's fiction drives itself toward a revelation he cannot or will not accept," that "the root of all evil is us absolutely, and the only absolute resolution lies in self-destruction, an apotheosis worthy of such a corrosive if consciously avoided vision" (522).

36. Cologne-Brookes, "Appendix," in *Novels of William Styron,* 215.

37. West, *William Styron,* 268.

CHAPTER FIVE

1. William Styron, *The Long March* (New York: Random House, 1968), 60. Subsequent in-text references are to this edition.

2. Cologne-Brookes, "Appendix," in *Novels of William Styron,* 223.

3. Georgann Eubanks, "William Styron: The Confessions of a Southern Writer," in West, ed., *Conversations,* 274; Louis D. Rubin, "An Artist in Bonds," in Casciato and West, eds., *Critical Essays on William Styron,* 94.

4. Georg Lukács, *Writer and Critic, and Other Essays*, trans. Arthur Kahn (London: Merlin, 1978), 18.

5. Judith Ruderman, *William Styron* (New York: Ungar, 1987), 53. On the novel's composition, see West, *William Styron*, 278–305.

6. Norman Mailer, *Cannibals and Christians* (New York: Dial, 1966; repr., London: André Deutsch, 1967), 103.

7. Matthiessen and Plimpton, "The Art of Fiction V," in West, ed., *Conversations*, 9. See Styron, *Letters to My Father*, 137, with regard to Cass's spectator's rather than practitioner's view of art. In a 1952 letter, Styron describes "an excellent trip" to Florence, Siena, Ravenna, Urbino, and Assisi that was "thoroughly illuminating because my companions were painters or, better yet, art historians who gave me first-hand scholarship or information about the Art (with a capital A) we were seeing."

8. F. Scott Fitzgerald, "The Rich Boy," in *The Bodley Head F. Scott Fitzgerald*, vol. 5, *Short Stories*, ed. Malcolm Cowley (London: Bodley Head, 1963), 286. See also West, *William Styron*, 299–300; and Alexandra Styron, *Reading My Father*, 147–48. Evidently, late in the creative process Styron gave Mason interests that coincided with Mailer's, and some words Mailer had used in a letter. But, in West's words, the talentless "fraud" Mason "was fundamentally unlike" the "serious and gifted" Mailer. For Styron's private comments on Mailer's attacks, see chap. 3, n. 2.

9. Cologne-Brookes, "Looking Back," 506.

10. Charles Monaghan, "Portrait of a Man Reading," in West, ed., *Conversations*, 112; Daniel W. Ross, introduction to Ross, ed., *Critical Response to William Styron*, 5; Joyce Carol Oates, "The Double Vision of *The Brothers Karamazov*," *Journal of Aesthetics and Criticism* 27, no. 2 (1968): 207. See also Robert Kanters, "On the Sin of Being American," *Figaroliteraire*, 10 March 1962, typescript translation, Box PM 15, Styron Papers, Duke; and Radoslav Nenadál, "The Patterning of a Modern Hero in William Styron's *Set This House on Fire*," *Prague Studies in English* 15 (1973): 83–97.

11. Fyodor Dostoevsky, *Crime and Punishment*, trans. Jessie Coulson (Oxford: Oxford World's Classics, 1981), 52.

12. A comparison of *Crime and Punishment* and Albert Camus's *L'Etranger* can be found in William Styron, "State of Writers in America," unpublished holograph, Container 8, William Styron Papers, Manuscript Division, Library of Congress, Washington, DC (hereafter Styron Papers, Library of Congress). I discuss this essay in chapter 8.

13. William Styron, "William Styron to *Publishers Weekly*," *Publishers Weekly*, 30 May 1960, 55; Matthiessen and Plimpton, "Art of Fiction V," 14–19; Cologne-Brookes, "Appendix," in *Novels of William Styron*, 221–22.

14. West, *William Styron*, 279, 301, 397–98; Wolf, *Reader and the Writer*, 43.

15. Fyodor Dostoevsky, notebooks for 1880–81, in *Polnoe sobranie sochinenii v tridtsati tomakh* [Complete works in thirty volumes] (Leningrad: Nauka, 1972–90), 27:65, trans. and quoted in James P. Scanlan, *Dostoevsky the Thinker* (Ithaca, NY: Cornell University Press, 2002), 139, and *The Brothers Karamazov*, trans. David Magarshack (London: Folio Society, 1964), 13–14.

16. West, *William Styron*, 269.

17. Cologne-Brookes, "Appendix," in *Novels of William Styron*, 228; Tolstoy, *Anna Karenina*, 811. The word *intuitions* in my quotation is printed as *institutions* in *The Novels of William Styron*, but that is an error.

18. Cologne-Brookes, "Appendix," in *Novels of William Styron*, 221.

19. Chaim Potok, *My Name is Asher Lev* (New York: Alfred A. Knopf, 1972; repr., Harmondsworth, UK: Penguin, 1994), 186.

CHAPTER SIX

1. Scot French, *The Rebellious Slave: Nat Turner in American History* (New York: Houghton-Mifflin, 2004), 4, 274.

2. Mary Kemp Davis, *Nat Turner Before the Bar of Judgment: Fictional Treatments of the Southampton Slave Insurrection* (Baton Rouge: Louisiana State University Press, 1999), 240, xiii, 249.

3. French, *Rebellious Slave*, 272, 10; Davis, *Nat Turner Before the Bar of Judgment*, 45–46; Henry Louis Gates Jr., letter to the author, 17 July 2009. For an essay that discusses the question of authorial motive, see James Harold, "Flexing the Imagination," *Journal of Aesthetics and Art Criticism* 61, no. 3 (2003): 247–57. Harold addresses the question of Styron's experience, which he suggests "is simply too distant from Turner's" and thus Styron "cannot hope to understand Turner, and neither can most of his contemporary white readers." For Harold, therefore, an author's "race is one significant barrier" to his or her likely success in dealing with the subject matter (250). He goes on to say that "whether or not his critics approve of Styron's project in *Nat Turner* will depend in part, I think, on whether they judge him to have the appropriate internally directed motives, and the humility and carefulness that those motives engender" (255).

4. West, *William Styron*, 334.

5. James Baldwin, interview by Mavis Nicholson, *Mavis on Four*, British television, shown as an obituary tribute, 3 December 1987; Friedrich Nietzsche, *Beyond Good and Evil*, in *Basic Writings of Nietzsche*, trans. Walter Kaufmann (New York: Random House, 1967; repr., New York: Modern Library, 2000), 278.

6. Joyce Carol Oates, *The Faith of a Writer: Life, Craft, Art* (New York: Ecco, 2003), 33.

7. Charles Burnett, Frank Christopher, and Kenneth S. Greenberg, *Nat Turner: A Troublesome Property*, dir. Charles Burnett (San Francisco: California Newsreel, 2002), DVD. This is Styron's version of James Baldwin's challenge to him: "What you should do, as a white writer, is to be bold and take on the persona of a black man, Nat Turner," just as Baldwin, in Styron's words, had himself "begun to deal with the idea of writing about white people from an intimate point of view."

8. Baldwin, quoted in Raymond A. Sokolov, "Into the Mind of Nat Turner," *Newsweek*, 16 October 1967, 69; Toni Morrison, in answer to my question about Styron's novel, City Hall, Sheffield, UK, 2 March 1988; Gates, letter to the author, 17 July 2009.

9. Barzelay and Sussman, "William Styron on *The Confessions of Nat Turner*," in West, ed., *Conversations*, 96.

10. Trouard, "Styron's Historical Pre-Text," 492; Cologne-Brookes, "Appendix," in *Novels of William Styron*, 218.

11. West, *William Styron*, 397–98; Cologne-Brookes, "Appendix," in *Novels of William Styron*, 219.

12. See Crane, *Root of All Evil*, 151–54.

13. Toni Morrison, *Playing in the Dark: Whiteness and the Literary Imagination* (Cambridge, MA: Harvard University Press, 1992), 69.

14. Barry Hannah to Styron, 9 May 1994, Box C 13, Styron Papers, Duke.

15. Davis, *Nat Turner Before the Bar of Judgment*, 262.

16. Wallace Stevens, "The Idea of Order at Key West," in *The Collected Poems of*

Wallace Stevens (London: Faber, 1955), 130; Claudia Tate, *Black Women Writers at Work* (Harpenden, UK: Oldcastle, 1985), 121.

17. Trouard, "Styron's Historical Pre-Text," 492; Fuentes, "Unslavish Fidelity," 505; Daniel S. Fabricant, "Thomas R. Gray and William Styron: Finally, A Critical Look at the 1831 *Confessions of Nat Turner*," *American Journal of Legal History* 37, no. 3 (1993): 334, 355; Gates, letter to the author, 17 July 2009. See also Fabricant, "Thomas R. Gray and William Styron," 361, 335–36, for a detailed examination of the veracity of Gray's document and its role in the court proceedings. Fabricant notes a range of factual inaccuracies, arguing that Styron's deeply skeptical examination of Gray "points to the need to scrutinize the bases of other divisive social perceptions in order to bring about more honest recountings of history, free of racist understructures dictated by individual whim and political and economic concerns." For Fabricant, "careful examination of Gray's *Confessions* yields better understanding of the systematic victimization of blacks that was carried out under the guise of law and justice in early nineteenth-century Virginia."

18. Trouard, "Styron's Historical Pre-Text," 493.

19. Ruderman, *William Styron*, 20.

20. Richard Dawkins, *The God Delusion* (London: Bantam, 2006; repr., London: Black Swan, 2007).

21. Cologne-Brookes, "Appendix," in *Novels of William Styron*, 223, 221, 228–29.

22. Albert Camus, *L'Etranger*, trans. Joseph Loredo (Harmondsworth, UK: Penguin, 1983), 99.

23. This comment is scrawled across the title page of chapter 4 of the holographic manuscript of *Sophie's Choice*, Box WS 5, Styron Papers, Duke. The page is reproduced in Gavin Cologne-Brookes, "Sophie's Voice, Tolstoy, Film, Music: Interpreting a Leaf from the Manuscript of *Sophie's Choice*," *Mississippi Quarterly* 62, no. 4 (2009): 512.

24. Alexandra Styron, *Reading My Father*, 13.

25. Ibid., 15.

26. For charges of "emasculation," see especially several of the contributions to *William Styron's Nat Turner: Ten Black Writers Respond*, ed. John Henrik Clarke (Boston: Beacon, 1968), including Lerone Bennett Jr., "Nat's Last White Man" (8); Alvin F. Poussaint, "The Confessions of Nat Turner and the Dilemma of William Styron" (22); Vincent Harding "You've Taken My Nat and Gone" (24); and Loyle Hairston "William Styron's *Nat Turner*—Rogue-Nigger" (71). All use the word *emasculation* or *emasculate*. John Oliver Killens implies emasculation in his title, "The Confessions of Willie Styron," and then compares Styron's version of Nat Turner to Laurence Olivier's movie version of Othello, which Killens sees as a reduction of "Shakespeare's magnificent Moor" into "a shuffling, stupid-cunning whining idiot, half man and half faggot" (35). Examples of critics labeling the *Sophie's Choice* narrator a chauvinist or misogynist include Georgiana M. M. Colville, "Killing the Dead Mother: Women in *Sophie's Choice*," *Delta* (Montpellier) 23 (January 1986): 113; and Joan Smith, *Misogynies: Reflections on Myths and Malice* (London: Faber, 1989), 89–90.

27. Cologne-Brookes, "Appendix," in *Novels of William Styron*, 228.

28. Ibid., 217, 222, 224.

29. See Styron, *Sophie's Choice*, 67. In Sophie and Nathan's company one morning, Stingo achieves "a benign, tingling high so surprisingly intense" that he becomes "a little uneasy trying to manage" his "euphoria." He feels "buoyed up by fraternal arms," even though aware that this is partly the result of "the coarse clutch of alcohol."

30. William Styron, *A Tidewater Morning: Three Tales from Youth* (New York: Random House, 1993), 37. Subsequent in-text references are to this edition.

CHAPTER SEVEN

1. Tadeusz Borowski, *This Way for the Gas, Ladies and Gentlemen,* trans. Barbara Vedder (London: Penguin, 1976), 16.

2. Primo Levi, "Afterword: The Author's Answers to His Readers' Questions," in *If This is a Man/The Truce,* trans. Stuart Woolf (London: Abacus, 1987), 389–90.

3. See Franz Link, "Auschwitz and the Literary Imagination: William Styron's *Sophie's Choice,*" in Sirlin and West, eds., *"Sophie's Choice,"* 144. Evidently this is an example of Styron's artistic license; the professors were not executed, but freed in March 1940.

4. Shlomo Venezia, *Inside the Gas Chambers: Eight Months in the Sonderkommando of Auschwitz,* trans. Andrew Brown (Cambridge: Polity, 2009), 69.

5. Julia Kristeva, *Powers of Horror: An Essay in Abjection,* trans. Leon S. Roudiez (New York: Columbia University Press, 1982), 2–3.

6. Ibid., 4.

7. Ibid.

8. Venezia, *Inside the Gas Chambers,* 66–67.

9. Bartosz Bartyzel et al., eds. *Auschwitz-Birkenau State Museum Report 2010,* trans. William Brand (Oświęcim, Poland: Pańtswowe Muzeum Auschwitz-Birkenau w Oświęcimiu, 2010), 57.

10. Levi, *Drowned and the Saved,* 26.

11. Alan J. Pakula, director's commentary track on the *Sophie's Choice* DVD (Santa Monica, CA: Artisan Home Entertainment, 1999), cited in Jared Brown, *Alan J. Pakula: His Films and His Life* (New York: Backstage Books, 2005), 239.

12. Gardner, "Novel of Evil," in Casciato and West, eds., *Critical Essays on William Styron,* 247–48, 251, 245–46. "When Dostoyevsky published Crime and Punishment (I think it was) somebody important—I forget who—made a long trip to him (I think) to tell him, 'You are the savior of all Russia!' After *Sophie's Choice,* I wish I had said, instead of what I did say, or at least in addition to what I did say, 'You are the savior of all America!'" (247). Styron's friend Willie Morris was unimpressed by Gardner's about-turn. He wrote to Styron on 12 August 1981: "No, I won't go along with it, John Gardner's reneging on *Sophie's Choice.* After all, he was the man who wrote the first-page review in the *Times.* Living in Mississippi, I will not tolerate this vicious acrimony. *Sophie* is the finest novel of our generation. Gardner's disclaimer wants me to throw up [*sic*]. For those of us who care for literature, without the nonsense, his second thoughts are dishonest and untrue. Thanks for sending his second thoughts to me. They only make me mad, so I don't want to hear from him again." Box C 9, Styron Papers, Duke. See *Selected Letters* for Styron's response to Morris on 16 August: "Your observations on John Gardner, received today, were right on target. Why the fuck couldn't he have said all that originally, the fink?" (552).

13. Cologne-Brookes, "Looking Back," 509.

14. Alexandra Styron, e-mail to James L. W. West III, 29 November 2010.

15. "We all know that art is not truth. Art is a lie that makes us realize truth. At least the truth that is given us to understand." "Picasso Speaks: Statement to Marius de Zayas," *The Arts* (New York), May 1923, 315, reprinted in Alfred H. Barr, *Picasso: Fifty Years of His Art* (New York: Museum of Modern Art, 1946), 270–71.

16. My subject is the novel, but clearly Alan J. Pakula's 1982 film not only utilized the novel's cinematic potential, just as Nicholas Maw's 2001 opera brought out the operatic, but also helped to sustain it as a bestseller. See also Cologne-Brookes, "Sophie's Voice," 511–26. Discussions specifically about the film include Benjamin Dunlap, "Pakula's Choice," *Papers on Language and Literature* 23, no. 4 (1987): 531–43; and Barbara Tepa Lupack, *"Sophie's Choice,* Pakula's Choices," in *Take Two: Adapting the Contemporary Novel to Film,* ed. Lupack (Bowling Green, OH: Bowling Green State University Popular Press, 1994), 91–111. For commentary on the genesis and making of the film and the novel's impact on Pakula and his cast, see Brown, *Alan J. Pakula,* 235–80.

17. Slavoj Žižek, *The Pervert's Guide to Cinema 1, 2, 3,* dir. Sophie Fiennes (London: P. Guide, 2006). All subsequent references are to this DVD.

18. Stendhal, *Red and the Black,* 11.

19. Styron increased the sensuous element, adding the phrases: "in the grip of an aching, devouring love. And at the same time joy—joy that was inexplicably both delicious and despairing swept across her skin in a cool blaze." Styron, *Sophie's Choice* holographic manuscript, 40.

20. Olga Lengyel, *Five Chimneys: A Woman Survivor's True Story of Auschwitz* (Chicago: Ziff-Davis, 1947; repr. Chicago: Academy Chicago, 1995), 160.

21. Susan Sontag, *Under the Sign of Saturn* (Harmondsworth, UK: Penguin, 2009), 93. See also Cologne-Brookes, "Appendix," in *Novels of William Styron,* 229–30: "I took enormous pains *not* to . . . describe any erotic connection of any importance between Sophie and the commandant. I could have chosen to have him have relations with her if I had wanted to, but I chose not to . . . because I thought it *would* be a total jarring." He said "it was a temptation" he had "very briefly," a fact corroborated by a handwritten note on the holograph title page: "After fucking Sophie Höss is cold & remote, sexual guilt."

22. Sontag, *Under the Sign of Saturn,* 93; George Steiner, "Speech as Translation," in *George Steiner: A Reader* (Harmondsworth, UK: Penguin, 1984), 376.

23. "His mirror shows the mire, and you accuse the mirror!" Stendhal, *Red and the Black,* 371.

24. Žižek, *Pervert's Guide to Cinema.*

25. Ibid.

26. See West, *William Styron,* 386–87.

27. Žižek, *Pervert's Guide to Cinema.* See also Kristeva, *Powers of Horror,* 55. Kristeva refers to "the erotization of abjection," a term one might apply to Stingo's attraction to Sophie. For instance, after hearing Sophie and Nathan having sex in the room above the night before he meets them, he recalls the nightmare he experienced soon after his mother's death. In it, he peers out of his bedroom window and sees "the open coffin down in the windswept, drenched garden" and his mother's "shrunken, cancer-ravaged face" beseech him "through eyes filmed over with indescribable torture" (46). Sophie's body, seen by Stingo for the first time, is in turn "not so much deficient as reassembled," and her skin possesses "the sickish plasticity . . . of one who has suffered severe emaciation and whose flesh is even now in the last stages of being restored" (51). Stingo's simultaneous admiration for its beauty "in its clinging summer dress," "with all the right prominences, curves, continuities and symmetries" (51), would seem, to use Kristeva's terms from *Powers of Horror,* 55, to be "an attempt at stopping the hemorrhage: threshold before death, a halt or a respite."

28. West, *William Styron,* 411.

29. Rebecca Parry, response journal for EN6039, In Search of America, Bath Spa University, 2011.

30. Small manuscript edits suggest that Styron had this notion of Nathan in mind. Of the original sentence, "He had managed to return in complete silence," he changed *complete* to *phantasmal*. Of the phrase "the most beguilingly tailored clothes," *beguilingly* becomes *bewitchingly*. "Oh what ghoulish opportunism are writers prone to!" is an insertion. Styron, *Sophie's Choice* holographic manuscript, 94, 121, 220.

31. Among the notes on the back of the title page of the holographic manuscript is evidence that Styron contemplated giving Stingo's father latent racist tendencies, which would have further paralleled Professor Biegański's anti-Semitism. The note reads: "Father's <u>racism</u> coming back: William, lawn clippings, nigger-ridden hospital." In his letter to Mary Buxton (see above, chap. 4, n. 22) Styron acknowledges that Stingo's father "was considerably idealized" and that Mary was "correct in saying that he kept most of the prejudices of his post-bellum Southern generation" (*Selected Letters*, 564).

32. See Crane, *Root of All Evil*, 9–39.

33. The fingertip motif is evident from Zaorski's flute demonstration and Sophie's experience with the figs to her digital rape in the subway. The manuscript shows that Styron sought to reinforce this motif during composition. Where, after calling her a rose, Nathan puts "his fingertips to her brow," the words *his fingertips* replaces the original word, *them*. Styron, *Sophie's Choice* holographic manuscript, 130.

34. William Styron, afterword to *The Confessions of Nat Turner* (New York: Vintage, 1993), 442; Henry Louis Gates Jr., *Loose Canons: Notes on the Culture Wars* (Oxford: Oxford University Press, 1993), 17.

35. Fay Weldon, "Words from the Wise: Lessons in Life from the Over-Sixties," *Times Magazine*, 7 November 2009, 12.

36. Franz Kafka to Oskar Pollak, 27 January 1904, in *Franz Kafka: Letters to Friends, Family and Editors*, trans. Richard and Clara Winston (New York: Schocken Books, 1977; repr. London: Oneworld Classics, 2011), 16.

CHAPTER EIGHT

1. Ted Geisel to William Styron, 3 December 1973, Box C 5, Styron Papers, Duke.

2. See chap. 3, n. 24.

3. Alexandra Styron, *Reading My Father*, 237.

4. Wolf, *Reader and the Writer*, 41, 44.

5. West, *William Styron*, 142.

6. Alexandra Styron, *Reading My Father*, 26–27, 3, 5.

7. Ibid., 14–15.

8. Ibid., 16; Cologne-Brookes, "Appendix," in *Novels of William Styron*, 244.

9. Alexandra Styron, "Reading My Father," *New Yorker*, 10 December 2007, 60.

10. Styron, *Sophie's Choice* holographic manuscript, 234. As is the case here, the page numbers of the manuscript are not always sequential and are sometimes repeated. The final two leaves, following this one, are both labeled 235.

11. Fitzgerald, *The Crack-Up*, 39.

12. Styron, *Letters to My Father*, 45.

13. West, "William Styron: Public Author," 148; Styron, *Sophie's Choice* holographic manuscript, 40, 195, 92.

14. Styron, *Sophie's Choice* holographic manuscript, 160; Matthiessen and Plimpton, "Art of Fiction V," in West, ed., *Conversations*, 16.

15. Ray Lane to William Styron, 5 February 1985, Box C, Congdon Papers.

16. This is from Joseph McCord, *The Piper's Tune* (Philadelphia: MacRae Smith, 1938). McCord's light romance was syndicated in newspapers, appearing, for instance, in the *Charleston Daily Mail* on Tuesday, 25 January 1938, 5.

17. "No evidence of rape or torture. Perhaps Nat has seen his wife seduced by Travis. Is yet determined to preclude rape in his campaign." Endpaper of copy of William S. Drewry, *The Southampton Insurrection*, Box WS 2, Styron Papers, Duke. The page is reproduced in West, *William Styron*, in the central selection of photographs.

18. "William Samuel Francis, son of Nathaniel Virginia Francis, his wife, was born 7th of September 1831 (EQ) 1 mo. 7 days after insurrection," quoted in "Nat Turner's Trail is Personal Quest: Man Who Lost Ancestors Keeps History," *Virginia-Pilot*, 26 March 2000, http://www.highbeam.com/doc/1G1=63241789.html.

19. Bertrand Russell, "Is There a God?" (1952), in *Collected Papers*, vol. 11, ed. J. C. Slater and P. Kollner (London: Routledge, 1997), 542–48.

20. Emily Dickinson, "I Years had been from Home," Poem 609, in *Complete Poems*, 299.

21. Styron, "State of Writers in America," Styron Papers, Library of Congress.

22. Wallace Stevens, "Of Modern Poetry," in *Collected Poems*, 239.

23. Gates, letter to the author, 17 July 2009, and *Loose Canons*, 32.

24. Cormac McCarthy, *The Road* (New York: Alfred A. Knopf, 2006; repr., London: Picador, 2007), 112–13.

25. Ibid., 192.

26. Morrison, *Playing in the Dark*, 69, and in answer to my question about Styron's novel, City Hall, Sheffield, UK, 2 March 1988. See also *Selected Letters*, which contains a lengthy footnote discussing Morrison's comments in her 1993 *Paris Review* interview defending his right to have created Nat Turner as he saw fit but querying his portrayal of Turner's attitude toward his own people (627).

27. Styron, "State of Writers in America," Styron Papers, Library of Congress.

28. Cologne-Brookes, "Appendix," in *Novels of William Styron*, 215.

29. Gardner, "Novel of Evil," in Casciato and West, eds., *Critical Essays on William Styron*, 246; Wallace Stevens, "Sunday Morning," in *Collected Poems*, 70; Cologne-Brookes, "Looking Back," 509.

30. Saul Bellow. *Henderson the Rain King* (New York: Viking, 1959; repr., Harmondsworth, UK: Penguin, 1981), 157.

SELECTED BIBLIOGRAPHY

WORKS BY WILLIAM STYRON

FICTION

Lie Down in Darkness. Indianapolis: Bobbs-Merrill, 1951.
The Long March. New York: Random House, 1968.
Set This House on Fire. New York: Random House, 1960.
The Confessions of Nat Turner. New York: Random House, 1967.
Sophie's Choice. New York: Random House, 1979.
A Tidewater Morning: Three Tales from Youth. New York: Random House, 1993.
The Suicide Run: Five Tales of the Marine Corps. New York: Random House, 2009.

NONFICTION

This Quiet Dust and Other Writings. New York: Random House, 1982. Revised and
    expanded ed. New York: Vintage, 1993.
Darkness Visible: A Memoir of Madness. New York: Random House, 1990.
Havanas in Camelot: Personal Essays. New York: Random House, 2008.
Letters to My Father. Edited by James L. W. West III. Baton Rouge: Louisiana
    State University Press, 2009.
Selected Letters of William Styron. Edited by Rose Styron with R. Blakeslee Gilpin.
    New York: Random House, 2012.

DRAMA

In the Clap Shack. New York: Random House, 1973.

UNCOLLECTED ESSAYS AND INTERVIEWS

"William Styron to *Publishers Weekly.*" *Publishers Weekly,* 30 May 1960, 55.
"Nat Turner Revisited." In *The Confessions of Nat Turner,* 431–55. New York:
    Vintage, 1992.
"A Wheel Come Full Circle: The Making of *Sophie's Choice.*" *Sewanee Review* 105,
    no. 3 (1997): 395–400.

SECONDARY SOURCES

BOOKS

Bakhtin, Mikhail M. *The Dialogic Imagination: Four Essays*. Translated by Caryl Emerson and Michael Holquist. Edited by Michael Holquist. Austin: University of Texas Press, 1981.

Baldwin, James. *The Fire Next Time*. New York: Dial, 1963. Reprint, Harmondsworth, UK: Penguin, 1964.

Bartyzel, Bartosz, et al., eds. *Auschwitz-Birkenau State Museum Report 2010*. Translated by William Brand. Oświęcim, Poland: Pańtswowe Muzeum Auschwitz-Birkenau w Oświęcimiu, 2010.

Bellow, Saul. *Henderson the Rain King*. New York: Viking, 1959. Reprint, Harmondsworth, UK: Penguin, 1981.

Berlin, Isaiah. *Russian Thinkers*. London: Hogarth, 1948. Reprint, Harmondsworth, UK: Penguin, 1994.

Bloom, Harold, ed. *William Styron's "Sophie's Choice."* Modern Critical Interpretations Series. Philadelphia: Chelsea House, 2002.

Borges, Jorge Luis. *Labyrinths: Selected Stories and Other Writings*. Edited by Donald Yates and James Irby. 1964. Reprint, Harmondsworth, UK: Penguin, 1987.

Borowski, Tadeusz. *This Way for the Gas, Ladies and Gentlemen*. Translated by Barbara Vedder. London: Penguin, 1976.

Brown, Jared. *Alan J. Pakula: His Films and His Life*. New York: Backstage Books, 2005.

Camus, Albert. *L'Etranger*. Translated by Joseph Loredo. Harmondsworth, UK: Penguin, 1983.

Casciato, Arthur D., and James L. W. West III, eds. *Critical Essays on William Styron*. Boston: G. K. Hall, 1982.

Clarke, John Henrik, ed. *William Styron's Nat Turner: Ten Black Writers Respond*. Boston: Beacon, 1968.

Claude-Emonde, Magny. *The Age of the American Novel: The Film Aesthetic of Fiction between the Two Wars*. Translated by Eleanor Hochman. 1948. Reprint, New York: Ungar, 1972.

Coale, Samuel Chase. *William Styron Revisited*. Boston: Twayne, 1991.

Cologne-Brookes, Gavin. *Dark Eyes on America: The Novels of Joyce Carol Oates*. Baton Rouge: Louisiana State University Press, 2005.

———. *The Novels of William Styron: From Harmony to History*. Baton Rouge: Louisiana State University Press, 1995.

Crane, John Kenny. *The Root of All Evil: The Thematic Unity of William Styron's Fiction*. Columbia: University of South Carolina Press, 1984.

Davis, Mary Kemp. *Nat Turner Before the Bar of Judgment: Fictional Treatments of the Southampton Slave Insurrection*. Baton Rouge: Louisiana State University Press, 1999.

Dawkins, Richard. *The God Delusion*. London: Bantam, 2006. Reprint, London: Black Swan, 2007.

Dickinson, Emily. *The Complete Poems of Emily Dickinson*. Edited by Thomas H. Johnson. 1890. Reprint, London: Faber & Faber, 1960.

Dickstein, Morris, ed. *The Revival of Pragmatism: New Essays on Social Thought, Law, and Culture*. Durham, NC: Duke University Press, 1998.

Didion, Joan. *A Year of Magical Thinking*. New York: Alfred A. Knopf, 2005. Reprint, London: Harper Perennial, 2006.

Dostoevsky, Fyodor. *The Brothers Karamazov*. Translated by David Magarshack. London: Folio Society, 1964.

———. *Crime and Punishment*. Translated by Jessie Coulson. Oxford: Oxford World's Classics, 1981.

Duff, John B., and Peter M. Mitchell, eds. *The Nat Turner Rebellion: The Historical Event and the Modern Controversy*. New York: Harper & Row, 1971.

Fitzgerald, F. Scott. *The Crack-Up, and Other Pieces and Stories*. Harmondsworth, UK: Penguin, 1965.

———. *The Great Gatsby*. 1925. Reprint, New York: Charles Scribner's Sons, 1953.

Flaubert, Gustave. *Madame Bovary*. Translated by Margaret Mauldon. Oxford: Oxford World's Classics, 2004.

Fossum, Robert H. *William Styron: A Critical Essay*. Grand Rapids, MI: W. B. Eerdmans, 1968.

French, Scot. *The Rebellious Slave: Nat Turner in American History*. New York: Houghton-Mifflin, 2004.

Friedman, Melvin J. *William Styron: An Interim Appraisal*. Bowling Green, OH: Bowling Green University Popular Press, 1974.

Friedman, Melvin J., and Irving Malin, eds. *William Styron's "The Confessions of Nat Turner": A Critical Handbook*. Belmont, CA: Wadsworth, 1970.

Friedman, Melvin J., and August Nigro, eds. *Configuration Critique de William Styron*. Paris: M. J. Minard, 1967.

Friedman, Melvin J., and Ben Siegel, eds. *Traditions, Voices, and Dreams: The American Novel since the 1960s*. Newark: University of Delaware Press, 1995.

Gates, Henry Louis, Jr. *Loose Canons: Notes on the Culture Wars*. Oxford: Oxford University Press, 1993.

Greenberg, Kenneth S., ed. *Nat Turner: A Slave Rebellion in History and Memory*. New York: Oxford University Press, 2002.

Gutman, Yisrael, and Michael Berenbaum, eds. *Anatomy of the Auschwitz Death Camp*. Bloomington: Indiana University Press, 1994.

Hadaller, David. *Gynicide: Women in the Novels of William Styron*. Cranbury, NJ: Farleigh Dickinson University Press, 1996.

James, Henry. *The House of Fiction: Essays on the Novel*. Edited by Leon Edel. London: Rupert Hart-Davis, 1957. Reprint, London: Mercury, 1962.

Kristeva, Julia. *Powers of Horror: An Essay in Abjection.* Translated by Leon S. Roudiez. New York: Columbia University Press, 1982.

Langer, Lawrence L. *The Holocaust and the Literary Imagination.* New Haven, CT: Yale University Press, 1975.

Lengyel, Olga. *Five Chimneys: A Woman Survivor's True Story of Auschwitz.* Chicago: Ziff-Davis, 1947. Reprint, Chicago: Academy Chicago, 1995.

Leon, Philip W. *William Styron: An Annotated Bibliography of Criticism.* Westwood, CT: Greenwood, 1978.

Levi, Primo. *The Drowned and the Saved.* Translated by Raymond Rosenthal. London: Abacus, 1988.

———. *If This is a Man / The Truce.* Translated by Stuart Woolf. London: Abacus, 1987.

Lukács, Georg. *Writer and Critic, and Other Essays.* Translated by Arthur Kahn. London: Merlin, 1978.

Lupack, Barbara Tepa, ed. *Take Two: Adapting the Contemporary Novel to Film.* Bowling Green, OH: Bowling Green State University Popular Press, 1994.

Mackin, Cooper. *William Styron.* Austin: Steck-Vaughn, 1969.

Mailer, Norman. *Advertisements for Myself.* New York: Putnam, 1959. Reprint, London: Panther, 1968.

———. *Cannibals and Christians.* New York: Dial, 1966. Reprint, London: André Deutsch, 1967.

McCarthy, Cormac. *The Road.* New York: Alfred A. Knopf, 2006. Reprint, London: Picador, 2007.

McGinniss, Joe. *Heroes.* New York: Viking, 1976. Reprint, New York: Touchstone / Simon & Schuster, 1990.

Merejkowski, Dmitri. *Tolstoy as Man and Artist.* Westminster, UK: Archibald Constable, 1902.

Mewshaw, Michael. *Do I Owe You Something? A Memoir of the Literary Life.* Baton Rouge: Louisiana State University Press, 2003.

Milazzo, Lee, ed. *Conversations with Joyce Carol Oates.* Jackson: University Press of Mississippi, 1989

Montaigne, Michel de. *The Essays of Michel de Montaigne.* Translated by Charles Cotton. London: G. Bell & Sons, 1913.

Morris, Christopher, and Susan A. Eacker, eds. *Southern Writers and Their Worlds.* College Station: Texas A&M University Press, 1996.

Morris, Robert K., and Irving Malin, eds. *The Achievement of William Styron.* Revised ed. Athens: University of Georgia Press, 1981.

Morrison, Toni. *Playing in the Dark: Whiteness and the Literary Imagination.* Cambridge, MA: Harvard University Press, 1992.

Murray, Edward. *The Cinematic Imagination: Writers and the Motion Pictures.* New York: Ungar, 1972.

Nabokov, Vladimir. *Lectures on Literature.* London: Weidenfeld & Nicolson, 1980. Reprint, London: Picador, 1983.

Nietzsche, Friedrich. *Basic Writings of Nietzsche*. Translated by Walter Kaufmann. New York: Random House, 1967. Reprint, New York: Modern Library, 2000.

Oates, Joyce Carol. *The Faith of a Writer: Life, Craft, Art*. New York: Ecco, 2003.

———. *New Heaven, New Earth: The Visionary Experience in Literature*. New York: Vanguard, 1974.

___. *A Widow's Story: A Memoir*. New York: Ecco, 2011; London: Fourth Estate, 2011.

Pascal, Blaise. *Pensées*. Translated by A. J. Krailsheimer. 1966. Revised ed. Harmondsworth, UK: Penguin, 1995.

Pearce, Richard. *William Styron*. Minneapolis: University of Minnesota Press, 1971.

Potok, Chaim. *My Name is Asher Lev*. New York: Alfred A. Knopf, 1972. Reprint, Harmondsworth, UK: Penguin, 1994.

Ratner, Marc L. *William Styron*. Boston: Twayne, 1972.

Reck, Rima Drell. *Literature and Responsibility: The French Novelist in the Twentieth Century*. Baton Rouge: Louisiana State University Press, 1969.

Ross, D. W., ed. *The Critical Response to William Styron*. Westport, CT: Greenwood, 1995.

Roth, Philip. *The Ghost Writer*. New York: Farrar, Straus & Giroux, 1979.

Rubenstein, Richard L. *The Cunning of History: The Holocaust and the American Future*. New York: Harper & Row, 1975. Reprint, New York: Harper Colophon, 1978.

Rubin, Louis D. *The Faraway Country: Writers of the Modern South*. Seattle: University of Washington Press, 1963.

Ruderman, Judith. *William Styron*. New York: Ungar, 1987.

Russell, Bertrand. *Collected Papers*. Vol. 11. Edited by J. C. Slater and P. Kollner. London: Routledge, 1997.

Ryan, Tim A. *Calls and Responses: The American Novel of Slavery since "Gone with the Wind."* Baton Rouge: Louisiana State University Press, 2008.

Scanlan, James P. *Dostoevsky the Thinker*. Ithaca, NY: Cornell University Press, 2002.

Sirlin, Rhoda. *William Styron's "Sophie's Choice": Crime and Self-Punishment*. Ann Arbor, MI: UMI Research, 1990.

Sirlin, Rhoda, and James L. W. West III, eds. *"Sophie's Choice": A Contemporary Casebook*. Newcastle, UK: Cambridge Scholars, 2007.

Sollors, Werner. *Beyond Ethnicity: Consent and Descent in American Culture*. Oxford: Oxford University Press, 1986.

Sontag, Susan. *Under the Sign of Saturn*. Harmondsworth, UK: Penguin, 2009.

Stafford, William, *Writing the Australian Crawl: Views on the Writer's Vocation*. Ann Arbor: University of Michigan Press, 1978.

Steegmuller, Francis. *Flaubert and Madame Bovary: A Double Portrait*. London: Robert Hale, 1939.

Steinbacher, Sybille. *Auschwitz: A History*. Translated by Shaun Whiteside. London: Penguin, 2005.

Steiner, George. *George Steiner: A Reader*. Harmondsworth, UK: Penguin, 1984.

———. *Language and Silence: Essays, 1958–1966*. London: Faber, 1967.

Stendhal [Marie-Henri Beyle]. *The Red and the Black*. Translated by Catherine Slater. Oxford: Oxford World's Classics, 1998.

Stevens, Wallace. *The Collected Poems of Wallace Stevens*. London: Faber, 1955.

———. *The Palm at the End of the Mind: Selected Poems and a Play*. Edited by Holly Stevens. New York: Alfred A. Knopf, 1971. Reprint, New York: Vintage, 1972.

Stone, Albert E. *The Return of Nat Turner: History, Literature, and Cultural Politics in Sixties America*. Athens: University of Georgia Press, 1992.

Styron, Alexandra. *Reading My Father*. New York: Charles Scribner's Sons, 2011.

Tolstoy, Leo. *Anna Karenina*. Translated by Louise Maude and Aylmer Maude. Oxford: Oxford World's Classics, 1995.

———. "Why Do Men Stupefy Themselves?" In *Recollections and Essays*, translated by Aylmer Maude. 1937. Reprint, Oxford: Oxford University Press, 1946.

Tragle, Henry I. *The Southampton Slave Revolt of 1831: A Compilation of Source Material*. Amherst: University of Massachusetts Press, 1971.

Venezia, Shlomo. *Inside the Gas Chambers: Eight Months in the Sonderkommando of Auschwitz*. Translated by Andrew Brown. Cambridge: Polity, 2009.

Vonnegut, Kurt. *Slaughter-House Five*. New York: Delacorte, 1969. Reprint, London: Triad, 1983.

West, James L. W., III, ed. *Conversations with William Styron*. Jackson: University Press of Mississippi, 1985.

———, ed. *Inheritance of Night: Early Drafts of "Lie Down in Darkness*. Durham, NC: Duke University Press, 1993.

———. *William Styron, A Life*. New York: Random House, 1998.

Wilson, A. N. *Tolstoy*. London: Hamish Hamilton, 1988. Reprint, Harmondsworth, UK: Penguin, 1988.

Wolf, Christa. *The Reader and the Writer: Essays, Sketches, Memories*. Berlin: Seven Seas, 1977.

Woolf, Virginia. *Collected Essays*. Edited by Leonard Woolf. Vol. 2. New York: Harcourt, Brace & World, 1967.

Young, James E. *Writing and Rewriting the Holocaust: Narrative and the Consequences of Interpretation*. Bloomington: Indiana University Press, 1988.

ESSAYS, REVIEWS, AND INTERVIEWS

Arms, Valerie Meliotes. "A French View of William Styron: Topicality vs. Universality." *Southern Review* 29, no. 1 (1990): 47–69.

———. "An Interview with William Styron." *Contemporary Literature* 20, no. 1 (1979): 1–12.

Arnold, Edwin T., ed. "The William Styron–Donald Harington Letters." *Southern Quarterly* 40, no. 2 (Winter 2002): 99–141.

Barth, John. "The Literature of Replenishment: Postmodernist Fiction." *Atlantic Monthly,* January 1980, 65–71.

Burgess, Anthony. "Brooklyn Liebestod." *Observer,* 9 September 1979, 15.

Campbell, James. "Styron's Voice." *Times Literary Supplement,* 15 January 2010, 3–4.

Caputo, Philip. "Styron's Choices." *Esquire,* December 1986, 136–59.

Cash, Jean W. "Styron's Use of the Bible in *The Confessions of Nat Turner.*" *Resources for American Literary Study* 12, no. 2 (1982): 134–42.

Coale, Samuel. "Styron's Choices: Hawthorne's Guilt in Poe's Palaces." *Papers on Language and Literature* 23, no. 4 (1987): 514–22.

Cologne-Brookes, Gavin. "Looking Back: A Conversation with William Styron." *Mississippi Quarterly* 62, no. 4 (2009): 499–510.

———. "Sophie's Voice, Tolstoy, Film, Music: Interpreting a Leaf from the Manuscript of *Sophie's Choice.*" *Mississippi Quarterly* 62, no. 4 (2009): 511–26.

———. "Written Interviews and a Conversation with Joyce Carol Oates." *Studies in the Novel* 38, no. 4 (2006): 547–65.

Coltrane, Robert. "The Unity of *This Quiet Dust.*" *Papers on Language and Literature* 23, no. 4 (1987): 480–88.

Fabricant, Daniel S. "Thomas R. Gray and William Styron: Finally, A Critical Look at the 1831 *Confessions of Nat Turner.*" *American Journal of Legal History* 37, no. 3 (1993): 332–61.

Fitzgerald, F. Scott. "The Rich Boy." In *The Bodley Head F. Scott Fitzgerald,* vol. 5, *Short Stories,* edited by Malcolm Cowley, 286–327. London: Bodley Head, 1963.

Friedman, Melvin J. "William Styron's Criticism: More French than American." *Delta* (Montpellier) 23 (January 1986): 61–75.

Fuentes, Carlos. "Unslavish Fidelity." *Times Literary Supplement,* 16 May 1968, 505.

Geduld, Carolyn. "Film and Literature." *Contemporary Literature* 15, no. 1 (1974): 123–30.

Harold, James. "Flexing the Imagination." *Journal of Aesthetics and Art Criticism* 61, no. 3 (2003): 247–57.

Lang, John. "The Alpha and the Omega: Styron's *The Confessions of Nat Turner.*" *American Literature* 53, no. 3 (1981): 499–503.

Love, Tamsen Douglass. "Defining Postmodernism: Styron's 'Complicitous Critique' of Faulkner." *Southern Literary Journal* 28, no. 1 (1995): 19–34.

Myers, D. G. "Jews without Memory: *Sophie's Choice* and the Ideology of Liberal Anti-Judaism." *American Literary History* 13, no. 3 (2001): 499–529.

Nagel, Gwen L. "Illusion and Identity in *Sophie's Choice.*" *Papers on Language and Literature* 23, no. 4 (1987): 498–513.

Nenadál, Radoslav. "The Patterning of a Modern Hero in William Styron's *Set This House on Fire.*" *Prague Studies in English* 15 (1973): 83–97.

Noland, Richard W. "Psychohistorical Themes in *Sophie's Choice.*" *Delta* (Montpellier) 23 (January 1986): 91–110.

Nostrandt, Jeanne R. "William Styron's *Lie Down in Darkness*: A Parable." *Southern Literary Journal* 28, no. 1 (1995): 58–66.

Oates, Joyce Carol. "The Double Vision of *The Brothers Karamazov*." *Journal of Aesthetics and Criticism* 27, no. 2 (1968): 203–13.

Reitz, Bernhard. "'Fearful Ambiguities of Time and History': *The Confessions of Nat Turner* and the Delineation of the Past in Postmodern Historical Narrative." *Papers on Language and Literature* 23, no. 4 (1987): 465–79.

Rosenshield, Gary. "Crime and Redemption, Russian and American Style: Dostoevsky, Buckley, Mailer, Styron and Their Wards." *Slavic and East European Journal* 42, no. 4 (1998): 677–709.

Sirlin, Rhoda. "William Styron's *A Tidewater Morning*: Disorder and Early Sorrow." *Southern Literary Journal* 28, no. 1 (1995): 85–93.

———. "William Styron's Uncollected Essays: History Collides with Literature." *Southern Literary Journal* 30, no. 2 (1998): 54–65.

Smith, Frederik N. "Bach vs Brooklyn's Clamorous Yawp: Sound in *Sophie's Choice*." *Papers on Language and Literature* 23, no. 4 (1987): 523–30.

Sokolov, Raymond A. "Into the Mind of Nat Turner." *Newsweek*, 16 October 1967, 69.

Styron, Alexandra. "Reading My Father." *New Yorker*, 10 December 2007, 50–60.

Trouard, Dawn. "Styron's Historical Pre-Text: Nat Turner, Sophie, and the Beginnings of a Postmodern Career." *Papers on Language and Literature* 23, no. 4 (1987): 489–97.

Weldon, Fay. "Words from the Wise: Lessons in Life from the Over-Sixties." *Times Magazine*, 7 November 2009, 12.

West, James L. W., III. "An Accidental Boswell: Writing the Life of William Styron." *Sewanee Review* 119, no. 3 (2011): 445–50.

———. "William Styron: Public Author." *Critique* 51, no. 2 (2010): 147–50.

———. "William Styron's *Inheritance of Night*: Predecessor to *Lie Down in Darkness*." *Delta* (Montpellier) 23 (January 1986): 1–17.

OTHER

Burnett, Charles, Frank Christopher, and Kenneth S. Greenberg. *Nat Turner: A Troublesome Property*. Directed by Charles Burnett. San Francisco: California Newsreel, 2002. DVD.

Žižek, Slavoj. *The Pervert's Guide to Cinema 1, 2, 3*. Directed by Sophie Fiennes. London: P. Guide, 2006. DVD.

INDEX